BEING
OSCAR

BEING
OSCAR

FROM MOB LAWYER TO MAYOR OF LAS VEGAS, ONLY IN AMERICA

OSCAR GOODMAN

WITH GEORGE ANASTASIA

WEINSTEIN
BOOKS

Printed in the United States of America.

Library of Congress Cataloging-in-Publication Data is available for this book.
ISBN 978-1-60286-188-6 (print)
ISBN 978-1-60286-189-3 (e-book)

Published by Weinstein Books
A member of the Perseus Books Group
www.weinsteinbooks.com

Weinstein Books are available at special discounts for bulk purchases in the U.S. by corporations, institutions and other organizations. For more information, please contact the Special Markets Department at the Perseus Books Group, 2300 Chestnut Street, Suite 200, Philadelphia, PA 19103, call (800) 810-4145, ext. 5000, or e-mail special.markets@perseusbooks.com.

Editorial production by *Marra*thon Production Services. www.marrathon.net
Book design by Jane Raese

First edition
10 9 8 7 6 5 4 3 2 1

FOR MY BRIDE, CAROLYN,
AND THE DYNASTY

CONTENTS

CONTENTS

PROLOGUE

Once in awhile there is a mayor whose personality defines his city. Richard Daley in Chicago. Fiorello LaGuardia in New York. Frank Rizzo in Philadelphia.

Oscar Goodman, who recently completed his third and by law final four-year term as mayor of Las Vegas, belongs on that list.

Vegas. Sin City.

Goodman. Mob Mouthpiece.

Could there be a better fit?

Oscar Goodman *is* Las Vegas at the neon-lit start of the twenty-first century. No excuses; no alibis. Life is short—grab it with both fists. Let others whine, moan and complain. Do your best. Be who you are.

Vegas is a town built on glitz and glitter. Its foundation is an industry that used to be illegal in most other states. The city offers people a chance to lose their money. In fact, it almost guarantees it. Yet millions flock there every year to live the fantasy—to roll the dice. To be, for just a few hours or a few days, somebody they're not: a high roller. A player.

Vegas is mostly make-believe. An adult fantasy world. Yet Oscar Goodman is for real—he embodies the city. Go figure.

This is his story, told in his own words and through his perspective. It's the way he saw things go down, the way he interpreted what happened, the way he played the hands that were dealt to him.

President Obama, casino executives, U.S. senators, federal prosecutors, and FBI agents will all have their own versions of these stories. Oscar Goodman doesn't care what they think. If they disagree, let them go write their own book.

Over the years, he's dealt with mobsters and moguls, pimps and politicos. His take on who they are and how they fit in society is fascinating. His is a unique look at life through a prism that only Las Vegas could provide.

The fiction, of course, is that the mob created Vegas. Gambling existed in the Nevada desert long before the wiseguys came along. But you could make an argument, and Oscar does, that it was the vision of men like Meyer Lansky and Benjamin "Bugsy" Siegel that turned the city into something special.

What Las Vegas got in return was the problem.

There was a time when organized crime had its hooks in some of the biggest gambling palaces in town—places like the Tropicana, the Stardust, the Hacienda, the Fremont, and the Marina. The skimming scandals of the 1970s and 1980s documented this. Mob families from Kansas City, Chicago, Detroit, and other parts of the country were said to be sharing in cash taken out of the counting rooms before any earnings were reported. Estimates put the annual take at anywhere from $7 million to $20 million.

In street corner terms, the mob was cooking the books at some of the city's biggest gambling halls. What grew out of these scandals was a push to clean up the industry. The exclusion list, the "Black Book" that contained the names of individuals whose very presence in a casino was deemed to be inimical to the integrity of the industry, was established, and individuals were banned.

Oscar Goodman was in the middle of dozens of legal battles and criminal cases that sprang from the controversy. Two of his major clients, Anthony "Tony the Ant" Spilotro and Frank "Lefty" Rosenthal, became the poster boys for all that the do-gooders said was wrong with casino gambling. He also represented reputed Kansas City mob boss Nick Civella and a dozen other wiseguys throughout the country, including Vinny Ferrara in Boston and Phil Leonetti in Philadelphia.

They were the "bad guys." But Oscar also dealt with a lot of so-called "good guys." Sometimes he had trouble telling the difference.

While he was doing all this, his persona and his reputation grew. His ego—and Oscar would be the first to acknowledge this—can fill up a room. Arrogant, self-deprecating, opinionated, understanding, aggressive, caring; they're all part of the package. His emotions are the pistons that drive his engine. But what sometimes gets lost in all the hype is his abiding belief in, and love of, the law.

The caricature—a martini in one hand, a showgirl on each arm—is sometimes so strong that people miss the person behind it.

Twelve years in City Hall and nearly twice as many bobble-head dolls fashioned in his likeness. What other mayor in America can make that claim? Goodman loved the attention. It made him feel, he has often said, "like a rock star."

When he defeated a tic-tac-toe-playing chicken at a media event, he quipped, "I don't cluck around." When the College of Southern Nevada asked him to teach a class on mixing martinis, he jumped at the chance.

But his three terms were more than just headlines and photo ops; more than show girls and martinis. In a political world where form is often more important than substance, Oscar delivered the goods. Las Vegas is a better place now than when he was first elected. That sometimes gets overlooked in the hype and sizzle that he brought to local government.

What he said sometimes overshadowed what he did. He could often be outlandish in an effort to make a point or, his detractors might argue, to call attention to himself. The point is, becoming mayor didn't change the way Oscar Goodman operated. He was as aggressive an advocate for the city as he had been for his criminal clients.

After 9/11, when the economy was tanking and Las Vegas casinos laid off 30,000 workers, he railed against the industry, arguing that it was taking advantage of a bad situation to enhance its own bottom line. Then he stood in front of the media and suggested that every man should get a lap dance in order to boost the economy.

When a local health clinic was endangering its patients through the faulty use of products in colon cancer testing, Goodman didn't hesitate to act. Nearly 14,000 patients had been warned of their potential exposure to hepatitis because of the questionable practices of the clinic, but neither the health department nor the medical board thought it had the power to do anything about the situation. Oscar ordered the city to pull the clinic's business license, effectively shutting down the facility.

When the FBI exposed a little known Arab-American as a publicity seeker who sought to stir a media firestorm by falsely claiming that he knew of a terrorist plot targeting the gambling capital of America, Goodman suggested the guy should be "whacked." It was a sentiment no doubt shared by many, but one that you might not expect would come out of the mouth of the mayor of the city.

Every day, no matter what he's doing or where he's doing it, Oscar Goodman brings it all to the table. He loves life. There is probably not a better way to describe him.

After his battle with federal authorities in the impeachment of his good friend, the late Judge Harry Claiborne, one of Goodman's former junior high school teachers wrote a letter to the *Philadelphia Inquirer,* Oscar's hometown newspaper. The teacher, Joseph L. Pollock, had this to say about Oscar:

"He is a . . . lawyer who combines the scholarship of a Sam Dash, the forensic skills of F. Lee Bailey, and the poise of Melvin Belli. He is in the proud tradition of what is called 'a Philadelphia lawyer.' . . . I was Oscar Goodman's American history and government teacher at the William L. Sayre Junior High School in 1952. In 40 years as a teacher, principal, and superintendent I met few pupils who are his equal in ability, talent, and social consciousness. Philadelphia should be proud of its native son who performed his legal services in a difficult case."

Oscar Goodman's roots are in Philadelphia, even if he has come to epitomize Las Vegas. Part of what he brought west is what Philadelphians often refer to as attitude. So while the comment of his former teacher was well-deserved praise, the more telling point was that the praise came not after a great courtroom victory—and God knows Oscar has had many of those—but after a grueling battle that ended in defeat.

Philadelphia can appreciate that. It's part of the city's DNA, part of what Sylvester Stallone captured so perfectly in *Rocky*. Life is not about winning, but about going the distance; not about throwing a punch, but taking one; not about getting knocked down, but about getting back up.

Oscar Goodman always gets back up.

—*George Anastasia*

BEING
OSCAR

PART ONE
LAS VEGAS

CHAPTER 1
THE MAN AND THE BRAND

The crowd was on its feet cheering. Nine thousand fans rising to salute me.

If this was what being mayor was all about, I thought, bring it on. I loved every minute of it. I had only been in office a couple of years and was still feeling my way in the job when I was asked to throw out the first pitch at a game for the Las Vegas 51s, then the triple-A affiliate of the Los Angeles Dodgers. This was our team and this was my city. I couldn't wait.

My wife Carolyn had driven me to the game at Cashman Field that night. We were running a little late, so she dropped me off before parking the car. Everyone was waiting for me. I emerged in a pinstriped suit, shirt, and tie, the kind of outfit I often wore during my days as a criminal defense attorney. But on this night it fit the image I was to project. They handed me a martini and arranged for Jen and Porsha—two beautiful showgirls wearing four-inch heels and sequined gowns festooned with ten pounds of white feathers—to escort me out to the mound.

While no one knew it at the time, they were witnessing the birth of a brand. On August 17, 2002, I made my first public appearance as the symbol of Las Vegas. I had been a mob lawyer for years and was proud of it. That was my reputation. I also loved martinis, and on any given night, once I had finished work, I was quite capable of knocking back several.

Martinis, the mayor, and the mob.

How's that for the city's image?

On this night, my detractors might have been thinking that, but no one in a position to promote the city, least of all myself, had realized how perfect that image could be. But I'm getting a little ahead of myself.

I walked out to the mound and the overflow crowd—the exact figure was 8,861, about 4,000 more than the normal turnout for a game—rose to cheer me. I nodded in acknowledgment. I couldn't wave because I had my arms entwined with those of the showgirls. And I didn't want to spill my martini.

Now I was on the mound and ready to do my stuff. I handed Jen my drink. I slipped out of my suit coat and handed it to Porsha. They both smiled and peeled away. I was alone, center stage, ready to throw out the first pitch.

Did I mention that the first 2,500 fans to arrive that night were given bobblehead dolls of me? The caricature, which I thought looked more like Dr. Martin Luther King, Jr., was wearing the same pinstriped suit I had on that night and was holding a baseball bat. It was another first. During my three terms as mayor I would be "bobbleheaded"—is that a word?—about twenty more times.

But as they say, the first is the one you always remember.

I'm on the mound. Ready to pitch. I've watched hundreds of baseball games in my lifetime. I played the game. I'm a fan of the game. And, truth be told, I've bet on the game. I grew up in Philadelphia where, during my youth, the Phillies were doormats. But that didn't stop me from embracing the sport. As I was standing on the mound I began channeling the great pitcher Robin Roberts, a star with the Whiz Kids, the only really good

Phillies teams I ever saw growing up. Fastball or curve? What do I want to serve up?

But first I pause and reach for the rosin bag like I've seen hundreds of other pitchers do. I load up. The sweat from my hand mixes with the rosin to form a sticky, gooey paste. I take the shiny white baseball and go into my windup. The fans continue to cheer. I rear back and follow through.

Nothing!

The baseball sticks to my hand. No trajectory. The fans grow still. The ball falls from my hand and plunks me on my big left toe. Then it rolls, oh, so slowly, toward first base.

The cheers are now replaced by eight thousand moans. As one voice I hear, "Aggggghhhhhhhhhhhh."

I think of Charlie Brown when Lucy lifts up the football.

My wife, who was entering the stadium at the time, later talked about the horrible sound. To her it was all audio: first applause and cheering, and then this terrible sound; this group exclamation of disappointment.

What could I do? I bowed, waved, and walked off the mound.

As we all know, there is no crying in baseball. But my wife Carolyn vowed never to go to another game where I threw out the first pitch.

I think it says a lot about me that I was undaunted by the experience. I would be invited twenty-five more times while mayor to throw out the first pitch at a baseball game. The great Greg Maddux, a future member of the Baseball Hall of Fame, even coached me before one game. It was no help. I have thrown out twenty-six pitches. After that first one trickled off my hand, just two of the next twenty-five, all of which made it to the general vicinity of home plate, were strikes.

That's the beauty of baseball, however. There's always another chance. Baseball, more than any other sport, teaches us about life. It teaches us patience and perseverance and something else that is very important; something that we used to learn in kindergarten; something that we seem to have lost sight of in twenty-first century America.

Baseball teaches us that we all have to wait our turn; that we'll all get a chance, and that the secret to life is to be ready when that chance comes.

My life has been built around chances and opportunities. I've taken advantage and succeeded when they presented themselves. In the courtroom and in City Hall, I never backed down, never shied away, never failed to take my cuts.

And I think I can say with certainty that the only time I dropped the ball as mayor of Las Vegas was that night in August, 2002, when I took the mound in Cashman Field.

I had three terms in office, twelve years, and I enjoyed almost every minute of it. Before that I had a career as a criminal defense attorney that spanned more than four decades. I've accomplished a lot, but there was more I wished I had done. Anyone who knows me knows I've always been a risk-taker, and that I don't shy away from unpopular positions. For starters, I wish I could have legalized prostitution and drugs . . . all drugs, not just marijuana. More on those issues later in this book.

To me, Las Vegas is unique, unlike any other city in the country—unlike any other city in the world. That's what I love about the place, and that's what I've always tried to promote.

Sin City? I'll take it.

Built by the mob? Yeah. So what?

Guys came here with jackets—long criminal arrest records. And when given a second chance, some of them became our founding fathers. Guys like Benny Binion and Moe Dalitz. They were community leaders. They built churches and synagogues and some of the fanciest gambling palaces the world has ever seen. That distinguished us. Now forty-eight different jurisdictions have some form of gambling. Dozens of places have casinos. But I still consider Atlantic City and those other places the industry equivalent of the 51s—minor leaguers.

Las Vegas, my town, is the major leagues.

CHAPTER 2

NEVER BACK DOWN

Over my forty-year career as a defense attorney, I regularly came into contact with people who lied, cheated, and tried to bend the system so that they would come out on top.

Most of them worked for the government.

I've never shied away from being called a mob lawyer. That's what I was. But—and this is important—the men I represented were my clients. They were entitled to a lawyer, the same as any other citizen.

That's one of the things that always bothered me about the federal government. Strike Force attorneys and FBI agents acted like they were doing God's work, and therefore they didn't have to play by the rules. They thought the guys I was representing were evil, and even if there wasn't enough evidence to prove the charges, it didn't matter because they were guilty of something. The agents felt that the ends justified the means.

That's not what the Constitution says, nor is it what the Bill of Rights is about.

My clients were some of the most notorious mobsters in the country, but the guys in the white hats were the ones who I saw breaking the law. In almost every case I tried—and I tried hundreds—Federal prosecutors and FBI agents thought nothing of withholding evidence, distorting the facts, or making deals with despicable individuals who would get up on the witness stand and say whatever they were told.

I was the guy who tried to make the government play by the rules. Sometimes I succeeded. And when I did—and I really mean this—I felt as though I had done something good for the country. I was helping to guarantee the fundamental rights that we're all entitled to. The grocer, the librarian, the trash collector, and the accountant are all the same under the law. And so is an alleged member or leader of an organized crime family. Just because his name ends in a vowel doesn't mean some snot-nosed prosecutor with a law degree from Harvard can come along and take away his rights as a citizen.

Maybe that feeling that we're all equal has more to do with where I came from than where I was when I started practicing law. I grew up in a tough neighborhood in West Philadelphia, a Jewish kid among a lot of Irish Catholics. We'd fight a lot. Sometimes I'd win, most of the time I'd lose, but I wouldn't back down. Eventually I ended up playing football with a lot of the Catholic guys, and we became friends.

That's one of those life lessons you learn over time—lessons that you're not even aware you're learning. Mine was this: never back down. It's the way I lived my life as a lawyer, and later as the mayor of Las Vegas.

I had other things going for me, of course. My father, A. Allan Goodman, was a lawyer who worked in the Philadelphia District Attorney's Office, and my mother was into the arts. I was the oldest of three children, and I received tremendous support from my family. My parents always made me feel I was the handsomest, the smartest, and the best at whatever I did. You can't underestimate the power of liking who you are if you're going to make it in the world.

My dad was a nice, decent man who was treated with respect and admiration wherever he went. He came to watch me play ball, and he took me to Phillies and Eagles games. I remember classic pitching duels between Robin Roberts, the Phillies great right-hander, and Don Newcombe of the Brooklyn Dodgers, both excellent hitters as well. I also remember Eagles' games at Franklin Field and the great middle-linebacker Chuck Bednarik. They called him "Concrete Charlie" because he was so tough.

We lived on Christian Street in West Philadelphia, where my dad set up a blackboard in the basement. Every night my sisters and I had to do our homework in chalk on the blackboard first. Once it was perfect, we could copy it onto paper that we would turn in at school the next day. My dad was a stern taskmaster who knew how important education was, and that's how he instilled its importance in us.

I loved both my parents very much, and I'm who I am because of them. My mother, Laura, was a card who took over any room she entered; I inherited my dramatic gene from her. Her father, Oscar Baylin, for whom I was named, came from Russia and settled in Chester, Pennsylvania. He started out with a pickle barrel and ended up the wealthy owner of a giant food market. He lost it all in the Great Depression, but his philosophy was that it was better to have had it and lost it than to have never had it at all.

My mother was the oldest of five daughters. She was a remarkable artist and sculptress who studied with the greats— Hans Hoffman, Milton Avery, Wharton Esherick, and Jacques Lipchitz. She was a graduate of the Moore School of Art, and for a time she taught the blind how to sculpt and also used art as a tool to counsel troubled teenagers. Remarkably, in her eighties, she earned a Ph.D. Her talents were passed on to my sisters. Lona is an actress, and Ericka was a prima ballerina with the Joffrey Ballet and danced for George Balanchine in New York City.

My mother lived in Philadelphia for most of her adult life, but at age ninety-one and a few years after my dad passed away, I finally convinced her to move to Las Vegas where it was warmer and where she wouldn't have to deal with the ice and snow. We moved her into a senior citizen facility across the street from the private school that my wife Carolyn founded. A few weeks after we moved her in, I got a call at my City Hall office.

"Mayor, your mother is causing a riot," one of the administrators said. "Talk to her, or we'll have no choice but to ask her to leave."

I rushed down there to see what was going on.

"Mom, what's the problem?" I asked.

"Oscar, they don't have any live food," she said.

I had heard that expression once before from a Boston mobster, "Champagne" Dennis Lepore, who was complaining about the meals he was being served in prison.

"They don't have baked potatoes or broccoli," my mother complained. "All they serve is that powdered stuff and boxed stuff."

I asked my mother what she had done to get the staff so upset.

"Well," she said. "I organized everybody who lives here, and we're on a hunger strike until they serve live food."

The families of the other tenants began to call the complex and ask the administrators what was going on. Some threatened to move their mother or father to another complex. Laura Goodman led a revolution. From that day on, and until she passed away at ninety-three while exercising, she had all the baked potatoes and broccoli she could eat.

Those are my roots, my bloodlines. That kind of support gave me great self-confidence. I was never afraid to make a decision or express my opinion. More often than not, I believe I was right, but not always.

✳︎   ✳︎   ✳︎

When I was at Haverford College, which at the time was ranked the number one liberal arts college in the nation by *U.S. News and World Report*, I was part of a class that boasted some of the smartest people of my generation. In a student body of fewer than five hundred, I had classmates who would become the CEO of Time-Warner, the editor-in-chief of the *Los Angeles Times*, a judge on the First Circuit Court of Appeals, the editor-in-chief of *Time* Magazine, and the leading researcher of Tay-Sachs disease. Some of these guys played football, and so did I. I think the coach was afraid to put me in an actual game, but I practiced every day. I was a center and a linebacker, and a very good long snapper, by the way. In one practice, on three straight plays I tackled an All-America running back who was on our team.

In the classroom, I thought of myself as a student of letters. I took a creative writing course, and my Dad, who was very proud of the fact that I was attending Haverford, would listen as I spoke of the theater arts. At the time, some friends of his had been invited to invest in a show that was heading for Broadway. My father, who was considering investing, asked me to attend a reading of the script. I think the price was $5,000 for a point in the production.

My father was told that if the play lasted a week on Broadway, it would get picked up and be made into a movie, and investors would also have a piece of that. I went up to New York City and attended the reading, along with a lot of very rich potential investors. After listening to a half hour of the script, I left and told my Dad the play was so bad that it wouldn't last five minutes on Broadway.

He relied on my counsel and passed on the investment.

You might have heard of the play. It was Neil Simon's first: *Come Blow Your Horn*. It ran for 677 performances, and Frank

Sinatra starred in the movie. The investment returned tens of thousands of dollars on the one point.

It was the last time my father asked for my advice.

But you have to have confidence; I always did. I had something else, too. The Yiddish word is *bashert*. It's a sense that even though the odds look insurmountable—even though there's no way in the world you can win this thing—somehow you're gonna do it. I went into a lot of criminal cases with the attitude that I would find a way to win; that somehow I'd catch lightning in a bottle. Often, I got lucky.

I believe in two expressions that say a lot about luck. Ben Franklin, another Philadelphian, supposedly once said, "The harder I work, the luckier I get." There's something to that. It's a different spin on that other great expression, "Luck is the meeting of preparation with opportunity."

I guess, in a way, I was prepared when I came out here. And Las Vegas in the 1960s provided me with all kinds of opportunities.

How we got here, Carolyn and I, is where this story starts. Neither one of us knows yet where it's going to end.

I'm a gambler. I have been all my life. I'll bet on anything: baseball, football, basketball. Two cockroaches having a race. I just like the action. It gets my adrenaline going. I remember my first bet. I was in grammar school in Philadelphia, and this bookie used to come around the school yard during the baseball season. You could bet ten cents and you got to pick three players. If they combined for a total of six hits in that day's game, you won. It paid ten-to-one. I was one of his best customers.

My Dad sensed that I liked to gamble. Early on, he wanted to teach me a lesson that the odds were always against you. When

I was eleven years old, he took me to the Chester County Fair, just outside of Philadelphia. The carnies were out and about, the smell of cotton candy floated on the air, and there were all kinds of "games of chance" waiting for suckers.

We played the one where you pitched a quarter at a stack of plates. If your quarter landed on a plate and didn't fall off, you won. The higher the plate, the better the prize. Well, I was a big winner. One of my quarters (and I must have spent five dollars that night) landed on a top plate.

"What prize do ya' want, young man?" the operator of the game asked.

With great pride, I chose a "very expensive perfume."

"I'm going to give it to Mom," I told my Dad.

When we got home that night, I couldn't wait for her to open the carton with the perfume in it. With great aplomb she took out this bottle of "perfume." It smelled like tap water sprinkled with two cloves.

A gambling lesson learned: even when you win, you may not come out on top.

But it didn't stop me from placing bets. And the problem was, very often I won.

In college at Haverford, I remember betting on a horse named Sherluck in the Belmont Stakes. Sherluck had finished fifth in the Kentucky Derby and in the Preakness, which I had watched on TV. And even though he had only won once in ten starts that year, I had a feeling about him. He went off at 65-to-1 in the Belmont. The track was damp, and I thought anything could happen.

I bet $10 on him and he won going away. He creamed the favorites. He paid an astounding $132.10. I won $650 based on my $10 bet. It was a veritable fortune to me at the time. I've been betting horses ever since—Del Mar, Santa Anita, Fairplex—and I have never seen another horse pay 65-to-1.

I think I spent most of my winnings at the Blue Comet, a diner near campus that we used to call the "Blue Vomit." Carolyn and I ate a lot of hamburgers there on Sherluck.

I'm also a drinker; I tell everyone not to call me after five o'clock. When I finish working, I enjoy a martini or two. You call me on the phone and I'll be perfectly lucid, but there's a good chance I won't remember our conversation in the morning. That's who I am, and I've never tried to hide any of this. I was the same person when I was a defense attorney, trying big cases all over the country, and after I became mayor. I guess when you look at it that way, it made sense that I ended up in Las Vegas.

But when I was young, Vegas wasn't even a glint in my eye. In 1964, I was working as a clerk in the Philadelphia District Attorney's Office while I was in my third year of law school at the University of Pennsylvania. The third year of law school is really a waste of time; in essence, you're just waiting to take the bar exam.

There was a case in which a woman named Lulabell Rossman had been murdered. The two suspects had stolen $300,000 that she had hidden under a mattress, and they went to Las Vegas because it was the ideal place to launder money. For some reason, these were all new bills. So these two guys went to the casinos, bought chips, played for a while, and then cashed out.

They ended up in Omaha, where they got arrested and were brought back to Philadelphia to await trial. In preparation, two detectives from Las Vegas came to Philadelphia. Arlen Specter, who was an assistant district attorney at the time, assigned me to debrief the detectives. I was just a law clerk, so that was my only involvement with the case. We were on the seventh floor of City Hall, the wind was blowing through the walls, and it was dank and dreary. As we were going over the cops' story, one of the two detectives said to me, "What's a young guy like you doing here?" I said, "Where else am I gonna be?" And they said, "Why don't you come to Vegas?"

Vegas wasn't a place I had ever thought about. Carolyn and I were living in an apartment in West Philadelphia, not far from the University of Pennsylvania Law School. It wasn't the greatest neighborhood; we would routinely hear gunshots at night, and I bought Carolyn a container of Mace that she carried when she went to work. That night at home I asked her, "How would you like to go to the land of milk and honey?" She said, "What, Israel?"

I couldn't wait to get out of law school. I sent letters out to district attorneys' offices all over the country, but I didn't get a whole lot of offers since I wasn't the best student in school. I had a chance to go to work for Frank Hogan, the D.A. in Manhattan, but we would have been no better off financially than we were in Philadelphia. I married a princess, but she wasn't a rich princess.

I didn't want to stay in Philadelphia. My father had been in the district attorney's office there, and later he had his own law practice. I loved my Dad, but I didn't want to go to work for him and potentially strain our relationship. And I was intrigued by Las Vegas.

I could care less that the Flamingo was Meyer Lansky's and Bugsy Siegel's baby. At the time, I had barely heard the words "organized crime." Back then, J. Edgar Hoover was still telling everyone that there was no Mafia. All that mattered to me was whether we should relocate to the desert.

I was looking for some adventure; something different. So I decided to write to the district attorney in Las Vegas about a job. Turns out there wasn't a D.A. in Las Vegas; he was in Clark County. Luckily the letter got to the right place and I was offered a job. Before we decided, we went for a weekend to check it out.

We went on a junket run by the B'nai Brith. Carolyn was ill with mono the whole time we were there, so she just stayed in the hotel room at the Flamingo. I walked around downtown on a Saturday morning. People were friendly. I stopped in some lawyers' offices and asked what kind of opportunities were there, and everyone encouraged me. Most of their practices were divorce and civil cases, of course, but I liked the place.

To a person, they told me the opportunities were limitless. There weren't that many criminal cases, but every once in a while somebody would shoot somebody. It was a relatively safe city, in hindsight perhaps because the mob was there.

Carolyn was feeling better by Saturday, so I took her to the Flamingo's "Candlelight Room." I ordered a martini, and Jimmy Blake, the bartender, served one with a pickled Brussels sprout as a garnish. I never saw one before, and never saw one since.

By that point, I had made up my mind that I'd rather risk starting a career in Las Vegas than stay in Philadelphia. If I had stayed in Philly, I probably would have gone to work for Arlen Specter, and eventually would have become a federal judge. It was clear that Arlen was a shining light and that he was going to go places. Had I stayed, my whole life would have been different. I might have been as successful, but I wouldn't have had the romance, the thrill of what I did in Las Vegas.

Later, when Specter was the U.S. senator and I was the mayor, he would always talk about that case he had assigned me when I was a kid. I was in Washington once with some politicians, and we were walking around the Senate offices meeting different senators. When we ran into Arlen, he told the story again. He said he sent me to Las Vegas to collect the money from the Lulabell Rossman case, and I never came back.

I accepted an offer to clerk for the Clark County District Attorney's Office in Vegas, and we left Philadelphia right after I took the bar exam in August 1964. We drove out in an Oldsmobile

Cutlass convertible and took the old Route 66. I drove during the day, and Carolyn drove during the night; it took us three and a half days to get there. We stopped in St. Louis one night and in New Mexico another night. When we drove up on Las Vegas, we stopped on a mesa overlooking the valley. We could see a few flickering lights blinking in the desert. But not many big buildings. This wasn't Philadelphia. I swear, some tumbleweed rolled across the highway in front of us. The only time either of us had ever seen tumbleweed was in a Roy Rogers movie.

My wife looked at me and said, "My parents were right. I should never have married you. Where have you taken me?" She was prescient. When she was taking courses at UNLV, where she got a Masters in counseling, one of her professors asked for a definition of cultural deprivation. Carolyn asked me what I thought. I said it was anyone in Las Vegas who couldn't afford a round-trip ticket to San Francisco.

There were no fancy, boutique clothing stores or gourmet restaurants back then. There was a JC Penney's, which we jokingly pronounced with a French accent—*Pen-nay*. But there was just something about Las Vegas. It was either the most real or the most unreal place I have ever been. I didn't know whether this was what life was supposed to be like, or whether it was an aberration. For many, the only reason to come here was the promise of financial success. It was a new frontier, and it appealed to me.

Philadelphia's society was steeped in tradition; there was almost a caste system in effect. In Las Vegas there was just a bunch of characters who mingled with one another. Social life seemed to revolve around Vegas Village, which was a supermarket. This wasn't like any supermarket I was used to; it was open

24 hours, and on Saturdays and Sundays it was a meeting place. You'd see senators, lawyers, bookmakers, showgirls, prostitutes—everybody interacting.

When we got to Vegas, my wife wanted to move into a nice apartment, so we got a place at the Palms for $185 a month. It had a beautiful little patio and was full of interesting people. But for the first six weeks, nobody talked to us. We couldn't figure it out. Then on the seventh week, everybody opened up. Later we found out that couples came there for six weeks to establish residence so they could file for divorce. Once we were there for seven weeks, they knew we were staying.

Carolyn and I both came from pretty staid backgrounds, but now we were living in this apartment building with showgirls, dealers, casino workers, and probably some hookers, too. There was a woman who used to walk her poodle every day wearing the skimpiest bikini I'd even seen. Nobody thought anything of it; she was a hooker or a showgirl, maybe both. Nobody cared. You've gotta love a place like that.

At first I worked in the civil division of the Clark County District Attorney's office while waiting to take the Nevada bar exam, which wasn't scheduled again until November of the following year. The job was interesting and allowed me to get to know a lot of people in the legal community. The people in the D.A.'s office took a liking to me. I think they respected the fact that I was from an Ivy League law school. Among other things, I became the ghostwriter for one of the judges, who used me to craft his opinions.

After I was clerking for six months, I got a call asking me to come back to Philadelphia to work for Arlen Specter, who had been elected district attorney. They offered me a salary of $17,000, and at the time I was making $7,200. But I made the decision to stay, and I've never regretted it. I've always felt that you can make your own mark in Las Vegas, since the city's founding fathers all came from somewhere else.

When I took the bar, I got the number one grade, so I was a shining star. The judge who supervised the group had nice things to say about me. It was said that Harry Reid was the best young civil lawyer, and Oscar Goodman was the best young criminal lawyer among the batch admitted during those years.

Carolyn got a job right away in advertising and publicity at the Riviera. Part of her job was to go out every night to the lounges and the showrooms to socialize with other people in the business. Sometimes she'd schlep me along. The first time we went to the Thunderbird, Frankie Laine and Sarah Vaughn were playing the lounge. It was free, and the casino was giving away drinks. They just hoped you would gamble.

Carolyn had a number of jobs. She worked PR for Louis Prima, and later she was the first executive secretary for two of the three founders of Caesars Palace. Nate Jacobson, one of those founders, asked her why she had married scrambled eggs when she could have roast beef, the little prick. I think that if she had stayed in the business, she would have become a casino president.

Carolyn also was a card counter before the gamers ever dreamed up that term. Today they would ban her from the casinos, but back then they didn't. And they played blackjack with one deck of fifty-two cards. One of her favorite games as a kid involved spreading out all the cards in a deck face-up, then turning them all over and trying to match them: a Queen with a Queen, a five with a five. She was very good at that game, and very good at counting cards. The dealers used to look at her like she was a mystic.

My mom and dad spent my whole youth teaching me to learn how to "fly," but when it came time to "fly away," they balked.

My dad had read *The Green Felt Jungle*, and he was disturbed by its depiction of the underworld in Las Vegas. For years, he told everyone that his son had moved to Phoenix. Even so, he would send me $25 every week, with the caveat that I had to spend that money for something we enjoyed. It wasn't to pay bills or to put in the bank. We would go over to the Hacienda for dinner and afterward Carolyn would go to the blackjack table with whatever was left over from the check. She usually won, put what she started with in her purse, and spent the rest of the night playing with the house's money.

After I passed the bar, I opened my office and started practicing law. From that point on, I've never worked for anyone except myself. I got the opportunity to practice law in a way that no other young lawyer ever has. It was because of the clientele, and because I was in Las Vegas. Because there was no society, no caste system, you made your own mark. The cream rose to the top, and I liked that. Still, you could be the smartest guy in the world, but without a client, nobody would know it.

CHAPTER 3
WHAT THEY DON'T TEACH IN LAW SCHOOL

I didn't set out to be a mob lawyer—they don't teach a course on that in law school. But I knew I wanted to practice criminal law because I thought it was meaningful.

I've always looked at life in terms of David versus Goliath. I identify with the underdog. When I was a boy attending religious school, stories involving fights against injustice and oppression made a big impression on me. Anyone who's ever read the Bible knows there are plenty of those in the Good Book.

At this time horrific stories were coming out about the concentration camps. This was post–World War II, and Americans were finding out about the atrocities perpetrated by Hitler. Six million Jews had been slaughtered because of a maniac who spewed a philosophy of hatred and intolerance.

All of that shaped who I was, and what kind of lawyer I would become.

It's no secret that I became a lawyer because of my dad. I saw him practice law, and I knew what it meant to see justice served. When I was about twelve years old, he took me to court with him one day. By this time he had left the district attorney's office and was in private practice. He was representing a woman in a civil case. When I think about it now, it still sends chills down my spine.

She had been a survivor of Auschwitz, the Nazi concentration camp in Poland. She had those horrible numbers tattooed on her arm. Some family members wanted to have her lobotomized so that she would forget the shock and terror that she had experienced.

But she was against it. She thought it was important that people remember.

My father had taken me to hearings held in police districts when he was with the D.A., but this was the first time he ever took me to City Hall, and the first time I was ever in a real courtroom. I was there for closing arguments in the case. I think he wanted me to understand what being a lawyer was. He was emotionally involved because of the principled position his client had taken; so involved, in fact, that he was getting physically ill.

But when he made his closing argument, he was awesome, passionate, and eloquent. The point he made was that while those were horrific times, forgetting them would be an utter tragedy. The judge ruled right from the bench in his client's favor. There would be no lobotomy.

Whenever I think about that case, I remember my dad's passion and conviction. From that point on, I knew that a lawyer—in particular, a lawyer who cared about what he was doing—was in the business of fighting for righteousness. It may sound trite, but when I was practicing law, I really saw myself as a defender and protector of the Constitution. My father had taught me that attitude, and as a result, I took my work very seriously.

Trial law is fascinating. You never know where it's going to take you. In one of my cases in Las Vegas, I found myself again dealing with a concentration camp survivor. Only this time I was on the other side of the courtroom.

This wasn't a headline case, and it didn't involve a high-profile client. I used to get my hair cut at a barbershop owned by a young man named Dino. He was a hardworking kid, in his early twenties. Handsome in a Stanley Kowalski kind of way. In fact, he wore those sleeveless t-shirts in the barbershop. He had a girlfriend and was planning to get married. I knew his family, and they were nice people.

One night when he was driving home from work, an elderly women stepped out of the shadows in front of his car. Dino knocked the old lady down. He panicked and continued driving. Two blocks away, he pulled into a convenience store and called his father from a pay phone. Sobbing, he told his dad what had happened. His dad told him to go back to the scene of the accident, which he did.

When he got there, he learned that the elderly woman had died. He was distraught. He told the police he was the driver. He was arrested and charged with manslaughter and leaving the scene of an accident.

His family posted bail and hired me to defend him. I was able to get the manslaughter charge dismissed. It was dark, and the woman clearly stepped out in front of him. It was tragic, but it was an accident.

To his credit, Dino told me not to contest the leaving the scene of an accident charge. He did that, he said. There was no disputing that fact.

In Nevada, a victim's family is permitted to address the judge at sentencing. When we went to court, the elderly woman's family packed the courtroom. In all my years of practicing law, that hearing might have been my most harrowing experience. One family member after another got up to address the judge. They all told the same story. The woman had been a Holocaust survivor. The victim's daughter was shouting and crying, pointing at Dino, who sat at the defense table with his head in his hands.

"He did what Hitler couldn't do!" the woman screamed. "My mother was in Auschwitz. The Nazis tattooed her. Hitler couldn't kill her."

Then she pointed at Dino and said, "But he did. Put him away forever."

A chill went through me. My knees were buckling. Part of it may have been the memories of that case my father defended. But part of it was also my concern that justice might be distorted by emotion. Dino didn't deserve jail time. It was an accident. He was a kid who momentarily panicked, but who ultimately did the right thing and was ready to take his punishment. But not this.

I started to make an argument, but Judge Tom Foley, who later became a good friend, stopped me.

"I know how the family must feel," he said to everyone in the courtroom, "but if ever there was an accident, this was it."

He said Dino's action in coming back to the scene showed that he had a conscience. And he said prison wasn't the answer. Probation, he said, was designed for cases like this, and that is what he imposed.

The judge said he knew that the thought of having caused someone's death, even accidentally, was something that Dino would have to live with for the rest of his life. That, Judge Foley said, was punishment enough.

I thought of my father and his case. In both instances, I believe, justice was served. That's what being a lawyer and being part of the legal system is all about. I've had many other bigger, high-profile cases, but probably none were more important in demonstrating how important our legal system is, and what it means to be a part of it.

My first law office was over a flower shop at Las Vegas Boulevard and Bridger, and as soon as I hung out my shingle, I started earning a living. In the beginning I didn't have any big cases, but to me and my clients, they were all important. Every day was a learning experience. People watch television and think that's the way it happens in the courtroom: *Perry Mason* and *Law and Order* are the common perception of the criminal justice system. They think that cases get presented in a neat and orderly fashion, and then the jury comes back with a verdict. Maybe sometimes there's a dramatic confession, and then the innocent person goes free.

It's a lot more complicated than that.

Sometimes you practice law the way they teach it in the textbooks. Sometimes you practice law with a baseball bat. I learned that difference in the beginning of my career. I was court-appointed to represent Lewis "Brown" Crockett, a black man and a suspected drug dealer accused of killing a guy who was going to testify against him in a narcotics case.

I never asked my clients if they were guilty or innocent. Most of the time they wouldn't know the answer anyway. The law is both art and science. For instance, imagine that you get home from work one day and your front door has been jimmied open, your house has been ransacked, and you're missing a lot of valuables.

The first thing you do is call 9-1-1 and tell the police dispatcher, "I've been . . ." Most people will say, "robbed." Wrong! You've been burglarized. Robbery is taking something by force or threat of force, but burglary is an illegal entry. What's the practical difference? For a defendant, about ten years. A robbery conviction carries a lot more time than a burglary conviction.

When I first get involved with a client, the only thing I really want to know from them is if they have an alibi. That's something you can work with in court. However, most times they don't.

Lewis Crockett didn't have an alibi, but he insisted he was innocent. Crockett was thought by law enforcement officers to be a major drug dealer on the West Side of Las Vegas, which was the black community. In the 1960s, Las Vegas was the "Mississippi of the West." Back then, communities were segregated. There were still a lot of Jim Crow laws on the books in several states, and in Nevada there were people with Jim Crow attitudes. A lot of that has changed for the better.

Crockett came from a well-known family in his part of town. His dad, Johnnie, owned a barbershop, and the family had status in the community. Of course the police said the family's power and influence came because of drug dealing. There might have been something to that, but there was also a hint of racism. When I first started practicing law, that attitude was part of every case involving a person charged with a crime from the West Side.

Crockett was a young guy, fairly well-spoken, and easygoing. He was charged with killing a guy named Curtis Wheeler who was planning to testify against him in a drug case. Wheeler drove a delivery truck for Dot's Dry Cleaners and was making a pickup at an apartment in North Las Vegas one morning. When he went to the door, he was greeted with a shotgun blast to the chest. That eliminated Wheeler as a witness in the drug case, and a short time later Crockett was arrested for murder.

The key witness to Wheeler's murder was a guy named Bingham who had been painting parking lines at the apartment complex that day. Bingham was from a prominent Mormon family in town, which added another dynamic to the case. As the only one at the scene to testify, he swore that he saw Crockett climb out of a window carrying a shotgun. He said Crockett then ran to a car and took off. The identification was based on about twelve seconds' time and from a distance of maybe fifty yards.

I wasn't involved in Crockett's first trial, which ended with a hung jury. The vote was eleven-to-one to convict. One female juror had locked herself in a bathroom during deliberations and refused to be a part of the process. Maybe she was scared, or maybe she decided she didn't want to be involved in a death penalty case. But the judge threw the case out and set a date for a retrial.

The judge appointed me along with another lawyer to represent Crockett. Although I was supposed to be second chair, I ended up handling most of the case. I was paid about $900, which was the fee for a court appointment on a murder case back then. We contested everything during the trial: cross-racial eye-witness identification, withholding evidence by the prosecution. But Bingham's testimony was overwhelming.

There was one juror, Mrs. Homer Black, who kept making eye contact with me. She seemed like a nice lady. But when the jury came back with its verdict, I looked at her and saw that there were tears in her eyes, and I knew we had a problem.

There's a rule of thumb that most defense attorneys agree is a fairly accurate assessment of the jury process. If the jurors return to the courtroom to announce their verdict and they don't look at the defendant, it means they're coming back with a guilty verdict. When I see a juror crying, particularly after a hotly contested trial, I know my client is in serious trouble. That certainly was the case in this trial.

In Crockett's case, the verdict was guilty of first-degree murder. In those days, that left the judge to impose the sentence, and the only option was the death penalty.

The judge was Tom O'Donnell. He came from coal country, Tamaqua, Pennsylvania, and he was tough but fair. He was a Catholic who I don't think believed in capital punishment. I was distraught over the verdict and was desperate to find a way to get it undone. Knowing the judge's propensities, I needed to figure out a way to get the case back before him; the concept of the judge as the thirteenth juror. I wanted to get him to nullify the verdict.

I knew the judge was ticked off at the Mormons for having taken a position in "The Book of Mormon" that the Catholic Church was the "abominable whore" of the earth. He used to quote that phrase, citing the page number and paragraph where he said it was stated. He also felt the Mormons considered the blacks to be inferior and relegated to a position at the bottom rung of the societal ladder. Therefore I had a feeling he wasn't thrilled with Bingham's testimony.

Carolyn was in the courtroom when the verdict came in. She could see how disappointed I was. Afterward I told her I wanted to go back and talk to Brown. She waited outside the visiting room just off the courtroom, and she heard all this sobbing and crying. When I came out, she was standing there.

"He took it badly," she said.

"No," I said. "That was me."

I was beside myself, angry and disappointed. I needed to do something. I spent the whole night researching the law. I stayed in the law library, drinking water, eating crackers, and reading. The next morning I was leaving, exhausted, and a reporter from the newspaper came up to me and asked about the case.

"My client's gutsy," I said. "He has a lot of guts." Then I mumbled some other stuff about an appeal and what I was trying to do.

Either the reporter didn't hear me or I was so tired I wasn't making sense, but the next day in the paper the headline read:

LAWYER SAYS CLIENT IS GUILTY

Now I was even more upset. I went down to the jail to see Crockett and explain what had happened. He was very understanding. Given the circumstances, I'm not sure many clients would have been. But he said, "I knew you wouldn't say anything like that."

Then he told me that he wanted me to meet somebody who was in jail with him, a fellow named Floyd Hamlet. I had been trying to find Hamlet during the trial because Crockett had said Hamlet was the guy who went out the window with the shotgun. But Hamlet had been released from prison, and he was nowhere to be found. I figured that was the way the prosecution kept me from getting to him.

Now he was back in jail on some other charge. I met him and it was amazing; he was the spitting image of Crockett. Hamlet told me that he was the guy leaving the apartment that day with the shotgun. He said that he didn't shoot Wheeler, but he was the guy that Bingham saw.

Even though it was a Sunday, I got a court stenographer to take down Hamlet's statement, and I used it in a motion for a new trial based on new evidence. Judge O'Donnell scoffed at the mistaken-identity theory after reading my motion. I was getting nowhere, until one day when the judge met the undersheriff, Lloyd Bell. They were friends, and they would go to lunch together. O'Donnell was down there one day and he saw a familiar-looking inmate. He said, "Hi, Brown. How ya' doin'?"

The murder trial had gone on for several weeks, and the judge looked at Crockett day after day sitting at the defense table. But at this moment, the inmate he was talking to was Floyd Hamlet. The next day, the judge granted my motion.

But my work was far from over.

The prosecution appealed and eventually the Nevada Supreme Court ruled three-to-two in my favor, granting the new trial. One of the dissenting justices, Jon Collins, asked me during the hearing, "What if Hamlet doesn't testify? What's to guarantee that he will?"

I couldn't believe it. Collins's question was puerile and, I thought, cavalier. We were talking about a death penalty case. A man's life was literally on the line. It wasn't time to be splitting hairs and speaking hypothetically. I sneered, looked him right in the eye, and said, "What guarantees are there in life?"

The granting of a new trial was good news and bad news, of course.

I got the word from Judge O'Donnell, who had been notified by the clerk of the State Supreme Court. The trial judge is always the first to be informed. When he called me on the phone, he sounded as relieved as I was. The burden of ordering Crockett's execution had been lifted off his shoulders, at least temporarily. I asked the judge if he'd like to join me for a drink to celebrate. We had several, and out of that grew a lasting friendship.

I know it might sound strange—the idea of a defense attorney having a drink with a judge after a criminal case he was involved in, but I could care less. To be brutally frank, the ethical issue wasn't something I was concerned with. It just seemed to be the right thing to do.

That night, the judge and I got completely sloshed. We ended up passed out on the living room floor in my apartment. In the morning, Carolyn came downstairs and cooked us corned beef hash and eggs. We also had a couple of beers to sober us up. From that day forward, we were fast friends.

But I still had to put the case in front of a jury. Remember, the first jury was going to convict Crockett if the woman hadn't locked herself in the bathroom. And the second jury had buried him. Even with this new evidence, we still had an uphill battle. And there was always the question of racism. I didn't know what Bingham, the only witness, was going to say about the likeness of Hamlet and Crockett.

The prosecutor in the case was the district attorney himself, a guy named George Franklin, and he was livid. He was a pompous megalomaniac who really enjoyed playing the role of the top law enforcement official in the city. From his perspective, both his office and the police department had been upstaged and embarrassed by a young punk lawyer who was an outsider. Franklin was convinced that Crockett was guilty.

So there was a lot at stake, and not all of it had to do with truth and justice. Too often for the prosecution, it's about winning. That's not the way it's supposed to be, but unfortunately that's the reality. I was new to the game at that point—just a baby lawyer—but I could see how it worked.

So I offered Franklin a deal. I told him my client would take a polygraph, and if he passed, the prosecution would drop the charges. If not, he would plead guilty. Franklin said okay.

But I wasn't going to use one of his polygraph experts. I brought in Leonard Harrelson, a guy with a national reputation from the Keeler Institute in Chicago. He turned out to be the uncle of the actor Woody Harrelson, who at that time was only five or six years old. Leonard was the brother of Charles Harrelson, Woody's father, who was later found to be an underworld hit man—but that's getting ahead of the story.

I set up Leonard Harrelson at the Fremont Hotel. He spent three days testing Crockett, and when he was done, Harrelson told me the lie detector results were pristine. Crockett passed with flying colors. He had nothing to do with the murder of Wheeler.

I took the information to Franklin, the prosecutor, thinking I'd done pretty well for my client. And the prosecutor backtracked.

"I'm not going to drop the charges," he said. "No deal."

I couldn't believe it. "You son of a bitch," I said. "You gave me your word."

He didn't care. He never thought Crockett would pass the polygraph, and he knew I couldn't use it in court. So he was still going to take my client to trial. Now I was really hot.

But I was lucky.

The National Conference of District Attorneys was holding its annual convention in Las Vegas, and Franklin was the host. He loved playing that role.

And that's when I stopped being a young lawyer, a boy, and became a man. I look back on it now as a rite of passage. Again, it wasn't something they taught you in law school, but something you had to learn if you were going to make it as a defense attorney. I confronted Franklin.

"If you don't honor our agreement," I said, "I'm calling a press conference and I'm going to announce exactly what you did. I'm going to call you a liar in front of every D.A. in the country. I'm going to tell them you care more about winning cases than justice, that truth doesn't matter to you, and that you're not a man of your word."

The charges against Crockett were dropped.

Interestingly, later on I heard that the jury in the second trial was torn on the identification issue and how it fit in with reasonable doubt. Would you believe it was resolved by a woman juror who examined the evidence in their deliberation room and announced to the others that when Crockett was arrested, the cuffs on his trousers matched the stitching on the drapes from the window the person carrying the shotgun came through? She said they must have come from the same sewing machine. Not in a million years do you figure a case gets decided that way, totally out of left field. Absolutely nuts! Her assumption could have put Brown in the electric chair.

Crockett and his family thought I was the greatest lawyer in the city. That's how I started building my criminal practice.

Was he innocent? He passed the test. But he went right back into the drug underworld, and I would have another encounter with him later that wasn't as pleasant.

In the end, you could say I won the case, but it wasn't based on anything they taught me in law school. I didn't get the district attorney to go along with the agreement based on the legal issues or the facts, which he should have done. That was the right thing to do. Instead, he went along because he was worried about his image and about all the negative publicity I was threatening to bring. I had to hit him over the head.

As I said earlier, sometimes you have to practice law with a baseball bat.

I did all kinds of cases back then. There was a dealer over at the Hacienda that Carolyn and I knew in our early years in Las Vegas. Carolyn would often play at his table after we had gone to dinner on my Dad's $25. His name was Bob Butler, and I had helped him with some financial problems by filing a bankruptcy petition for him.

One day while Butler was working, the phone rang. The pit boss answered it and then cupped his hand over the receiver and asked everyone, "Who's the best criminal defense attorney in Las Vegas?"

Butler thought of me. "I don't know if he practices criminal law, but Oscar Goodman's a great guy," he said.

The pit boss got back on the phone and told the caller, "Oscar Goodman is the best criminal defense lawyer in town."

Little did I know I was about to take my first step toward becoming a mob lawyer.

The caller was Mel Horowitz, who I didn't know from Adam. He was a major underworld figure supposedly involved in pornography, which was a big mob money-maker back in the 1960s. He had a vast bookmaking operation in the Northeast and

Canada, and he moved around in the best of mob circles. He knew people like Meyer Lansky, who the FBI said was the financial genius behind the national crime syndicate; Raymond Patriarca, the Mafia boss who oversaw all organized crime in New England; and Fat Tony Salerno, who was head of the Genovese crime family in New York, the family originally headed by the late Charles "Lucky" Luciano, who with Lansky had set up the national organization. These were heavyweights in a world where I was clearly a novice.

Horowitz's stepbrother had been arrested in Las Vegas driving a stolen car. He needed a lawyer. The case was pretty much open-and-shut; there wasn't much of a defense. The car was stolen, and he was driving it. He had crossed several state lines, which was a federal offense.

I got a call and was told to go to an address on South Fifteenth Street. I was so nervous that I accepted Carolyn's suggestion that she drive me—very brave of me. I knocked on the door, and the guy who answered handed me an envelope.

"There's three dimes in there, kid," he said in a hoarse, gruff voice. "You'd better win the case."

I didn't know it at the time, but the fellow who handed me the envelope was Bob Martin, probably the most astute odds maker in the whole country. He set the sports line that everyone in the world followed. Apparently he was tight with Horowitz.

I returned to the car, and as Carolyn drove around the corner, I opened the envelope. I had never seen so much money at one time in my life. Three dimes is street talk for three thousand dollars; thirty one-hundred-dollar bills. That was a fortune to me.

This was my first federal case, which was held at the old federal courthouse on Stewart Street. To be honest, I had no idea what I was going to do for a defense.

The case was set for February 14, Valentine's Day. I didn't want it to turn into another massacre. Horowitz flew into town to meet me the night before the trial was to begin. He came to my office with Bob Martin. One look, and I immediately understood why friends referred to Horowitz as "the Professor." He looked like an Ivy League academician, impeccably dressed. Nothing flashy. No one wore an overcoat in Las Vegas, but Horowitz wore a Chesterfield and a Homburg. And when he spoke, he sounded like a teacher. He would pause to make a point, and everything he said had a purpose. During the meeting, they reminded me again how important it was for me to win the case.

"He's my brother," Horowitz said.

"No problem," I replied, again not having any idea what I was going to do.

I was a nervous wreck that night. I couldn't sleep. The bed was soaked with sweat, at least on my side. When I went to the courthouse very early the next morning, I saw the judge's secretary and said I wanted to have a non-jury trial. I figured I had a better shot trying to talk my way around things without a jury. But she told me the judge had summoned a jury panel for the trial, and the case would start at 9 A.M. I panicked. I went outside and threw up on the courthouse steps—interestingly enough, now the site of the Mob Museum. The client was the brother of some underworld big shot, and I was told again and again that I had to win it.

The case wasn't complicated. The prosecution called two witnesses, the owner of the stolen car and the cop who arrested the younger Horowitz behind the wheel of the vehicle. I did something I don't do very often: I put my client on the stand, as well as his friend who was a passenger in the car at the time of the arrest. I had them both dressed like prep school kids, with rep ties, white shirts, blue blazers, and khakis. Each told a story about having borrowed the car. The prosecution witnesses, the car owner, and the cop, contradicted their testimony. That was the entire case, which lasted only one day. The bottom line was whether the jury chose to believe the boys or the prosecutor's witnesses.

We left the courthouse after closing arguments that afternoon and walked back to my office.

"Is it better when the jury comes back with a quick verdict, or is it better when they're out for a long time?" my client asked me.

"The quicker they return, the worse it usually is for the defense," I said.

Twenty minutes later, we got back to the office and the phone was ringing.

The jury had a verdict. I figured this can't be good.

We hustled back to the courthouse.

When they announced their decision, I couldn't believe it: Not guilty. Either the jury had enough reasonable doubt to acquit, or they might have just felt sorry for me. I could have tried that case a thousand times and would have lost 999 times, even with experience.

I didn't think I had a shot, but we won. Better lucky than good—*bashert!*

And that's how I became a mob lawyer.

CHAPTER 4

PLAYING FAST AND LOOSE

The Horowitz case opened doors for me that I didn't even know existed. Word got out—I don't want to say in the underworld, but my name started to get mentioned in certain circles where guys worked in businesses that required criminal defense representation.

And my phone started to ring.

Life was good and getting better, both in professional terms and on a personal level.

Carolyn and I had tried to start a family, but it just didn't happen. So we decided to go in another direction. We set up an appointment with Catholic Welfare, an agency that dealt in adoption. We met with Sister Margaret and Sister Joseph, two lovely ladies who seemed to take a liking to us. They knew we were Jewish and said they would respect that. They would find children from Jewish birth mothers for us.

In a little less than four years, we adopted four children: Oscar Jr., Ross, Eric, and Cara. No matter how well I did as a lawyer, nothing could ever compare to what those children meant to Carolyn and me.

She was an amazing mother, raising four children who were all under the age of four. The diaper changing and potty training alone were gargantuan tasks. I spent a lot of time out of town on cases, so most of the child rearing fell to her. She'd just tell me, "Go earn." That was my job.

When one of the kids got the chicken pox, she put the other three in bed with him. They all got it, which she knew was inevitable anyway. This just allowed her to deal with it in a compressed time period. Brilliant!

Now is as good a time as any to put this on record: Of all the decisions I've made in my life, and of all the things I've accomplished, nothing compares to marrying Carolyn.

She was a freshman at Bryn Mawr College when I was at Haverford. I had met her roommate at a mixer and the roommate mentioned me to Carolyn. She told her she had met this interesting fellow that she thought Carolyn might like.

It was not love at first sight, at least not from Carolyn's perspective. In fact, she thought I was a conceited jerk. A couple of years later I was at the library at Bryn Mawr doing some research for a paper when I saw her again. I still remember her wearing this short, kilt-like skirt. I think I fell in love with her legs first.

I called her at her dorm. Back in those days there was a pay phone in the "smoker" room of the dormitory lobby. Whoever answered called her and told her who was on the line. As she was walking toward the phone I heard her say, "Not that jerk."

I hung up.

But I wasn't ready to give up yet. She ended up taking a sociology course where I was working as a teacher's assistant. I couldn't take my eyes off her, so I called again. After some bantering back and forth, she finally agreed to go out with me.

That night we stopped at a bar on City Avenue in Philadelphia, and I asked her what she'd like to drink. She said whatever I was having. Ever the sophisticate, I ordered up two boilermakers, a shot of whiskey washed down with a cold beer.

Despite her initial misgivings, we hit it off. That night we stopped by my house and she met my sister Ericka. They liked each other, and I think that's when she started to see me in a different light. She got past my reputation for being somewhat arrogant and cocky and saw who I really was. We started dating, and that was it. We saw each other almost every day.

Once we had gotten serious, she said that if I wanted to marry her, I would have to ask her father for her hand. Dr. Carl Goldmark, Jr., was an imposing man. He was the OB/GYN to the stars at Lenox Hill Hospital in New York City. He was tall, handsome, and very self-assured. And he was not too anxious to give his daughter's hand to some cocky kid from Philadelphia.

Carolyn's mother, Hazel Seligman Goldmark, was from New York as well. She came from a cultured family. Her father, Carolyn's grandfather, was a full professor at Columbia and a noted scholar in the field of economics and taxation. Hazel kind of liked me. Carl, not so much.

We were walking on 75th Street when he asked me how I intended to support his daughter. I said at first I didn't intend to. The plan was for me to go to law school while Carolyn worked.

"You'd better support her in the style to which she's become accustomed," her father told me, "or I'll kick your ass from here to 76th Street."

"If you're big enough," I said.

It was a rocky start, but we got past it. I spent the summer in New York after graduating from Haverford. I stayed in the Goldmarks' home and got a job working as a janitor in a community center in Harlem. Carolyn had a job there, too, working the telephone switchboard.

I got to know her family and they got to know me. Dr. Goldmark had asked us to wait a year before we got married, so we weren't wed until the following summer, after I had finished my first year at the University of Pennsylvania Law School.

Our anniversary is June 6, 1962. Most people of my generation know June 6 as D-Day, the day Allied troops invaded France and the tide began to turn in World War II. But for me, June 6 has a different meaning. I look at it as the best day of my life.

Carolyn is not only my wife, but the person I most admire and trust in the world. She's the only one whose advice I will always listen to. She cuts through the bull. She tells me what she thinks and why. She also knows me better than anyone. And despite that, she apparently loves me.

When the kids were young, we took a trip to Disneyland. Carolyn drove. When we got there, she left me with the four of them while she parked the car. As we stood in line, I suddenly felt petrified that one of them might take off. I spent days dealing with important criminal issues and fighting big legal battles, but I'd never experienced that kind of fear or anxiety.

We were waiting in line. Nothing was happening. Then Carolyn came strolling up after parking the car and said, "What are you doing?"

"Waiting in line," I said.

She looked at me and shook her head.

"Oscar," she said. "This is a bus stop."

Then she pointed in the opposite direction to a sign that said Disneyland.

"The entrance is over there," she said, taking the kids by the hands and leading the way.

Like I said, she loves me.

✳ ✳ ✳

I was much more adept in court. And the more I worked at it, the better I became.

One day I got a call from John DePasquale, a bartender at the Golden Nugget in downtown Las Vegas. He had been indicted in a big federal bookmaking case out of Miami. It was the first national case built around the use of the new wiretap laws, part of the Omnibus Crime Bill of 1968. DePasquale was a minor player, but he had been picked up on some wires and got charged along with some fairly significant bookmakers from other parts of the country.

John was accused of using the phones to provide bookmakers information about the morning betting line. One of the big targets was Little Marty Sklaroff and his father, Jesse, a bar owner in Miami, who had been a major figure in sports betting, too. The feds were very familiar with them. The FBI had put a tap on a public pay phone at the Miami airport that Little Marty used.

Marty, a dapper, well-dressed fella with a huge pompadour, was an associate of Gil "The Brain" Beckley, who at the time was considered the number one bookmaker in the country. Beckley was based in New York City. I visited him there once. He lived in a circular-shaped apartment building on Central Park, and I was struck by the fact that every apartment unit on his floor had a pay phone. Whether each unit was part of his gambling operation was something I didn't bother asking about. There are things that a lawyer doesn't need—or want—to know.

Young Marty was enthralled with Beckley. You could see that he was trying to emulate the Brain in the way he did business. Whenever Beckley was in Miami, they'd go to dinner at Joe's Stone Crab—Beckley would hold court there. He was used to being center stage. The word in the gambling world was that Beckley had sources in the locker rooms of several teams and was able to get inside information that he used to set his betting lines. He did a lot of the complex computations in his head. There were rumors that he had been able to bribe athletes and referees to fix basketball games.

Marty Sklaroff loved those stories and never hesitated to share them with me. I think he saw himself as an up-and-comer in the business. He wanted to be Gil Beckley. There was, of course, a down side to that life and those aspirations. According to most law enforcement reports, Beckley was killed in 1970 because some people in the Patriarca crime family out of New England believed he was cooperating with the FBI. No one knows for sure because Beckley just disappeared. His body has never been found.

In the Miami case, the FBI set up surveillance from a cargo container in which they had cut peepholes. That's how they watched the pay phone. In the middle of this investigation, a couple of airport porters came along and were moving the container. All of a sudden they heard, "Stop! FBI."

The porters took off running, their eyes wide as saucers.

As a result of that phone tap, a dozen major bookmakers must have been indicted. John DePasquale's indictment was returned in Miami. Little Marty was represented by a fine lawyer, Dave Rosen, whose reputation preceded him since he had also represented Meyer Lansky. Dave told Marty to tell John to hire me because Mel Horowitz had told him about my "win" in Las Vegas. I flew down there to represent John at trial.

In reviewing the case, I saw that John was hardly even mentioned in the indictment. He was clearly a small fish in the scheme of things. I argued that he should be granted a severance. I filed a motion saying that he was entitled to be tried based on the evidence against him, and that to stand trial with the other defendants, with all that the government alleged against *them*, would be unfair and would create an undue prejudice. It was a pretty standard severance argument, and in this case I think it was righteous.

After hearing two or three days of evidence without John's name being mentioned, the judge agreed. John headed back home to Las Vegas, and he was severed from the case. Dave Rosen, who took me under his wing, asked me to stick around. I did, but there wasn't much for me to do, so I listened and learned.

* * *

Spending a lot of time around Marty Sklaroff was the beginning of a life lesson for me. It was the first time I was around one of the "fellas" who I came to represent over the years. And I learned that no matter how the government and its handmaiden, the media, came to characterize my clients, putting them in the worst light, the people I represented had redeeming qualities and were worthy of salvation.

Marty told me that when he was a young man, he experimented with drugs and ended up a heroin addict. I had heard how hard it was to get that monkey off your back. He told me firsthand how he did it. He locked himself in a room and made sure no one came in until he broke the addiction. He said it was like a bad case of the flu, but it could be done.

He also was a great father. He gave his daughter a confirmation party at the Fountainebleau Hotel in Miami, to which I was invited. These fellas had the best of everything. Each table offered the best scotch, the best gin, the best rye whiskey; you made your own drinks. His daughter made a speech about her father, how much she loved him and all that he had done for her. I realized there was more to this guy than the prosecution and the FBI were saying. I ended up thinking that way about many of my clients, and that's one of the reasons I worked so hard to defend them.

On a personal level, and there's no point in denying this, I was impressed by the way he and the other guys lived. I told myself that when I gave a party for my daughter, Cara, I wanted it to be just like the one at the Fountainebleau. No expense was spared, the guys were all dressed as if they were going to a fancy wedding, and the women were dripping with diamonds. It was a scene right out of a Damon Runyon short story, "Guys and Dolls," set in Miami.

The cast of characters included a guy named "Wingy," who had one arm shorter than the other; "The Camel," who had a noticeable hump on his back; and "Lefty," which I assumed meant he was a southpaw. This was a world I had never seen before. It was fascinating and seductive, but as I was sitting there enjoying the party, a voice in the back of my head—my wife Carolyn's voice, actually—kept saying, "Don't become your client."

That was something she told me again and again as I got more deeply involved in representing high-profile criminals. "Who would want to live like that?" she would ask. "You have the glamour and the luxury, but you're on the cusp of illegality. That's not who we want to be."

Wiretaps can be devastating—ask any defense attorney who has had to deal with them. The problem is, you're sitting at the table with your client, and the jury members have their headphones on. The next thing you know, they're listening to your guy, in his own words, substantiate the charges against him.

You can't cross-examine a tape, so the best defense is keeping the recording out of the trial, finding a way to get the incriminating evidence ruled inadmissible. To do that, you have to understand the wiretap laws. I became the guru of defense attorneys when it came to the wiretap statutes. I knew them upside down, inside out, and backwards. The DePasquale case was one of my first experiences with an electronic surveillance case, and, as I said, I really didn't do much, other than get my client severed.

But the law works in funny ways sometimes.

The trial in Miami ended with Sklaroff and the others convicted, but my guy walked away. The government never came after him, and I eventually got the charges dropped.

No big deal. In the greater scheme of things, John DePasquale was a small cog, not someone the feds really cared about. In certain circles, however, the bottom line was that I had once again gotten somebody off. That translated to being a wiretap expert, even though John's dismissal had nothing to do with the wiretap aspect of the case. But the word started to spread that the only defendant to beat a big wiretap case was Oscar Goodman's client.

I got a phone call from Rosen, the attorney who befriended me when I was down in Florida. His client, Meyer Lansky, had been indicted along with Morris Lansburgh and Sam Cohen, the owners of the Fountainebleau, for being part of a skimming operation at the Flamingo Hotel-Casino in Las Vegas.

Skimming was a big part of the mob's game when it ran several of the major casinos. It's not a really complicated crime, when you think about it. Anyone in a cash business could understand the principle. In essence, the mobsters owned the casino (although their names never showed up on any papers), and what they were taking by skimming was their own money.

But they took it before the casino's earnings had been reported to state regulators. Of course, money that was reported was subject to taxes. It was the cost of doing business; part of the deal a casino struck with the state in order to be licensed. Simply put, the mobsters who had their hooks into certain casinos wanted their money—or at least a piece of their money—*before* taxes.

This kind of stuff happens every day in the business world. People are always looking to get one over on the tax man. In Las Vegas, at least in mob-controlled Las Vegas casinos, the skims totaled millions of dollars and involved mob families from Chicago, Kansas City, and several other jurisdictions.

When I got the call from Rosen asking me to represent Lansky, I jumped at the chance. This was the number one criminal in the underworld, according to the FBI. He was the financial genius who grew up poor on the Lower East Side of New York City and rose to the top of his chosen field. One of his best friends was Bugsy Siegel. They built the Flamingo, and in doing so turned Las Vegas into the gambling capital of America. Say what you will about Lansky and Siegel, but there's no denying when it came to Las Vegas, they were visionaries.

"Would you be Lansky's local counsel?" Rosen asked.

"You bet."

Once again luck shone on me. I received a handsome retainer from the man reputed to be the financial genius behind organized crime.

As the case moved forward, I sought delays because of Lansky's purported bad health. His Miami doctors said he'd risk death if he traveled to Las Vegas for a court appearance, and that his condition made it impossible for him to withstand the rigors of a trial.

I worked on the case for several months, but I never met Lansky or had a conversation with him. All my contacts were with Rosen, Lansky's primary lawyer, or with Lansky's doctors. Looking back on it now, I realize that it would have been fascinating to sit down and have a discussion with Meyer, but the reality is if that did happen, we would never have talked about his reputation or background. It would have been presumptuous of me to ask him about that, or about any of the people he did business with. It just didn't work that way. As a lawyer for such clients, all you have to know are the facts in the case, and then figure out a way to use them to win an acquittal. In this case, the only thing I really needed to know was his medical condition. Could he withstand the stress of a trial? His doctors said again and again that he could not. That's what I had to work with.

As the trial date came closer and closer, the government prosecutors got more and more frustrated. They had photographs of Lansky walking his puppy on Collins Avenue in Miami Beach.

"Certainly he can't be that sick," they said.

But I kept on presenting medical records to Judge Roger Foley in Las Vegas, and he became more and more convinced that Lansky's condition was very serious. Edward Bennett Williams, the great trial attorney from Washington, and Bill Hundley, Robert Kennedy's right-hand man, were representing the owners of the Fountainebleau. They got a kick out of my driving the prosecutors nuts. The trial came and went. Their clients were convicted, but Meyer Lansky was still walking his dog in Miami.

Finally, Judge Foley said, "Enough is enough," and dismissed the indictment against Meyer. Another "win." This time my client was the biggest name in the criminal underworld.

You can't buy that kind of advertising. Now I started getting more phone calls, from guys in Cleveland, in Chicago, in Detroit. Would I be available to come out and represent them? My practice took off.

This eventually led to my involvement in one of the biggest wiretap cases the U.S. Justice Department had ever brought. And it got me face to face with John Mitchell, the pipe-smoking attorney general of the United States under Richard Nixon.

I think I was drawn to these wiretap cases because of the fundamental issue that was involved. To overhear a person's words and thoughts through a listening device is clearly a violation of an American's right to privacy, and it's not something that should be handled in a cavalier fashion. The law was supposed to provide safeguards. The idea was that a wiretap was an investigative tool of last resort. When all else failed—when there was no other way to get the information and when the case was of significance—then, and only then, could a judge be asked to consider approving a wiretap on a phone. Only then would investigators be allowed to listen in on private conversations.

That was the theory of the law, but the practice was something else. FBI agents would file sworn affidavits seeking wiretap orders, and judges would rubber-stamp them. Instead of being an investigative tool of last resort, wiretaps became the opening salvo in building a case, and thus the feds became Orwell's "Big Brother." The government got to enter our homes and listen to our conversations, and this was usually based on the caprice of FBI agents who were only interested in building a case.

In 1970, the FBI conducted a series of raids targeting a national bookmaking operation with supposed ties to organized crime. Mitchell, the attorney general, bragged that these were the "largest coordinated gambling raids ever." They took part in eleven different states and in twenty-six different cities, including Las Vegas.

Marty Kane, one of the most successful sports bettors in Vegas, asked me to get involved on behalf of a friend of his, Frank "Lefty" Rosenthal. Rosenthal had been indicted as the result of a wiretap that had been placed on a phone used in connection with the race and sports book in Las Vegas. He had a reputation as being one of the sharpest gamblers ever.

Marty Kane was old-school like Bob Martin and Mel Horowitz. Everybody who was anybody in the gambling business knew he was tops in the field. His opinions on how a game would turn out could, and usually did, change the betting line substantially. This is no small thing in the bookmaking business. As someone who likes to bet sports, I appreciated what that meant.

They called Kane "Marty the Jew." He had friends like Marty Sklaroff in Miami and Gil Beckley in New York. By this point I was starting to get a sense of who some of these people were. These were the major players in the sports betting world, a world that fascinated me long before I became a lawyer and that provided me with clients through my entire legal career.

I genuinely liked Marty. He was a little gruff, but we spoke the same language, especially when it came to sports betting. I was fascinated with what he did, and how he was able to do it. Marty was a little portly, and he had permanent dark circles around his eyes, which made him look like a woeful raccoon. But he was an educated guy. I think he had a degree in journalism, of all things, from New York University.

He used to hang out with some of my other clients, guys like gamblers Ruby Goldstein, Joey Boston, and Frank Rosenthal. Marty, Ruby, and Joey were major players in the sports betting business. They would work at it all day long, booking and betting and setting the lines. They knew more about sports than the athletes who played the game or the businessmen who owned the teams. I loved watching them operate. It was a skill that few people had, and that even fewer people appreciated. As someone who loved to bet, I felt I was in the presence of genius.

Marty had asked me to represent him in a case a few years earlier, and it turned out pretty well. He had been indicted in Mineola, New York, and for two years we fought extradition. There was no way I was going to let him go back there to face gambling charges. They were trying to tie him to a $100-million-a-year illegal sports betting operation with alleged mob ties. Mike O'Callaghan was the governor of Nevada at the time. He listened to my pleas on Marty's behalf and refused to sign the order that would have required Marty to surrender in New York. I threw up every roadblock I could think of and sparred with the prosecutors back there over every issue. I didn't give an inch. Finally, I think they knew they were going nowhere fast and just got tired. So they proposed a deal.

The New York district attorney, Bill Cahn, from Nassau County, came out to Las Vegas. We didn't get along. In fact, we ended up getting into a pushing match in the law library. But a deal's a deal, and he kept his word.

He said, "Here's the New York penal code. Pick a crime and we'll let your guy plead out." I picked walking a dog without a leash on the streets of New York. Marty paid a fine of $50 and beat the $100 million bookmaking case.

I've never been a good winner. I crowed about the victory, putting my thumb on my big nose and wiggling my fingers at the New York D.A.

When the big bookmaking case dropped, Marty asked for my help for some of his friends who had heard about our victory. It was another case built around wiretaps, and by now I had a reputation for knowing how to defend those kinds of cases. So I signed on and got involved with Lefty Rosenthal.

Marty said that Frank—no one who knew him called him "Lefty"—was facing serious charges, and it would be a feather in my cap if I was his lawyer.

The feds had made these kinds of cases into the essence of their war on organized crime. Almost every defendant's name, aside from Rosenthal, ended in a vowel. I know we're not talking model citizens here, but the government's targets in reality were just bookmakers. And the Justice Department was using the wiretap statutes to bring them down.

The allegation was that all the defendants were using telephones to receive information and place or accept bets. The phone calls were from one state to another, making the communications a form of interstate commerce and creating a violation of federal law.

There were twenty-six cities where these electronic surveillances had led to indictments, and defendants hired me in nineteen of those cities. I went all over the country for preliminary hearings. A lot of the legal arguments that prosecutors used to get wiretap orders were boilerplate. But in order to comply with the law, Mitchell, or one of his nine top assistants, had to personally sign the authorization requests. That was the only way they could be valid.

If I had had just one client, instead of nineteen clients with nineteen separate case files, I never would have found the legal jackpot that I did. I was sitting in a hotel room one night in Detroit with one of my clients going over some documents. There were papers from nineteen different cases strewn about the room, and he started rummaging through them. After a while, he said to me, "Oscar, this doesn't look right."

Since I was preparing for court the next day, I was only listening with one ear, but he persisted.

"You gotta look at this," he said. "They're the same name, but different signatures. One doesn't look like the other."

I started to compare one city's paperwork to another city's paperwork.

My client was talking about the signature of a guy named Will Wilson, the assistant attorney general in charge of the Criminal Division and one of Mitchell's top assistants. And his "signatures" on the authorizations were strikingly different. We started to check the other documents from the other cases, and we found more discrepancies. The feds were just playing fast and loose with the wiretap rules. Apparently, it didn't matter to them.

I ended up deposing John Mitchell. I brought him to my friend Byron Fox's law office in Kansas City. Byron had a co-defendant in a wiretap case in which one of my clients, Nick Civella, was involved. Mitchell sat down with his pipe and I questioned him. Under oath he admitted it wasn't his signature on any of the documents, and that it wasn't Will Wilson's signature either. It turned out that one of Wilson's assistants had signed his name on all the paperwork.

None of the authorizations were signed by the appropriate official. We filed motions to suppress in all nineteen cities, and every case was thrown out. Every defendant in every city walked. And with that, my "legend" grew: apparently I couldn't lose a case.

Now here's my question—and unfortunately, I could ask this in almost every case I was ever involved in: Was anybody in government penalized for breaking the law, for perpetrating a fraud to get judges to sign orders for wiretaps? Was anybody held accountable?

Maybe Mitchell was punished enough being married to Martha, but what about the others?

If a defense attorney violated a criminal statute in that way, there would be Bar Association actions and possible criminal charges. But time and again, it's been the same old story: the government disregards the rules and nothing happens.

There was a mob case in Philadelphia where the government had a videotape of several gangsters meeting on the boardwalk in Atlantic City outside the Resorts International Casino-Hotel. One of the gangsters was Nicky "The Crow" Caramandi. He became a government informant and testified in a half dozen cases.

Caramandi was a consummate con man who became a hit man for the Philadelphia crime family in the 1980s. They called him "The Crow," he said, because "a crow is a shrewd bird." He was always getting one over on people, scamming them out of their money. But I think his ultimate scam was getting a deal with the government. He ended up doing less than five years after admitting to his involvement in four gangland homicides.

The prosecutors paraded him at almost every mob trial in Philadelphia in the late 1980s. I got to know him from the witness stand. He was the typical government witness, willing to say whatever it was the prosecution needed to make its case. And it seemed like they used that stinking videotape from Atlantic City every time he was on the stand.

There he was, on the boardwalk, meeting with the mob boss, Nicodemo "Little Nicky" Scarfo and two other gangsters. There was no audio of the meeting. And in every case the government had Caramandi, under oath, tell a different version of what was being discussed; a version that fit with the prosecution's theory of that particular trial. They used the same video, but in one case they're talking about whacking *this* guy, and in another case they're talking about whacking *that* guy.

It was outrageous!

FBI agents used their informants as puppets and made them say anything they wanted. It was like a sinister courtroom version of *Sesame Street*. The witnesses were like Oscar the Grouch or Kermit the Frog. The prosecutors and the FBI were out of sight, manipulating the characters behind the scenes, literally putting words in their mouths.

During my closing arguments to the jury, I would try to make that point by creating my own "puppet." I'd take a black magic marker and draw two eyes on the fleshy part of my left hand above my thumb and index finger. Then I'd use a red marker to draw a mouth. I'd hold my hand up, with the eyes and mouth facing the jury, and I'd play the role of the prosecutor. I'd tell the jury this is what they've heard. I'd pretend to be a courtroom ventriloquist. I'd ask my hand questions and then respond with an answer favorable to the government. It was a show-and-tell way to make the point.

Prosecutors would roll their eyes, but I didn't care. The government used the same techniques and offered the same justifications for what they did in almost every trial.

I've cross-examined numerous FBI agents about the way they debrief cooperating witnesses and record that information. Every time it's the same mind-boggling story. Agents are required to file a memo after every debriefing session with a cooperator. The report is a written synopsis of what was discussed. It's called a "302" because that's the filing number that the FBI uses to designate this type of memo. Agents swear by those memos, sometimes to the point of absurdity.

When I cross-examine an agent about a 302, my line of questioning usually goes like this:

"When you did this interview, did you have a tape recorder?"

"No."

"Did you have access to a tape recorder?"

"Yes, I did."

"Wouldn't it have been more accurate to record the witness's statement verbatim, rather than simply jot down some notes?"

"No."

"No? Wouldn't a tape recording have more accurately reflected what the witness said?"

"No, the 302 is more accurate."

I just shook my head in amazement. I wondered if some of these agents really believed what they said, or if they had just been brainwashed to resort to that statement whenever they were on the witness stand.

The 302 memo let the agent shape the witness's statement to fit the government's theory of the case. The witness got to review that memo before he was called to testify, so at the end of the day, everyone—the prosecutor, the investigating agent, and the witness—were on the same page.

It may not have been the truth, but it was consistent. And unfortunately, in many cases that was all the government cared about.

John Mitchell sat smugly puffing on his pipe while I deposed him and shamelessly acknowledged that his office had violated the requirements of the federal wiretap law. But he didn't seem to care, and neither did anyone else.

You could make the argument that I got more than a dozen major organized crime figures off the hook in that case. That certainly was the government's reaction when we had everything thrown out. They said, "Oscar Goodman won on a technicality."

This cavalier attitude and the lack of any penalties for prosecutorial misconduct came into play again and again, but it was never more dramatically illustrated than in the case of Manny Baker.

Manny lived in the "'hood" in Las Vegas. Everyone knew his house; it was the one with the surveillance cameras outside and a couple of Caddies parked in the driveway. Law enforcement described Manny as a kingpin heroin dealer. He might have been, but the cops still had to make the case.

Manny's appearance wasn't impressive; he dressed as if he were out for a casual stroll on a sunny day. He wore brightly colored Hawaiian shirts that hung loosely over the baggy trousers that were part of his regular outfit. And he loved to wear boots, usually white boots made out of the skin of a snake or an ostrich. He was relaxed and casual, never in a hurry. If you didn't know he was on his way to court, you'd think he was going fishing.

He tended to mumble when he spoke, but if I listened, I was always able to understand what he was saying. You wouldn't know it to look at him, but he was one of my savviest clients. He was street-smart. As soon as he opened his mouth, you realized that. And he was good at playing the game. He loved to go fishing, and he used his boat to thumb his nose at law enforcement, christening it "Catch Me If You Can."

I got involved with Manny after some state troopers down in Texarkana, Arkansas, thought they had done just that. They had staked out the airport there after getting a tip that Manny had a load of drugs come up from Mexico. They had the airport under surveillance and even knew the supposed pick-up point. They saw Manny being handed a bag and watched as he walked back to his car, which was parked by the curb. After a series of events, Manny was arrested and brought back to Las Vegas to stand trial, and that was when he hired me.

I filed a motion to suppress the evidence seized during the search at the airport, arguing that it was the fruit of a violation of the Fourth Amendment's guarantee against unreasonable searches and seizures. At a hearing before Judge Roger Hunt, I moved to exclude witnesses from the courtroom so that they wouldn't hear the testimony of other witnesses. Three big redneck guys got up and went out into the hallway. The prosecutor called a fourth, just as big and with a neck just as red, to the stand, where he took the oath.

He identified himself as a state trooper and said he had gotten a tip that a drug deal was going to go down at the airport. He said that he and the other three who had just left the courtroom went to the Texarkana Airport and approached a car that they saw parked at the curb.

"That gentleman," he said, pointing to Manny, "was behind the wheel."

I have to believe it was one of the first, and maybe the only time someone in law enforcement referred to Manny Baker as a gentleman.

"What happened next?" asked the prosecutor.

"We asked him to step out of the car."

"What happened next?"

"He said 'Certainly,' and stepped out."

That didn't sound like Manny to me.

"What happened next?"

"We asked him whether we could retrieve the key from the ignition."

"What happened next?"

"He said 'Certainly,' and we removed the key."

At that point, Manny poked me in the ribs with his elbow and whispered, "Mister Goodman, they lyin'.'"

I said, "Shhh," but Manny kept saying, "They lyin'. They lyin'.'"

"What happened next?" continued the prosecutor.

"We asked whether we could open the trunk, and Mister Baker said, 'Yes.'"

"They lyin', Mister Goodman," Manny said yet again.

"And then?"

"We opened the trunk and saw a bag. We asked Mister Baker for permission to open the bag."

"He lyin'."

"Manny, be quiet," I said.

"What happened next?"

"After receiving Mister Baker's permission, we opened the bag and saw what looked like over $150,000 in twenty-dollar bills. We placed him under arrest."

Next witness. A second fat redneck took the stand, and by God, his testimony was virtually verbatim of what the first witness had said.

"They lyin', Mister Goodman," Manny said once again.

Next witness, a third fat redneck, told the same story all over again.

Finally, I looked at Manny and said, "Three white cops swearing to tell the truth against a black heroin dealer. Who's going to believe you?"

The fourth cop came in and offered more of the same testimony.

"They all lyin'," Manny said. "The people in the van will tell you."

"What van, Manny?" I said.

"You know, the one that picks up the pilot and crew after the plane lands."

"You saw them?" I asked.

"Yeah. And I'm sure they saw what happened."

With that, I asked the judge for a two-day continuance. He wanted to know why. I said I wanted time to research something that my client had come up with that might be very important. The judge granted the request, but only until the following afternoon.

There was an audible groan from the courtroom. The prosecutor had stacked the room with people from his office. This was a tactic I've seen often at hearings. It's a not-so-subtle way to put the judge on notice, an attempt to intimidate him. But Judge Hunt wasn't the kind of guy to be intimidated by that kind of petty ruse.

I rushed back to my office and called Vinnie Montalto, who worked on wiretap cases for me and who listened to the tapes. I asked him to find out the airline, the flight number, and the name of the pilot whose plane Manny was waiting for at the Texarkana Airport. About an hour later, Vinnie reported back: mission accomplished.

The airline was Golden Eagle. I called the pilot, who lived in San Francisco. I introduced myself and asked him if he had seen what had happened. He said he had and told me the story. I told him to fly to Vegas and charge his ticket to me. I would get him a room and if he brought a friend with him, I'd buy them dinner at one of the best restaurants in town. The next day, the pilot joined me in court.

I put him on the stand. He took the same oath the cops had. After some preliminary questions, I said, "Tell the judge what you saw."

"It was like *Miami Vice,*" he said. "These four cops stormed the guy over there," he continued, pointing to Manny. "They ran with their guns drawn, ripped him out of his car, threw him on the ground, cuffed him, put guns to his head. One of them kicked him while he was on the ground.

"Then another one took the keys out of the car ignition and opened the trunk. He pulled out a valise, which he opened and then screamed, 'Jackpot!' It was like the Gestapo. I never saw anybody brutalized that way."

Judge Hunt looked at the prosecutor, expecting him to do the right thing, to concede my motion to suppress. But all the prosecutor said was that his office intended "to investigate Mister Goodman for bribing this witness."

With that, Judge Hunt threw out the evidence.

A technicality? No. It was the Fourth Amendment of the United States Constitution.

Manny Baker was right. They were lying pieces of shit. Was anything ever done to those cops to deter that from ever happening again? You probably know the answer to that question.

PART TWO
GOODFELLAS

CHAPTER 5
THE BLACK BOOK

The waiting room in my law office had become a legalistic melting pot. Clients from many different backgrounds would spend time there waiting to speak with me. Some were alleged Mafia bosses and capos. There was also an oral surgeon indicted for sexually molesting seven patients while they were under the influence of an anesthetic "cocktail," a federal judge accused of accepting a bribe from a pimp and whoremonger, and a suspected drug dealer charged with having a judge in Texas assassinated.

Then there was Bobby Kay, perhaps my smallest client. Bobby was a little person, but he was a big player in the gambling world. He used to hang outside one of the bookie joints in town and transmit information about betting lines and wagers to gamblers throughout the country. He used a pay phone outside one of the betting parlors. He was so short, he had to jump up to drop a dime in the slot before he could make the call.

He was a real operator with a great sense of humor. He would often joke about his stature. One of his favorite lines was that while many of the guys he knew took the fifth (the Fifth Amendment against self-incrimination) and refused to testify when called before a federal grand jury, because of his size, he couldn't do that.

When I asked why, he replied, "I had to take the two and a half."

I guess you could say I had it all—the short and tall, the alpha and omega of criminal jurisprudence.

I never had a problem accepting these cases. We had a saying in my office, "Where there's a fee, there's a remedy." There was more to practicing law than that, of course, but my practice was also my business. It was the way I supported my family. I didn't bring moral judgments into my decisions about accepting cases or defending clients. I was providing a service, and they were willing to pay for it. I was also honoring the Constitution. For me, it was a win-win.

These were all high-profile cases. They kept me busy and, unfortunately, often kept me away from home. Carolyn and I had developed a routine, however, that seemed to work.

Growing up, I don't think our kids had any real concept of what kind of criminal law I was practicing. And that's probably as it should be. When I had a big case out of town, I would usually leave on a Sunday night and return Friday evening. For my kids, that was just Daddy's job.

On Sundays Carolyn would cook breakfast, and everyone got their favorite. Pancakes. Eggs. Cereal. Even hot dogs and spaghetti, which was Eric's choice. I'd be gone all week, so Carolyn had the responsibility for the kids. I've said this before, but I can't say it enough: she did an outstanding job. I would convince myself that I was providing quality time with my family, rather than quantitative time. That was the reality of my work schedule.

I'd come back home on Friday nights and Carolyn would pick me up at the airport. She'd have a babysitter at the house and we'd go out to dinner, usually to The Bootlegger, a local pizzeria. It was a date night for us, and in some ways that hectic schedule kept the spark going in our marriage. We made the best of the time we had together.

Saturdays were always devoted to the kids. I went to soccer games, viola recitals, plays, whatever they had going. Then we'd all go out to dinner together. Even when they were young, we took them out. They were all well behaved—again, thanks to their mother's influence—and we never hesitated to bring them to a nice restaurant, never worried about them acting up or causing problems that might upset other customers.

After dinner on Saturday night we'd head home, put the kids to bed, and just relax. I'd usually have a martini or two. Carolyn might join me. Then Sunday morning we'd get up and start the routine all over again.

Sometimes the kids might meet one of my clients, and without exception, the clients always went out of their way to make the kids feel comfortable. I think they got a kick out of them. My clients were seeing a different side of me, and I think it made my job easier. They knew I was more than just a mouthpiece looking for a legal fee.

Chris Petti, supposedly the mob's guy in San Diego, used to refer to the boys as "Huey, Louie, and Dewey," the Disney duck characters. Kansas City mob boss Nick Civella called Oscar Jr. "Grunt" because the first time he met my oldest son, he was just a baby. We were at the Venetian restaurant eating dinner and Oscar was napping. He was grunting as he slept, and Nick always remembered that.

Joe Blasko, a rogue Metropolitan police officer in Las Vegas who got tied up with the mob, taught my son Ross how to pitch. Joe had played minor league baseball before taking his life in another direction. Jack Binion, the son of legendary casino owner Benny Binion, once took my son Eric on a three-day ski trip.

All my clients and friends were great with my children, and I think they and the kids all benefited from the relationship. I had degrees and higher education, but I still learned a lot from my clients.

Prosecutors and FBI agents might label them criminals.

I saw them as people.

* * *

There was one client, however, who had an influence on me like no other—Tony Spilotro.

Talk to the feds and they'll tell you "Tony the Ant" was sent to Las Vegas by the guys who run the Chicago Outfit. He was there to look out for their interests. His background, from the resume the FBI put together, included nearly two dozen murders. One particularly gruesome killing allegedly involved placing his victim's head in a vise and tightened it until the guy's eye popped out, not to mention part of his brain matter.

That was Tony's rep, although I didn't know any of that when he walked into my office one day and asked me to go over one of his contracts. Tony had purchased a gift shop at Circus Circus from a guy named Willie Cohen. Willie was friends with Jack Gordon, who later married La Toya Jackson, Michael Jackson's sister. I have her photograph in my office, autographed "La Toya Gordon."

I had represented Jack Gordon in a prostitution case in California. He had some massage parlors there, and he also had one of those shops where you could get a quick oil change for your car. Turns out if you used your credit card at the massage parlor, it would show up as an oil change. I guess that gave new meaning to the term "lube job."

When Spilotro took over the gift shop, he changed its name to "Anthony Stuart's." Stuart was his wife Nancy's maiden name. It was a legitimate business as far as I could tell, and the contract was strictly on the up-and-up.

Tony showed up at my office dressed very professionally in a jacket and tie. I looked over his paperwork. The meeting only lasted fifteen minutes. To me it was not a big deal, but people in law enforcement were watching Tony's every move. This was just the start of a ten-year run where it seemed like every day I was fighting some battle on his behalf.

The gaming regulators were putting pressure on Jay Sarno, the owner of Circus Circus. They told him he had to get Spilotro out of the place or Sarno would lose his casino license.

Sarno was a visionary. Prior to Circus Circus, he created Caesars Palace, and probably had as much to do with shaping the modern theme-oriented Las Vegas as Steve Wynn or Howard Hughes. But he also was a libertine in his tastes and habits. He was a gourmand. He ate, womanized, and gambled to excess. He always wanted more. And as a client, he wouldn't listen.

I had represented Sarno in a bribery case that was a clear case of entrapment by the IRS. We beat it, but it was a struggle— not because of the evidence, but because of my client. He and I were constantly banging heads during the trial. He tried to tell me what questions to ask and how to cross-examine witnesses. I guess he was just used to being in charge. He would get angry and red in the face and start to sweat, and when he did, his toupee would start to slide off his head. Several jurors noticed and couldn't help themselves. They started to laugh. Maybe that helped us in deliberations; you never know. Maybe they felt sorry for him.

Because of his experience in that case, I knew that Sarno was leery of law enforcement. It's a shame that an individual has to feel that way. Most citizens never come in contact with the law, and they have this image of G-men as upstanding, honest, and all for God and country. A lot of agents are like that, I'm sure. But many of the ones I had to deal with were cut from a different cloth.

Sarno was a creative genius, but he still had to deal with the pettiness of the state gaming regulators. When they threatened his license because of Tony Spilotro's gift shop, Sarno had no choice but to buy him out. I think Tony paid $70,000 for the gift shop, and I believe Sarno had to pay $700,000 to buy him out. Not a bad profit for Tony. For me, it was the start of a fascinating relationship.

While I was representing Tony, he was a target of the Federal Organized Crime Strike Force, the Justice Department, the FBI, the IRS, the Metropolitan Police Department, Nevada gaming regulators, and the media. It seemed to be a tacit conspiracy in which they literally "created" this nefarious organized crime figure, this hit man and extortionist who wielded unbelievable power in an underworld that stretched from Chicago to Las Vegas. At least that was their version of who Tony was. That they couldn't prove any of this didn't seem to matter. As a result, Tony's problems became a big part of my criminal practice. Indictments, grand jury appearances, Gaming Control Board and Commission hearings, searches and seizures gave me a forum to litigate serious constitutional issues in courts and other legal forums.

In addition to my formal representation, and because of the extensive media attention, I became his "mouthpiece," attempting to temper the animus leveled against him by the pundits in the press and on TV.

Representing Tony Spilotro catapulted me to a whole different level in the practice of criminal law. For the first time, everything I did became personal. To my opponents I was the Prince of Darkness, the anti-Christ. From my perspective, they were suborners, liars, and anti-American. It was war, and I had to win it—not only for Tony Spilotro, and not only for myself. The real issue underlying almost every battle I fought for Tony was whether the U.S. Constitution was going to remain intact and stand inviolate. That's the way I saw it, and that's why I gave no quarter in any of the battles I fought.

My problem with law enforcement doesn't have anything to do with the law. It has to do with some of the people whose job it was to enforce the law. I don't like crusaders and true believers; I find them self-righteous and intolerant. I think they abuse the criminal justice system and undermine the Constitution.

Nobody better exemplified that than Special Agent in Charge Joseph Yablonsky. Don't you love those titles? He was sent to Las Vegas in 1980 to head the FBI office. He had previously worked in Cincinnati, among other places, and when he arrived he made no secret of his agenda. In his mind, Las Vegas was Sin City, and he was going to change it. He told some people that he intended to plant the American flag in the Nevada desert. Clearly he was a crusader, but he didn't care about the rules of law. He said he intended to get a white-haired senator, a little mobster, and a federal judge. That would be Paul Laxalt, one of President Ronald Reagan's best friends; Tony Spilotro; and Harry Claiborne. In the cases of Tony and Harry, I was the guy Yablonsky had to deal with.

I hope it wasn't a pleasant experience for him.

Tony Spilotro got to Las Vegas a few years before Yablonsky. He came to my office that first time because some of the people I had represented in gambling and wiretap cases recommended him to me. They called him "the little guy" or "the ant" because of his diminutive height. He was only about five-foot-five. But they never called him those names to his face. His name conjured up respect among a certain group of people who knew him, and among others, it instilled fear.

After selling the gift shop at Circus Circus, Tony opened a jewelry store called The Gold Rush and continued to receive lots of bad press.

Yablonsky and the crew he set loose to get Tony were only interested in making cases. Justice and truth weren't of any consequence. The more I got involved with Tony, the more I saw how the system worked, and I was sickened by it. Yablonsky had built a reputation in the FBI working and supervising undercover operations. He considered himself the "king of sting" and brought that same approach to Las Vegas.

He sent agents in to entrap and harass any and all who associated with Tony. I was no exception, and found myself targeted by an FBI undercover agent who sat across the desk from me in my law office and told me a tale of being threatened by the FBI if he didn't cooperate with them to "get" Tony.

Tony knew the guy as Rick Calise, but his real name was Rick Baken. He had gotten close to Tony. It was a classic FBI undercover operation; Calise was supposedly in the "diamond business" and started hanging around The Gold Rush, the jewelry store Tony had opened.

Now Calise came to my office with Tony and laid out this story about how the FBI had come to him and warned him that Tony was going to have him killed. They said that unless he cooperated against Tony, he was going to be indicted and would face serious charges. It was all bullshit, of course, but we didn't know it at the time.

"What should I do?" he asked, holding up a *Time* magazine cover that featured a picture of a gun and the screaming one-word headline, "MAFIA."

"Tell him what to do, Oscar," Tony said.

I shook my head.

"Fellas, there's no way I can give advice here," I said. "There's an inherent conflict of interest. I represent Tony." I looked right at Calise and said, "And the feds want you to help them get Tony. You need an independent lawyer to advise you. Do you have one?"

"No," he said.

"Would you like me to recommend one?"

"Yes."

With that, I gave him the names of three of the best attorneys I knew—ethical, tough advocates. I told him any one of them would be able to properly counsel him. I would find out a little while later that he left the office and ran to his FBI supervisors, telling them I was trying to obstruct justice. Either he was lying or just plain dumb. I think it might have been a combination of the two.

I got a phone call from the Strike Force attorney who was working with the undercover agent. He told me that if anything happened to the undercover—this is how we learned the guy was an agent—they'd hold me responsible. I went nuts.

"I'm not a fucking insurer," I screamed into the phone, "and I sure hope the bastard had a wire on him to record our conversation."

Thank God, he did. But that's the way these guys operated. Half-truths, entrapment, make it up as you go along—those were the rules of engagement in the war I was fighting.

I had been through this before. A few years earlier, Lewis "Brown" Crockett, the drug dealer whose charges were dropped in the murder case I had defended him in, came to my office unannounced. I hadn't seen him in a long time. We sat down and started chatting, but then Crockett went off. He started to talk about how he needed money, and could I invest in this venture he was involved in, and on and on. I knew right away that this was a setup, and I told him as much. He finally admitted he had gotten jammed up in another drug case and was trying to work out his own problem by cooperating. The police wanted him to set me up in a drug deal.

I told him to get out of my office. I never saw him again.

✳ ✳ ✳

The Black Book, the casino exclusion list, is another example of government abuse.

Several of my clients, including Tony Spilotro, ended up on the list and in the book. There's almost no way to defend against an allegation that doesn't have to be proven. Tony's reputation was what got him excluded, and there were dozens of others just like him. And it was no coincidence that most of those names in the Black Book ended in vowels. This was a government vendetta: keep the mob out of Las Vegas. Meanwhile, they weren't doing anything about the rampant street crime.

The media, of course, loved all of this hype. Reporters jumped on each action and allegation by any law enforcement agency. In many instances, they ignored or gave short shrift to what was really happening, and instead editorialized the event. Tony, it seemed, was the suspect in every unsolved murder in town. The myth took on the patina of truth. The gore sold papers and drove viewers to the evening news, where commentators pontificated. There were the M&M murders in Chicago, two alleged mobsters whose names started with "M" and who were tortured and killed. There was Danny Seifert, a potential witness blown away in front of his young son so he wouldn't testify in court. There was Tamara Rand, who purportedly loaned money to Allen Glick, the alleged front man for the mob-controlled Stardust casino. Rand was found murdered in her San Diego condo.

There was also a guy called "Action" Jackson who was found dead, hung by a meat hook stuck in his rectum. His knees had been smashed and his genitals had been poked and crushed with a cattle prod before he died. On and on it went. Every sensational murder always resulted in finger-pointing at Tony Spilotro.

The irony was that they could never convict him. I never lost a case representing him. Depending on who was telling the story, I would hear about how he was involved in twenty-two gangland murders, or twenty-six mob hits. If he did all this, then prove it.

If he was the nefarious mobster, then get the evidence and put him in jail. It never happened, but government agencies and the media loved to label him.

There was even a rumor, which I believe law enforcement had started, that Tony once plotted to poison all the members of a grand jury who were hearing evidence in a case the government was trying to build against him. Before an indictment could be handed up, according to the rumor, Tony planned to bribe the chef who prepared lunch for the grand jurors to lace their food with a lethal substance. Someone had a fertile imagination, but the whole thing was ridiculous.

Inclusion in the Black Book was the mark of Cain in the desert: no proof, but punishment nevertheless. After they placed his name in the book, Tony couldn't go in a casino. Not only could he not go in a casino, he couldn't go into any facility that was part of a casino—a restaurant, a bowling alley, a gift shop.

At first the banishment was so broad that anyone on the list was prohibited from going into any licensed gambling establishment. If Tony was driving from Las Vegas to Reno and there was a gas station with five slot machines on a highway out in the desert, Tony wouldn't have been permitted to stop there to use the restroom. I went to court and got that changed, but he still couldn't enter any of the casinos or casino-hotels in town.

I've never understood the rationale of the Black Book concept. It would be different if you said that someone who had been caught cheating at cards, or rigging a dice game, or had been convicted of defrauding a casino was barred from gambling. That would make sense. But what crime had some of these guys committed? Even if you accepted that some of them had criminal records—these were not choirboys, after all—if their crimes had nothing to do with casino gambling, why should they be barred?

Tony's only conviction, despite all these allegations, was for making a false loan application. He was fined one dollar, and the sentencing judge apologized because the case was so ridiculous.

I thought, and still think, that the Black Book is unconstitutional. But that was a battle that I fought and lost. I'd do it all again without a second thought. Those guys on the Gaming Commission thought I was the devil incarnate, but I didn't care.

Once there was a hearing when someone asked Shannon Bybee, who was chairman of the Gaming Control Board, to define organized crime. He said, "Organized crime is anyone who Oscar Goodman represents."

I thought this was a cheap shot, and I think it said more about him than it said about me. He wasn't a particularly bright fellow, but he was holier-than-thou. And it was very disturbing to think that he was calling the shots when it came to the Black Book, and in a position to make moral judgments based on some dime-store-novel-like stories that might have appeared in the media—stories without any evidence to back them up. I thought the whole thing was un-American.

That's the kind of mindset that existed when Spilotro came to Las Vegas. He and the guys around him were constantly under surveillance, either by the FBI or the Intelligence Unit—talk about an oxymoron—of the Metro Police.

A few months ago, I was given a copy of an Intelligence Unit surveillance log from 1979–80. Investigators working for the unit filed these daily reports. What a waste of taxpayers' money! It was just nonsense, following people around, going from casino to casino and reporting who was there. No one was immune from their invasive presence—judges, county commissioners, lawyers, everyday people, and, of course, Tony and anybody with whom he was in contact.

I loved the comments about me.

There was one from January 5, 1980, that read in part: "Pissed off Oscar Goodman." I have no idea what that was about, but on January 25 there was a second notation, "Oscar Goodman still pissed off."

Who gives a shit? This is what law enforcement is about? They were tracking my comings and goings. "Oscar is going to the airport. . . . Oscar is back in town."

When my daughter Cara turned 13, we had her bat mitzvah at a lodge outside of town. I invited everybody—state Supreme Court judges, senators, assemblymen, clients, family members, friends. At the bottom of the hill, Metro Police and the FBI set up surveillance. They took down the license plate numbers of every car heading for the lodge that day. It was ridiculous, like something out of *The Godfather*. And the saddest part was, some of the people I had invited turned away when they saw the authorities. Too bad for them—we had a great time. Tony was there, and so was Joey Cusumano and some of my other reputed wiseguy clients. They weren't worried about anybody taking down their license plate numbers.

FBI agents came up to the lodge and asked whether they could come in. I told them to drop dead.

Joey Cusumano was a really interesting guy. Originally from New York, the feds and the gaming regulators alleged that he was tied to the Chicago Outfit. Naturally, they wanted him excluded from the casinos. I represented him in that fight, but he still ended up in the Black Book.

He had one conviction tied to an alleged insurance scam involving the Culinary Union. I didn't think that proved he was a "career criminal," as the authorities alleged. I also pointed out that Joey had a great resume. He was one of the line producers for the movie *The Cotton Club* and had run a successful restaurant. He moved in circles that had nothing to do with the criminal underworld. He was an avid tennis player and a regular at the Las Vegas Country Club, where he mixed and mingled with the city's movers and shakers.

Why he shouldn't be allowed in the city's casinos was beyond me. I argued that he was targeted because his name ended in a vowel, like many listed in the Black Book, but the authorities didn't want to hear that.

Joey Cusumano never complained about the situation. He fought the fight, lost, and moved on. I appreciated that. He was the reason we held my daughter's bat mitzvah at the lodge and later her engagement party at our home, instead of in one of the casino-hotels. If we had had those events at a casino, Joey couldn't have attended. That's another example of how ridiculous and discriminatory the exclusion law was.

Joey's friendship meant a lot to me, and I wanted him there for those events. He and Tony were more than just clients. And it bothered me to see the way the law was able to abuse them.

Tony and the guys around him were stopped almost every single time a cop saw them in a car. The cops took them out of the car and harassed them. One associate of Tony's, Frankie Bluestein, was killed. He worked at the Hacienda as a maitre d' and was supposedly "with" Spilotro. The Hacienda was one of the casinos that the Chicago Outfit allegedly had an interest in. Bluestein was a thirty-five-year-old hotel worker driving home one night, not speeding or driving erratically. But he got stopped by two Metro detectives, and they shot him dead. They said he got out of his car with a gun in his hand, but that was bullshit. He was holding the keys to his car in his hand and didn't have a gun.

The cops were cowboys; the good guys were the bad guys. The FBI was no different. Yablonsky, their leader, was the kind of guy who would make J. Edgar Hoover roll over in his grave. This wasn't law enforcement; it was harassment. Wherever I went, there was Yablonsky's cigar-chomping ugly face.

He came to Vegas for the wrong reason, and did his job the wrong way. He retired in 1983, and I like to think I had something to do with that. I like to think I helped run him out of town.

He talked about law and order, but at the same time his wife had a business where she was selling shrimp and seafood to the casinos. Do you think the fact that her husband was the Special Agent in Charge of the Las Vegas FBI helped her make any sales? By mistake he received a huge payment from a bank one time. I think it was $40,000. Did he return it? Hell, no; not until it became a big issue three years later.

The FBI and the Organized Crime Strike Force were single-minded in their focus, but they lost sight of what their job was all about. Their brazenness toward Tony pervaded almost everything they did. Once I had a client who had been subpoenaed before a federal grand jury. I took him to the federal building and waited outside the grand jury room. In the hallway, up on the wall, there was a plaque with these caricatures of Nick Civella, one of my clients and the supposed mob boss of Kansas City; Lefty Rosenthal, another one of my clients; and Judge Harry Claiborne, a good friend of mine and one of the best defense lawyers to ever practice in Nevada. Harry was a federal judge at the time, and the Strike Force had a caricature of him as a clown up on the wall. This is what you saw when you were heading into the grand jury room.

It was intimidating and frightening. The message was clear: if you don't play ball and do what these guys want, you're going to end up targeted and your face will be on that wall.

I wasn't going to stand for that, so I did a most unusual thing. I applied as a citizen for a search warrant. Judge Roger Foley approved my application and sent federal marshals in. They took the thing off the wall. I think it was one of the few times—maybe the only time—a federal judge issued a search warrant based on an application from a citizen.

I made the plaque public, figuring what's good for the goose is good for the gander. I wanted people to know how these guys operated. I think it demonstrated the arrogance of the Strike

Force, the FBI, and the pieces of garbage in Washington who backed up everything they did.

* * *

When I first got to Las Vegas, it wasn't like that. The sheriff back then, the guy who headed the Metropolitan Police Department, was Ralph Lamb. He was a throwback to another time. He had been a rancher and a calf roper, a legitimate tough guy. This was his town, and he was the law.

He's now the subject of a television show written by Nicholas Pileggi, in which Dennis Quaid stars as Sheriff Lamb.

One of my favorite clients, Nick Civella, used to sneak into town all the time. Nick just loved Las Vegas. There was a restaurant, the Venetian, that made pork necks in vinegar just the way he liked them. He'd fly out for the food. He didn't care much about gambling, but he loved those pork necks. Sheriff Lamb would have his people waiting at the airport to turn Nick around and send him back.

There were probably two people in my life who should have been living in the days of ancient Rome. One was J. R. Russo from Boston, who I'll talk about a little later. The other was Nick Civella.

Nick was balding with white hair, thick lips, a prominent nose, and eyeglasses as thick as coke bottles. But there was just something about him. When he walked into a room, you got the sense that everyone should stand at attention. He had more street sense than anyone I ever saw.

Nick was intuitive, and he was also very well read in the classics and history. He was an intellectual. If Nick had gotten his hair cut, he could have been the president of IBM or AT&T. He would quote Shakespeare or Cicero. And he was around people who weren't intellectuals, certainly people who weren't going to engage him in an academic discussion. He liked to call me on the phone to talk about these kinds of things; Nick would wax eloquent about the classics. Or if he saw a movie, he would evaluate the script and the acting. We shared mutual interests along those lines. But in his world, people were at least smart enough to know not to mess with him.

Nick wanted me to file a civil rights lawsuit against Sheriff Lamb and the Metropolitan Police because they were denying his access to Las Vegas. I told him that before I did, I wanted to sit down with the sheriff. So I contacted Ralph Lamb and asked if we could meet. He said that he'd be at my law office at 5:30 the next day.

"Fine, I'll see you tomorrow night," I said.

"No," he said. "Five-thirty *in the morning*."

When I got to my office early the next day, he was already waiting at the front door. He walked in and sat down in my chair behind my desk, bigger than life. Before we started talking, he felt around under the desk. I think he was looking for a bug. I told him I had no intention of recording our conversation, and he said neither did he.

We hit it off. He said he didn't want any trouble, and I told him Nick Civella wasn't going to cause any trouble. He just liked those pork necks, and he wanted to come into town without having cops waiting for him at the airport ready to send him home. Nick Civella and Ralph Lamb never met, but they came from the same era. You gave your word and you stuck by it. I promised the sheriff that Nick wouldn't be a problem. And Lamb said as long as that was the case, his people wouldn't stop him from coming.

It was like those old cowboy movies where the sheriff has everybody check their guns when they come into town. That's what Las Vegas was always about, and Ralph Lamb understood that. And I think law enforcement was better served as a result.

Not so with Yablonsky, who was judgmental. Someone who understands and believes in the law doesn't operate the way Yablonsky did. It was as if he "knew" someone was guilty even before he had gathered any evidence. That's not the way the system is set up, but unfortunately, it's the way a lot of these guys operated. It made for great press. Yablonsky kept talking about Spilotro and the mob, but he never built a case against Tony. He used the media to get people excited and to act like he was doing the Lord's work, instead of solving the rapes, murders, and robberies that were taking place. It was easier simply to call people names.

Don't get me wrong: the system is supposed to be adversarial. Not everyone in law enforcement was a bad guy, and not everyone was abusing the system. But too often those in charge were allowing abuses to take place in "the interest of justice."

I didn't see it that way. I defended Tony Spilotro and, over a ten-year period, I was able to ensure that he didn't spend any time in jail because I was able to show that the government wasn't doing its job. When I did that, I saw it as protecting every American from similar abuse.

I can remember the newspaper headlines: "Spilotro says this . . . Spilotro says that." In fact, Tony never said anything. I did all the talking, and he was a great client that way. He let me be his mouthpiece. I genuinely enjoyed the company of guys like Tony and Nick. And the bottom line was that by representing them, I got a chance to keep the system honest.

In law enforcement circles, however, I was perceived as the bad guy. And somebody like Yablonsky, who—it seemed to me— didn't care about the law, was the good guy. That never made sense to me, and it still doesn't.

CHAPTER 6

HEAVYWEIGHTS
I HAVE KNOWN

Two of my favorite sports are baseball and boxing, and my criminal practice offered me opportunities to move in both those worlds.

In 1980, the Phillies played Kansas City in the World Series. Nick Civella, who by that point was one of my major criminal clients, arranged for me and my family to travel to Kansas City to take in a World Series game. The last time the Phillies had played in a World Series was 1950, and before that it was 1915—and they lost both times. So this was a very rare event and one that, as a longtime Phillies fan, I really looked forward to.

In 1964, the year Carolyn and I moved to Las Vegas, the Phillies had suffered one of the greatest all-time collapses in baseball history. They were leading the National League (back then there were no divisions, just a National and an American League) by six and one-half games, with just twelve games to play. Gene Mauch, the "Little General," was a genius manager who looked to bring the Phillies their first National League pennant since the days of the 1950 Whiz Kids. Then the bottom fell out. We were in Las Vegas, following it from a distance, because there wasn't the kind of daily national sports coverage or cable television network coverage that we have today. We would read about it in the paper and follow the sports reports on television and the radio. Still, it was agony, although certainly not as painful as it must have been for those in Philadelphia. Mauch's team lost ten straight games, and the St. Louis Cardinals got red-hot and won the pennant.

Phillies fans like me had been suffering ever since, and now the 1980 team—including Mike Schmidt, Pete Rose, Steve Carlton, Bob Boone—was in the World Series. Finally, we had arrived. So when Nick Civella asked if I wanted to bring my family out for a game, I jumped at the chance.

Carolyn and I and the kids, Oscar Jr., Ross, Eric, and Cara, were at the airport waiting for the plane to Kansas City. It turned out that Tommy Lasorda, the great manager of the Los Angeles Dodgers, and Bill Russell, the team's shortstop, were waiting for the same plane. I sent the kids over to get their autographs. Both men were very nice to the children and we exchanged pleasantries. I think the kids had lost the autographs by the time the plane landed, but that's beside the point. When we were leaving the airport in Kansas City, we ran into Lasorda and Russell again.

Nick Civella had sent a limo to pick us up, and I offered them a ride since they were staying at the same hotel. Tommy Lasorda and I exchanged business cards, and I guess he figured that would be the end of it.

That night we were at the game. We had great seats, front row right behind home plate. At one point I turned around, and about fifteen rows up I saw Lasorda. He was looking at us, and I could tell he was thinking, "Who the hell is this guy?"

After that first encounter, we became friends, and whenever he was in Las Vegas or I was in Los Angeles we would try to touch base. Several years later Carolyn held a charity fundraiser for the Meadows, the school she had founded, and Tommy was in town to help with the event.

The Meadows was entirely Carolyn's idea. She was never one to complain, but when she saw a problem, she'd try to figure out a way to correct it. It was clear to her in the late 1970s that the public school system in Las Vegas was a sure path to nowhere. She didn't think it could be fixed from within, so in 1984 she started her own private school. I was bouncing all over the country at the time representing clients in high profile cases. Our children were in school, although only Cara was young enough to attend the Meadows.

Carolyn started that school with some pre-fab classrooms for kindergarten through sixth grade and ended with a modern, 40-acre campus that is now the home to one of the best prep schools in the state, grades pre-K through 12. She did this as a labor of love and because she valued education for children, and she never took a salary.

At the time of the fundraiser, I was in the middle of a really difficult trial. My client was the previously mentioned oral surgeon who was accused of sexually assaulting patients while they were under anesthesia. The case was being tried in Carson City before Judge Archie Blake, and I could tell he wanted to give my client a zillion years. I couldn't catch one break: none of my motions were granted, and none of my arguments seemed to carry any weight.

But I knew Blake was a really big baseball fan, so I told Carolyn to have Tommy sign two baseballs. One he inscribed, "To Judge Archie Blake, the greatest legal mind of the century." And then I asked him to sign another one for the prosecutor, Noel Waters. Tommy signed it: "To Noel Waters, the fairest prosecutor in the land."

When I went back up to Carson City the next week for the trial to resume, I had both the baseballs with me and I told the judge I wanted to see him.

"I've got a gift for you, your honor," I said.

He was a little standoffish and said, "Wait until Mr. Waters gets here."

I knew he would do that. You couldn't have an ex-parte conversation with one side or the other during a trial. It wouldn't look right. That's why I had Tommy sign a ball for the prosecutor as well.

When Waters got to court that morning, the judge called us both up to the bench.

"Get on with this, Mister Goodman," he said.

But as soon as I handed him the baseball, his mood changed. After that, my motions were heard and some of them were even granted. I also received a very favorable jury instruction before the jury went out to begin deliberating. Did those things make a difference? I don't know. There was a lot of conflicting and circumstantial evidence in the case. What I do know is that my client was found not guilty. I also know the judge was a big baseball fan. In a criminal trial, you have to use whatever tools are available. In this case, one of them was Tommy Lasorda's autograph.

That's not the kind of thing they teach you in law school, but it's the kind of thing you have to use in order to give your client the best representation possible.

Over the years, my criminal law practice also brought me in contact with some of the major players in the boxing world. The experiences were both fascinating and rewarding.

I'd been a boxing fan since I was a kid in Philadelphia. I remember going to Old Man Willard's house. He lived a few doors down from us, and was one of the first people on the block to have a television set. It was black and white, of course, with a magnifying bowl placed over the screen to make the picture larger. One of my earliest memories is watching a boxing match on that TV. I remember this because it was also the first time I ever had a Coca-Cola. Old Man Willard mixed me the drink. He took some seltzer water and added syrup of coca-cola, which was great. I sat there watching Jersey Joe Walcott battle Rocky Marciano. It was a classic fight, and I enjoyed the soda as much as I did watching the bout.

My dad got me interested in boxing. He used to take me to Lew Tendler's, a famous restaurant on Broad Street. They featured steaks and chops, but the real draw for me were the pictures on the walls. Boxers were everywhere. And the thing I remember—and this is probably why my dad took me there—was that the boxers were Jewish.

Lew Tendler had been a pretty good boxer himself. They called him "Lefty Lew" since he was a southpaw, and he and some of the other guys in his restaurant loved to tell stories about their experiences and about the great fighters they had seen. I was in awe. I loved hearing about guys like Barney Ross, the lightweight champion. He was never knocked out in eighty-one fights, and he defeated some of the best boxers in his division, including Tough Tony Canzoneri.

Ross was not only a great boxer, but a great American. That was part of the story they told me. He had been a Marine and fought on Guadalcanal in the South Pacific, one of the bloodiest battles of World War II. Ross was awarded a Silver Star, one of the highest commendations. He and three of his fellow Marines came under attack from a larger group of Japanese soldiers. Ross and his three buddies were all wounded. He was the only one who could still fire a weapon, and he fought off the Japanese during a battle that lasted all night. He ended up killing two dozen enemy soldiers. Two of his Marine buddies died during the night, but he carried the third one to safety. Ross weighed about 140 pounds, and the guy he carried was 230 pounds.

After hearing that kind of story about the great Jewish boxers, I guess it was only natural that I developed an interest in the sport. And then, after I became a lawyer, I got a chance to represent some of boxing's more interesting characters. One of the first was the promoter Don King. He hired me to fight an injunction that would have barred a match between Roberto Duran and Esteban DeJesus. King was promoting the match, and at the eleventh hour I was able to get the injunction lifted. From that point on, I was his guy.

King was everything he appeared to be: outspoken, flamboyant, just a force of nature. It wasn't an act; it was who he was. He had a lot of connections in the boxing world and started to send me business. He also introduced me to Muhammad Ali, the greatest heavyweight ever, and we've remained friends. Every year I could count on earning about $100,000 from the action Don King sent my way. He had faith in me and never hesitated to call.

One night he called around two in the morning. I was asleep, but when I picked up the phone, I knew right away who it was.

"Oscar," he said. "I need to see you. It's urgent."

"What time is it?" I said.

"Don't matter," he replied. "We're at the Riviera. Can you get down here right away?"

I got dressed and drove over to the casino-hotel. When I walked into the lounge, I saw him sitting in a booth with Larry Holmes, the great heavyweight champion. King and Holmes had a contractual relationship that they wanted severed. It was all amicable, but they wanted it done right away. I drew up an agreement on a napkin and had them sign it. I was never really clear on why it was so urgent and why it couldn't have waited until morning, but that was Don King; one-of-a-kind. After they signed the napkin, I went home to bed.

A few months after that, Larry Holmes was subpoenaed to appear in front of a federal grand jury in the Southern District of

New York. Rudy Giuliani was the U.S. Attorney for the district at the time. The feds were investigating Don King for fraud, and they wanted Larry to testify. Larry was a standup guy. There was no way he was going to testify against King or anybody else.

Larry wouldn't budge. I made it clear that my client had nothing to say. Giuliani was frustrated, but there was nothing he could do about it.

Larry Holmes was a fascinating guy and one of my favorite people. I had a case once in Easton, Pennsylvania, his home-town, and a got a chance to spend some time with him while I was there. It's one thing to say that someone is a celebrity in his hometown, but Larry Holmes was more than that. He was revered. When we drove around town, it was like I was with the king. Everyone knew him; everyone called out to him. He owned that town, and I don't just mean that figuratively. He was a major property owner in Easton. The federal courthouse where my case was being tried was one of his properties; the government leased the building from him.

Later, I had another case, this time in New York, that led me to the great Joe Louis.

My client was a guy named Izzy Marion. Izzy was a charming guy. He was a hairdresser and had a business in Las Vegas. But he had been picked up on a federal wiretap talking about an unregistered gun. He was subpoenaed and went back to New York, where he appeared in front of a grand jury. I wasn't his lawyer at the time.

He was testifying under oath and was asked by a federal prosecutor why an unregistered handgun had been transported from New York to Las Vegas and ended up in his hands. It was a pretty straightforward question, but Izzy didn't give a straightforward answer. The simplest thing would have been for him to say that he needed the gun for protection. That might have been the end of it. Instead, Izzy offered about thirteen different explanations, several of which made no sense and which were contradictory. As a result, he got indicted for making inconsistent statements to a grand jury. The assumption was that some of them were false, and he was charged with perjury.

He hired me to represent him at the trial, and a few months later we flew back to New York. We stayed at the Park Lane Hotel. Izzy knew everybody. Two of his close friends were Joe Louis, the Brown Bomber, and Louis's wife Martha. Joe was going to be a character witness for Izzy, and as we were preparing for trial, I could see there was a problem.

We couldn't get Joe to enunciate; everything he said was garbled and incoherent. Izzy's daughter and Martha tried to help get the champ focused on what he was going to say. All we needed was for him to stand up, say who he was, and vouch for Izzy's good character and reputation for honesty. It was brutal; we couldn't get Joe to make sense. So we decided to use Martha instead, and have Joe walk into the courtroom with her. Joe didn't have any mental problems. It wasn't like he was punch-drunk or had been hit in the head too many times. He just swallowed his words when he spoke, and I didn't think he would be an effective advocate. If you couldn't understand him, what was the point of having him speak? But his presence turned out to be enough.

We went to court early that Friday morning. The prosecutor was a real jerk. He thought he had a guaranteed winner, and he finished his case by noon. We were to go on right after lunch. When we got back to court, Izzy's daughter came running up to me in a panic.

"Mister Louis ate fish in the cafeteria for lunch," she said.

I didn't see how that could be a problem.

"He ate everything, bones and all!" she said, nearly screaming.

But the champ was fine. He came walking up to us, and we were ready to go. We all went into the courtroom together. Judge Richard Owen was already on the bench, but he nearly fell off of it when he saw us.

"Mister Goodman, would you please come up here," he said.

Prior to that, everything had been pretty formal. When I got up to the bench, he said, "Is that who I think it is?"

"Yes," I said, figuring no other explanation was needed.

"Can you get me his autograph?" the judge asked.

At that point, I liked our chances with the perjury case. I knew Izzy would be found guilty. His statements to the grand jury were what they were; there was no way to fight that. The evidence made it a slam-dunk conviction. But the key was sentencing. Would he get hammered by the judge, or would he catch a break? I think the champ being in Izzy's corner turned the odds in our favor. The prosecutor had bragged about "doing a war dance on Izzy's grave" at sentencing, but the judge wasn't buying any of it.

He was a Joe Louis fan, and Joe Louis was Izzy's friend.

"Guilty," the judge said. Then, he added, "Probation."

We couldn't have asked for more.

Joe Louis wasn't my only heavyweight. I once represented Frans Botha, the South African boxer known as "The White Buffalo." Botha had defeated Axel Schulz in New Jersey to win the International Boxing Federation heavyweight title. But after the match, he had tested positive for a steroid. I represented Botha in a hearing before the New Jersey Boxing Commission, which planned to strip him of his title. Everyone thought we were going to concede and plead for mercy, but I put on a defense. We argued that the drug had been prescribed by a doctor for an arm injury, and that Frans had no idea it was a banned substance or that it was still in his system when he fought Schulz. Frans wasn't stripped of his title, and he went on to fight several other memorable matches. He was beating Mike Tyson, according to all three judges, when Tyson knocked him out in the fifth round of their match.

Tyson was another heavyweight whom I represented. You may have heard about the incident; Tyson bit off a piece of Evander Holyfield's ear during their heavyweight fight. I can't begin to offer an explanation for why he did that; "heat of the battle" doesn't come anywhere close to justifying it.

But from my perspective, after the fact, that wasn't the issue. Tyson had bitten off a piece of Holyfield's ear. That wasn't in dispute. What I was trying to do was save Tyson's career.

My good friend Mills Lane had been the referee at that fight. Mills and I went back a long way, trying cases against one another. He had been a prosecutor in the district attorney's office up in Reno, and then became a district court judge. He also had a part-time job as a fight referee. The fight was at the MGM Grand Arena. Many people might not remember this, but Tyson bit Holyfield twice. The first time, Mills stopped the fight temporarily and issued a warning. The second time, after a piece of Holyfield's right ear fell onto the canvas, Mills stopped the fight and awarded Holyfield the victory.

The Nevada Athletic Commission withheld $3 million from Tyson's $30 million purse, which was the most they could withhold. And then the commission scheduled a hearing to consider banning Tyson from the sport. Don King hired me to represent Iron Mike.

Dr. Elias Ghanem, another friend of mine, was the chairman of the Athletic Commission. I had successfully represented him in an IRS case many years before, and we had remained friends. He was also my doctor; he was the only one who could get my gout under control.

Everyone knew about our friendship, but everyone also knew that he was a straight-shooter who would call the issues as he saw them. This was another case where the evidence was not in dispute. Holyfield's ear—at least a piece of it—had been bitten off by Tyson. The state's attorney wanted Tyson's license suspended. This would have resulted in an indefinite suspension before he could box again, if ever.

The media, as you can imagine, was all over this case, and everyone was waiting to see what was going to happen. Tyson, who was considered one of the greatest heavyweights of all time, was now vilified as an animal.

Dr. Ghanem called me aside before the hearing started. He said that the best we could hope for, with all the heat this case had attracted, was license revocation and a fine of $3 million, which is what the commission had already withheld. Then he whispered to me, "With revocation, he can reapply in a year."

That sounded great to me, since I knew Tyson's entire life revolved around his ability to box. Without boxing, I don't know what he would have done. Say what you will about the incident, Mike Tyson was one of the faces of boxing. The bout with Holyfield had grossed $100 million. Boxing was a major event in Las Vegas, the "Fight Capital of the World," and Tyson, like it or not, was a big part of the sport. Events like heavyweight title bouts filled hotel rooms, brought thousands of people to the city, and drove the economy. Those were the kinds of things I was thinking of.

So we went for the revocation rather than the suspension. The revocation took effect on July 9, 1997. Tyson reapplied for a license, and the revocation was lifted on October 18, 1998. He was out of boxing for a little over a year. If his license had been suspended, we might still be appealing for its restoration.

Mike Tyson was a great boxer, but you could get into a serious debate about the other parts of his life. However, Barney Ross was a great man who happened to be a great boxer.

I love the sport, but I never lose sight of the difference.

CHAPTER 7
A NINETEEN-MINUTE DEFENSE

Many people in law enforcement tried to say that I was more than just the legal representative of the mobsters who were my clients. They wanted to make me out as a criminal "consigliere," a guy who counseled gangsters on illegal activities.

That's never who I was, but I have to admit there was one time when I did provide counsel that helped avoid a major underworld confrontation between two of the most dynamic and dangerous clients I ever represented.

Tony Spilotro used to hang out at a club on Paradise Road called Jubilation. It was a fancy bar-restaurant owned by the singer Paul Anka, and lots of important people would go there. Tony was a creature of habit and always sat in the same booth. It was toward the back of the room and up against a wall. If you sat there you could see the rest of the restaurant and everyone else in the room. Guys like Tony always had their own booth, usually up against a wall. There was no need to look over your shoulder.

One night, around midnight, Tony went into the club. Jimmy Chagra, another of my clients, was sitting in Tony's booth along with his entourage, including the usual sycophants and beautiful women. Tony told him to get out of the booth. Chagra had no idea who Tony was, and he refused. They had words. I think Jimmy called Tony "a midget" and said, "Get lost."

Tony left the place steaming. He had been embarrassed. If this had taken place in Chicago or Philadelphia, Chagra probably would have left the place in pieces. As it was, he was in more danger than he knew. But this was Las Vegas, and if anything was going to happen, it wasn't going to be in a public place.

Chagra was an interesting guy. The feds alleged he made his millions dealing drugs, but Jimmy liked to represent himself as a professional gambler, which explained his frequent visits to Las Vegas.

Chagra was the son of Lebanese immigrants, and growing up he had worked in his father's carpet store in El Paso, Texas. He looked like a handsome Saddam Hussein with soulful dark eyes that could be piercing when he looked at you. He was always personable, but I found him to be moody, and at times it seemed like he was depressed. He had an older and a younger brother, both of whom became lawyers. Jimmy was apparently the only non-student in the family. But he was entrepreneurial, and he liked being center stage and having a good time. He could also be aggressive and would sometimes shoot from the hip, which was at the heart of his confrontation with Spilotro. If Jimmy had known who he was dealing with, I doubt that he would have called Tony a "midget."

The next day Tony came to my law office. He stopped by most days, because so many things were going on that there was always some legal issue that had to be discussed. But all he could talk about that day was "this jerk who was sitting in my booth." As he was talking and describing the guy, I realized it was Jimmy Chagra. This was bad; I immediately got on the phone and called Chagra.

"Get down to my office now," I said. "It's very important."

"What's going on?" he said.

"Don't worry about it. Just get over here."

Chagra arrived, and before they could get into it, I made introductions and told them to resolve the problem right there, shake hands, and forget about it.

"You're both good guys," I said. "Let's not have any problems."

Some people think I saved Jimmy's life that day. If I did, it would have been the first, but not the last time.

I met Jimmy's brother Lee about a year before I met Jimmy. Lee was a prominent defense attorney in El Paso. He represented a lot of drug dealers and was involved in high-profile cases. He wasn't quite as flamboyant as Jimmy, but he lived the good life.

He was a regular at the Kentucky Derby, where he moved in the best circles. He placed his bets in the Colonel Winn Room, which was an exclusive dining area on the third floor of the clubhouse with its own betting windows. The minimum bet was $100. He'd be there dressed in a white suit, a cowboy hat, boots, and a fancy cane. When he bet, he'd go up to the window and tell the clerk to keep his hand on the button, running up bets in the thousands. Sometimes his actions alone would change the odds on a race.

I was familiar with the set-up because I had been there as a guest of the Chandler family. Happy Chandler, the patriarch of the family, had been the governor of Kentucky at one time, and later was the Commissioner of Major League Baseball.

The Chandlers had hired me to represent a family member who had been charged—and this was unbelievable—with possession of a small cannon that had been stolen from a military base in California. My client was Brad Bryant, a Chandler cousin. The cannon was in a storage locker leased by Bryant. The combination to the locker was Bryant's birth date, and Bryant's prints had been found on the cannon.

The case looked insurmountable, but somehow we got a jury to come back with a "Not guilty." I attacked the credibility of some witnesses and made a strong closing argument about reasonable doubt. You never know with a jury.

In fact, I wasn't even there when the verdict was announced. I had to fly to Kansas City for the start of jury selection in a case against Nick Civella. My co-counsel, a local attorney from Lexington, called me when the verdict came in. To tell the truth, I couldn't believe it.

Anyway, in appreciation, the Chandler family invited me to the Derby. I went with my friend Billy Walters, a legendary gambler. We were treated like royalty, and that's how I got to see the Colonel Winn Room.

While we were there, we went to a party and I met Phyllis George, the former Miss America who was married to the governor of Kentucky. I also ran into George Steinbrenner. We sat next to each other to watch the race. Lee Chagra, in all his sartorial splendor, probably fit right in with the Derby crowd. I didn't meet him until after this, but I could see how he would be in his element. I clearly wasn't in mine. But that didn't stop Billy Walters and me from having a great time.

The Chagras had plenty of money. The government, of course, implied that it came from drug dealing, even insinuating that Lee, who was a lawyer, had a role in his brother Jimmy's drug network. That was never proven.

The allegation was that Jimmy had a pipeline into Mexico and South America, and that he was a major distributor—a supplier to the suppliers—of marijuana and cocaine. Some speculated that he had direct ties to the Colombian cocaine cartels.

Lee Chagra had contacted me sometime in 1977 or 1978. He wanted me to represent him in a civil rights suit against a federal judge, John H. Wood, Jr., "Maximum John," they called him.

Lee had tried several cases in front of the judge, and he was convinced Wood harbored bias and that he wasn't giving Lee's clients, and other clients for that matter, a fair trial. To many in the defense bar, Judge Wood was viewed as a second prosecutor in the courtroom.

Wood seldom ruled in favor of any defense motions, and at sentencing, he could be brutal. I went down to El Paso, which is where Lee practiced law, and I met him to discuss the civil suit. I had been in enough courtrooms to know how the game was played, and like Lee, I had tried cases where I felt as if the deck was already stacked against me. Lee represented drug dealers; I represented mobsters. But both groups of clients got the same kind of treatment.

Lee also thought that Judge Wood didn't like him personally, and that that had an impact on the way the judge dealt with his clients at trial and at sentencing. Lee Chagra was one of the best defense attorneys in Texas. He could be colorful at times, and he certainly was fearless and controversial. But in a courtroom, he knew what he was doing.

I didn't know Jimmy at the time, but I knew of him. He was a regular in Las Vegas and had a reputation as a big-time gambler. He loved to throw his money around, and he had a lot of it. He would come into town with suitcases full of cash, check into the Frank Sinatra Suite at Caesars Palace, and gamble all his money away. Even if he won in the casinos, he was a sucker on the golf course. Guys would line up to play him. He'd lose $50,000 or $100,000 playing a round of golf, and be right out there the next day playing again. Then he'd hang out at the country club and get involved in a high-stakes rummy game where he'd drop even more cash.

Clearly he was a guy who liked the action. I could appreciate that, but the amounts he bet were staggering. He used to go to

Binion's Horseshoe all the time because he liked to shoot craps without any betting limits, and they'd let him do that there. One night, after I had gotten to know him, he asked me to go with him.

"Jimmy, I don't play craps," I said. "And I have no desire to learn. I lose enough with the vices I have, betting sports and the horses. I don't need another outlet."

"Come with me," he said, "just for luck."

So I went and I watched. By the end of the night he bet $700,000 on one roll of the dice. That kind of betting doesn't make sense to me, but money didn't seem to have much value to him. I'll bet $5,000 on the Super Bowl or maybe $1,500 on a football game, but to bet nearly three-quarters of a million dollars on one roll of the dice? It was nuts.

Even though he lost that roll, Jimmy did really well that night. As a "thank you" when he cashed out, he gave me $25,000.

"Is this a retainer?" I asked.

"No, it's for you. You brought me luck."

And I guess in a way I did. That situation with Tony was one example of Jimmy benefiting from an association with me. But I wasn't always able to keep him out of harm's way.

I can say with certainty that while I was Tony Spilotro's lawyer, he was never convicted and never spent any time in jail. I can't say the same for Jimmy Chagra, although you could make the argument that I saved his life at least twice.

Plans to file the civil law suit on behalf of Lee Chagra ended on December 23, 1978, when two men made their way into his law office and killed him. It was apparently a robbery gone bad, as reports said the shooters made off with about $450,000.

The murder occurred while the Sun Bowl was being played in El Paso. I've always wondered about the circumstances. Lee's office was impenetrable, with state-of-the-art security and surveillance. You had to be buzzed in, so Lee must have let them in, but why? The murder occurred while the game was being played. They shot him with a .22, and the bullet bounced off his clavicle and nicked his aorta so that he bled to death. They put cocaine in his mouth and took cash out of his safe.

The murder of Lee Chagra was just part of a murky Texas underworld that I wasn't familiar with. Some people thought Lee was the brains behind Jimmy's drug operation, but I don't think that was the case.

Did Lee keep some of Jimmy's money in his law office safe? I don't know, but if people thought that he did, it would explain why he was robbed. The Chagra brothers were portrayed in some law enforcement circles as a crime family; their own little Lebanese-American Mafia. It was an easy way for the government to label people and to affix blame, even when there wasn't enough evidence to make a case. The Chagras came up several times in an investigation into the attempted murder of a federal prosecutor a few years earlier, and Jimmy's name would come up again in the notorious assassination of Judge Wood.

It's funny how things overlap. I represented the relative of a friend of one of my bookmaker clients who was wanted for questioning in the Lee Chagra murder case. I brought him to the grand jury down in Texas. He was cleared of any involvement, but while I was there outside the grand jury room, I first met Jimmy Chagra.

Jimmy had moved from El Paso to Las Vegas with his wife Liz, a former fashion model, and their kids. They happened to move to the same street where Carolyn and I were living at the time, Viking Road. In fact, at one point he talked to me about wanting to buy another house on the block for his maid. The funny thing was, the house he was describing was our house!

In February 1979, Jimmy got indicted in Midland, Texas, in the cocaine and marijuana case that he knew was coming. He hired me to represent him. I got a $250,000 retainer, and I earned it. Bail was set at $1 million. We were able to get it knocked down to $400,000, and he was released pending trial. Eventually the government expanded the indictment to include a Continuing Criminal Enterprise charge. That made the potential penalties even higher.

It came as no surprise when the case was assigned to U.S. District Court Judge John H. Wood, Jr. There was speculation that the U.S. Attorney's Office brought the indictment in Midland, rather than another Texas jurisdiction, because they wanted Wood as the trial judge.

I filed dozens of pre-trial motions, including a motion to have Judge Wood recuse himself because I had been planning to file the civil rights suit against him on behalf of Lee Chagra. Every motion was denied, but for some reason I felt comfortable in his courtroom. His staff seemed to like me.

I'm not sure why, but several members of the office were nice to me in a motherly kind of way. I got the impression that they saw me as a nice guy who was about to be cut in half by the buzz-saw that their boss, the judge, was operating. No one figured I had a chance to win the case, so I guess they felt sorry for me.

When I went down there for the pre-trial hearings, I would stay at the Hilton Hotel near the courthouse. They had a restaurant called "Oscar's," which I took as a good sign. I still have a match-book from the place. I had gotten a continuance; the trial was supposed to begin in May, but I got it put off until July. And the judge also granted a request to move the venue to Austin.

I knew that it was going to be a David vs. Goliath battle. Jimmy was considered a major drug kingpin, and the government had several witnesses who had worked for him in the drug business. Prosecutors also had flipped a major player who had agreed to cooperate and testify against Jimmy.

On May 29, everything changed. That morning, Judge Wood walked out of his condo in San Antonio and into the line of fire of a rifleman who was hiding nearby. Two shots hit him, and he died instantly.

The murder attracted national attention. It was the first time in more than a century that a federal judge had been killed. Because of the kinds of cases Judge Wood heard, those in the drug business became the prime suspects. And of course, Jimmy Chagra was at the top of that list.

Jimmy was in Las Vegas at the time. He had an alibi, since he had been to see his pretrial service officer that day. I went over to his house to talk with him. To be honest, deep down inside, I had mixed emotions. I wanted to believe that because he had two brothers who were lawyers, Jimmy had a certain respect for the law. I also thought that because of the way his brother had died, Jimmy knew what it felt like to lose a loved one that way and wouldn't have been part of an assassination.

On the other hand . . .

The drug case got reassigned to Judge William Steele Sessions, who would later become head of the FBI under President Ronald Reagan. Sessions had a pretty inflated opinion of himself; he thought he was one of the finest judges in the land. To me, he wasn't as genuine as he would have liked people to believe. Prior to the start of the trial, I had some discussions with the prosecution, but we couldn't work anything out.

We went to trial, and the evidence was devastating. There was testimony from witnesses who said they worked for or with Jimmy. They talked about staggering amounts of money and drugs. They described a network for the importation of tons of marijuana and cocaine using boats and planes. From a defense perspective, we were looking at a potential disaster.

My best shot was a strong closing argument, but I wasn't sure that would be enough. The night before I was to sum up, I was in my hotel room going over what I planned to say when the phone rang.

It was my wife Carolyn. My father had died.

It's hard to describe how I felt. All I can say is, it was one of the saddest days in my life. My father was one of my best friends. He was just a great guy. Even though it took him a while to acknowledge that I had gone to Las Vegas, after I had established myself, he and my mother came out to visit. I think he was proud of what I was doing when he saw me in court.

My dad was a wonderful lawyer, and he loved the law. He had spent a career in the district attorney's office in Philadelphia and had hoped to become a judge. He was very active in the Republican Party and when a spot on the federal court opened up, he expected to get the position. But the political machine people told him he'd have to donate $10,000 to the party in order to have their support. He wouldn't do it; he felt he had earned the right to sit on the bench.

"I'm not going to buy it," he said.

I think it broke his heart. He left the district attorney's office after that and went into private practice. He was very successful and highly respected, but he was disappointed in the whole process.

I thought about all those things that night, and about all that he had meant to me. I couldn't believe he was gone. The next day I told Judge Sessions that I couldn't make my closing arguments. I asked for a delay so I could go to Philadelphia to bury my father. We're Jewish, I said, and our tradition is to have the burial the next day.

"Judge, I have to have a continuance," I said. "To be honest with you, I don't even know where I am."

"Oh, no," Sessions said. "You're a professional. We're going forward. You make your closing. Motion denied."

I made my closing argument to the jury that day, but I have no idea what I said. My mind was a million miles away from where it was supposed to be as a lawyer. I was a shell.

The closing argument in any trial is usually one of my strong points, but I doubt I did Jimmy Chagra any good that day. The jury was out for about two hours and came back with a guilty verdict.

Jimmy was unbelievably kind to me. He arranged for a private plane to fly me up to Philadelphia, and I left immediately. Maybe Sessions felt guilty because of what happened, because he allowed Jimmy to remain free pending sentencing. Jimmy was looking at thirty years.

I headed to Philadelphia and Jimmy went into hiding. He took his wife and kids and went on the lam. They settled somewhere in Kansas, got some phony identification with new names, and started to live a new life.

Despite all the flamboyance, Jimmy was a pretty simple guy. What he liked to do most was watch sports on TV. In Kansas he had his satellite dish and all the games he wanted. He was happy as a pig in mud.

He called me once or twice, and as a lawyer, I had to tell him to come back. He didn't take my advice, but eventually he surfaced. Evidently, TV sports weren't enough. He got the itch and decided he was going to come back to Las Vegas. He had called a plastic surgeon and was going to slip into town and have some work done. The doctor tipped the FBI agents, who were looking for him.

But before the feds could move in, Jimmy gave himself up. A police car had pulled him over for some reason when he was driving in town. He got out of the car and said, "I give up."

In the backseat, stuffed in a half dozen diaper bags, was thousands of dollars in cash. I don't know if that was money for the plastic surgeon or for the craps table; maybe both. But instead of rolling the dice, Jimmy ended up at the federal penitentiary in Leavenworth doing a thirty-year sentence for the drug conviction.

It's hard to believe, but his troubles were just beginning.

One of my other clients, Nick Civella, the mob boss from Kansas City, was also in Leavenworth at the time and was the focus of an ongoing investigation. The feds had the visiting room at the prison bugged with audio and video, because they wanted to know what Nick was saying and who he was saying it to.

The assumption the feds made was that he was still running his crime family from behind bars. One of the issues that the feds were really focusing on was a rumor that Nick had influence in the prison system and was going to help one of his nephews, also an inmate, get a transfer to a prison camp.

Jimmy Chagra knew nothing about the waiting room being bugged, and he had the misfortune of having some pretty candid discussions with his wife and his brother Joe, who both visited him there. One of the topics they discussed was the murder of Judge Wood.

The feds were already targeting Jimmy for that murder. A low-life named Charles Harrelson, who as I mentioned earlier was the father of the actor Woody Harrelson and the brother of the polygraph expert I had used in the Crockett case, had been making noise about the judge's murder. Harrelson was in jail on other charges, and was apparently trying to work a deal.

In addition to the conversations Jimmy was having with his wife, Liz, they were also passing notes back and forth. This was picked up on the surveillance cameras, and the feds eventually installed a trap in the sewer line from the visitor's room women's bathroom. Liz Chagra would take whatever note Jimmy gave her, read it, rip it up, and then flush it down the toilet.

The feds got the pieces of paper, put them back together, and had what they contended was even more incriminating evidence.

Eventually Jimmy, Liz, his brother Joe, Harrelson, and Harrelson's wife got indicted for conspiracy and murder in the assassination of Judge Wood. The two women were allegedly the conduits for the passing of money—supposedly $250,000 in cash—that Jimmy was accused of paying Harrelson to kill the judge.

Liz Chagra, who in her day was a beautiful woman, ended up in jail awaiting trial and apparently found Jesus while she was there. She had been born again. She wrote a letter to Judge Wood's widow asking for forgiveness and acknowledging her guilt. Among other things she wrote that her husband forced her to make the delivery, telling her she was the only one he could trust.

I felt sorry for Liz, and I knew a little about their relationship. Although she was his wife and the mother of his children, Jimmy wasn't shy about partying with other women. When he was out at the casinos or in the clubs in Las Vegas, he'd always be surrounded by an entourage of sexy ladies.

And Jimmy could be a domineering guy. So if you accepted the government version of the case, at worst what Liz Chagra did was deliver a briefcase. That was the extent of her involvement in this murder conspiracy.

But she and everyone involved faced insurmountable odds. First of all, the judge was William Sessions, the same judge who had sentenced Jimmy to thirty years in the drug case. Sessions had delivered the eulogy at Judge Wood's funeral. Second, the trial was to take place in the federal courthouse in San Antonio, which was now the John H. Wood, Jr., Courthouse, memorial plaque and all.

Talk about a stacked deck.

Liz Chagra's letter and her attempt to cut a deal didn't do her any good. She went to trial with the Harrelsons. They all were convicted; she got thirty years, and Jo Ann Harrelson got twenty-five years. Charles Harrelson got two consecutive life terms.

Joe Chagra had pleaded guilty before the trial to a conspiracy charge and was sentenced to ten years. He also lost his law license. His plea agreement stipulated that he would not have to testify against his brother.

I had gotten a severance for Jimmy because of the letter his wife sent to the widow, among other things. And I was fortunate that Judge Sessions also agreed to a change of venue. Jimmy was to be tried in Jacksonville, Florida, rather than in the John H. Wood, Jr., Courthouse. This was our first break.

The publicity in this case was unbelievable. Before it was moved to Florida, I was down in Texas for several pre-trial hearings, and you could almost feel the tension in the air. Everyone was talking about it. After one hearing, I was in a cab heading back to the airport and the driver surmised I was in town for the Wood murder case.

"Judge Wood was such a good man," the cabbie said. "He always gave the maximum sentence for all those filthy drug dealers. They should take that Chagra guy and raise him on the flagpole and put honey in his eyes and ants on the honey. Who are you with?"

"I'm with the FBI," I said.

I wasn't about to tell him I was Jimmy Chagra's lawyer.

Jacksonville wasn't much better. The prosecution was loaded and ready, and this conviction was going to be the icing on the cake. They had gotten Harrelson and the others, but Jimmy was the prime target. The talk was that they had a piñata and champagne in the office, and planned a big victory party once Jimmy was found guilty.

I had to work with the evidence. There were some things that couldn't be refuted, such as the taped conversations. The recorded words weren't going to change. And the government also had informants and prison snitches, including a guy named Jerry Ray James, a prison inmate who said Chagra had admitted to him that he had had the judge killed.

James was a very bad guy. He had led a prison riot in New Mexico where he stuck brooms into the orifices of the guards and inmates who he knew were rats, and burned them with welding torches. But he cut a deal with the authorities where he would not be penalized if he could help them get Jimmy Chagra.

In my opening statement, I argued that the charge didn't make sense. I told the jury to think about it. Jimmy was involved in a drug case in front of Judge Wood, and he was facing a possible thirty-year sentence. Killing the judge wasn't going to make that case go away. In fact, it didn't. So what was the point? And more important, Jimmy was in negotiations with the prosecution to resolve the drug case. The government wanted what amounted to a ten-year cap, and Jimmy insisted that the deal have a five-year cap.

You don't kill a judge for a five-year difference.

In a case like this, you attempt to get the jury thinking. If you can get one or two of the jurors to at least consider your position, then you have something to work with. That's why I always tried to pick jurors who seemed intelligent. You want jurors who have minds of their own, who aren't going to swallow everything the prosecution tries to feed them.

Then you try to chip away at the facts and hope you bring the jury along with you.

The tapes, of course, were a problem. As they were being played, Jimmy was concerned. He kept looking at me. I had told him that before the trial started, my wife Carolyn had listened to all the tapes. She was one of the few people I trusted, and this was one of the only times I ever asked her for help in a criminal trial. She had listened and told me I was going to win this case. I told that to Jimmy.

At the defense table, he wrote me a note.

"How the fuck does your wife think we can win this fucking case?"

I wrote him a note back that said, "Because I'm fucking brilliant."

One of the pieces of evidence the prosecution used was a diorama of the condominium complex where Judge Wood lived. There was a witness who the government hypnotized, who had testified about what she had seen from her unit. The diorama was so specific that it had the streets and the parking spaces, and even the trees that lined the parking area where the judge was standing when he was killed.

I had fought to exclude her testimony, arguing that there was inherent unreliability in anything said under hypnosis. It would be too easy for someone to suggest something to her under those conditions. But Judge Sessions didn't see it that way.

"Denied," he said to my motion to bar her testimony.

Now I had to deal not only with what she said, but also with this elaborate diorama that the prosecution was using to back up her story. Something bothered me about it. I kept looking and looking. Finally, when I got a chance to cross-examine the witness, I asked the judge's clerk if she had a pen, preferably a green one, that I could borrow. She did.

I could see Judge Sessions start to steam. I knew he was thinking, "What's Goodman doing here, wasting my time?"

I asked whether the clerk could hand me some Kleenex. With that I began to dab the Kleenex with the pen, wad them up and place them on the diorama's trees, which were barren of leaves.

The assassination took place in May. The trees would have been covered with leaves, so there was no way the witness could have seen what she said she had seen.

That was a small point, but nevertheless it was a way to begin raising some doubt about the prosecution's case.

I had bigger issues to deal with than leafy trees, however. One, which Jimmy clearly recognized, was his taped comments. Another was alleged statements he had made to fellow inmate Jerry Ray James admitting his involvement in the murder. James had been transferred from the New Mexico prison to Leavenworth so he could get next to Jimmy. What I argued was that Jimmy was puffing, making it up. I tried to get across to the jury the idea that Jimmy was smart; I said he was too smart to think he could get away with killing a federal judge. But once he was in prison for the drug conviction, he needed to survive. He wasn't a tough guy, but he could make himself out to be one by bragging that he'd had a federal judge killed.

It was a macho thing, a survival tactic. To make that point, I told Judge Sessions I wanted to subpoena over two dozen hardened inmates who were at Leavenworth, Florence, and Terre Haute, the government's high security locked-down prisons. I wanted to put them on the stand and ask them about reputation and survival in the prison system, and whether killing a federal judge would provide an inmate with status and give him prestige.

Sessions went nuts. A federal prison official had called Sessions and said, "Is this Goodman fucking nuts? There's no jail in the world that would hold these guys."

"You can't bring those inmates down here," Sessions said. "It's too big a security risk."

They would have had to be housed in a county facility while waiting to be called, and the judge saw the potential for a massive prison break. He agreed, however, to bring some of those inmates to the federal penitentiary in Atlanta, and allowed me to go up there and interview them.

The prison guards in Atlanta weren't too happy with me when I went up there. I was the reason these hard cases were now their responsibility, and I think they got a kick out of putting me in a room with all of these guys. I spoke with several of them. Some only spoke Spanish. All I could say was "abogado." I wanted to make sure they knew I wasn't a fed.

Ultimately, I decided not to call any of them.

The old adage in criminal law, "Don't ask a question unless you know what the answer is going to be," kept coming up as I thought about these prisoners as witnesses. They were loose cannons. They were telling me what I wanted to hear; that killing a judge would be a badge of honor in a federal prison. That backed up my argument that Jimmy was saying this to give himself status with hardened convicts. But I couldn't be sure what else they might say if I called them to testify.

I was putting together a surgically crafted defense. I didn't want to run the risk of any one of them undermining what I was trying to do. So in the end, and I think to the great relief of the prosecution and prison officials, I didn't call them as witnesses.

But another inmate provided me with a major break. A fellow from Las Vegas, Andy Granby Hanley, called me. I had known Hanley and his dad Tom, who had been charged with bombing supper clubs in Las Vegas that were non-union. At the time, I was representing the head of the Culinary Union, who was charged with conspiring with them.

It's amazing what prisoners learn; the network of information they have and the ability they have to get that information out. Granby said that James had already been advanced some of the $250,000 reward that had been offered by the feds and the Texas Bar Association for the arrest and *conviction* of persons in the Judge Wood murder. If that were true, I could use it to chal-lenge his credibility.

Not only had he gotten the money, Granby told me, but he had used some of it to buy his wife a $50,000 Mercedes Benz.

"Are you sure?" I asked.

"I'll get you the VIN number of the car and you can check the registration," he said.

In a couple of days he was back on the phone with the VIN. It checked out; the car was registered to Mrs. Jerry Ray James.

Amazing.

There was another part of James's story that didn't ring true. In addition to having Judge Wood killed, he said Jimmy Chagra had bragged about another killing. He also said Chagra claimed that he had personally murdered a drug dealer named Mark Finney.

Jimmy told me that was a lie. Finney rode with a biker gang, the Banditos, and I managed to get in contact with one of their leaders. He agreed to help me out.

When it came time to cross-examine James, I first focused on the reward money.

James did a lot of hemming and hawing when I asked him about the cash. At first he tried to deny that he had gotten any money, then he denied that he had used any of the money to buy his wife a Mercedes. When I told him I had the VIN number, he had to admit it. That raised questions about his credibility and his motivation for testifying.

When it was time for me to put on my defense, I recalled James as my first witness. The prosecution and the judge weren't sure where I was going, but I had a clear idea of what I wanted to do. My examination of James lasted about nine min-utes, but it might have been the turning point in the case.

After some preliminary discussion and questions and answers about what Jimmy Chagra had allegedly told him about the murders of Judge Wood and Mark Finney, I said to James, "Describe how Mister Chagra told you he killed Mark Finney."

"I think he said he shot him."

"Are you sure of that?"

"I'm sure he told me he offed him."

"As sure as you are that Mister Chagra had Judge Wood murdered?"

"That's right."

I looked at Judge Sessions and said no further questions. The prosecution had nothing for cross, so Sessions told me to call my next witness.

I stood up and said, "I call Mark Finney."

The biker gang leader had helped me locate Finney. Finney had called me at my hotel a few nights earlier. I told him what I needed, and he said he would be happy to help Jimmy. Finney wasn't on the stand very long. After I had him identify himself, I asked, "Do you know Jimmy Chagra?"

"Yes," he said, nodding toward the defense table.

"Did he kill you?"

Finney laughed, and so did some of the jurors.

"No further questions," I said.

I didn't call another witness. It was a nineteen-minute defense.

In summation, I tried to hammer on the same points I had made during the trial: their accusations didn't make any sense, the government witnesses were not credible, the tapes and the "confession" were just Jimmy boasting and bragging and trying to survive. My argument lasted close to six hours, the longest I ever made.

You hope that in a case like this, with everything stacked against you, one or two jurors will agree with you. Maybe you can get a hung jury and negotiate a plea deal for your client.

In this case, all twelve jurors heard what I was saying.

They found Jimmy Chagra not guilty of the murder of Judge John H. Wood, Jr.

*　*　*

To this day, I still get asked about that case. Invariably someone will want to know how I felt about "helping Chagra get away with murder." Or, "Doesn't it make you sick to know you helped him beat the case when you knew he was guilty?" There's no answer to that question, because whoever asks it doesn't understand the system.

Think about the O.J. Simpson case, in which I almost got involved. It's the same issue and the same post-verdict question. Unpopular clients still deserve representation. Our adversarial system is set up so that the accused is presumed innocent and must be proven guilty.

My answer to the question is that I don't defend the guilty or the innocent; I defend our system of justice and the U.S. Constitution. People don't want to hear that, though. They think I'm just spouting platitudes. But if you believe in this country and our system of justice, then you have to accept the truth in that old adage about how it's better for ten guilty men to go free than for one innocent man to be convicted.

Is it a perfect system? Of course not.

Is it the best system on earth? Probably.

Was Jimmy Chagra guilty? It really doesn't matter that I don't believe he was. Would I feel bad if I felt justice wasn't served by the jury's verdict? Hell no. My thoughts would be irrelevant. What I think, what I feel, is not part of the system. What matters is that "twelve good men tried and true" said that he was not guilty.

I think the system works. Most of the people I represented were never going to get offered a deal. The prosecution wanted them convicted and in jail, or sentenced to death. I had a unique practice in that sense. Some studies suggest that 96 percent of all criminal cases are pleaded out. Guys like Chagra or Tony Spilotro were never going to be part of that statistic, because any deal the government was going to offer them wasn't going to be palatable.

That being said, I was still happy to work the system and fight the fight. I enjoyed presenting a case to a jury. For the most part I think jurors are serious about what they do and try to listen and understand. That's all you can ask.

Could the system be improved? Maybe, but only slightly. I would like a third jury option in criminal cases; what's called the Scottish verdict. In Scotland, juries have three options: guilty, not guilty, or "not proven." What the jury found in the Jimmy Chagra murder trial, I believe, was that the prosecution hadn't proven its case.

CHAPTER 8

I NEVER REPRESENTED
A RAT

One night in October 1982, I had just finished a martini and was sitting at home relaxing when I got the phone call. I don't remember who it was, but I'll never forget the message. Someone had just tried to kill Lefty Rosenthal. Lefty had come out of Tony Roma's restaurant and his Cadillac was parked in front. They planted a bomb in his car and nearly blew him away. They replayed the scene in the movie *Casino*. As you might imagine, Lefty was angry. The caller said Lefty had miraculously survived, and he wanted to see me.

I lived only two miles away, so I drove right over. I remember thinking, "This kind of stuff happens in other cities, not Las Vegas."

When I drove up to the restaurant, there were black-and-whites all over the place. Flashing lights, yellow crime scene tape blocking the area. I never saw so many cops in one place.

Lefty was still there. They had him on a gurney and were in the process of transporting him to the hospital. His hair was completely singed, his face was blackened, and his eyes were glazed.

"What happened?" I asked.

"Whoever did this, we're gonna get this guy," he said.

His Cadillac was mangled. It looked like something from one of those World War II movies where the tanks get blown up. What a scene! All the windows in Tony Roma's were shattered. This happened around eight o'clock at night. This wasn't some remote location; the restaurant was right across the street from a busy shopping center. Whoever set this up knew what they were doing. If this had happened during the day, when shoppers and tourists were all over the place, there's no telling how many people might have been killed or injured. Parts of the car were found hundreds of feet away.

News accounts at the time said Lefty's life was saved because of a metal plate that had been installed under the driver's seat. The plate was put there to correct some kind of balancing problem, but it apparently served another purpose on the night the bomb went off by shielding Lefty from the explosion.

I was told, however, that what really saved Lefty was the fact that he reached in the car to turn on the key, rather than sliding behind the wheel. Why did he do this? Who knows? Maybe he wanted to get the air-conditioning working before he got in. Maybe he was being cautious. I never asked him.

That night he'd had dinner with Marty Kane and Ruby Goldstein, two local gamblers. He had left the restaurant intending to head home. Obviously, he didn't make it.

Naturally, the question was who had planted the bomb? And the follow-up was, why?

Lefty Rosenthal was a very interesting guy. Unlike a lot of my other clients who wouldn't say "boo" and who just listened, Rosenthal was very vocal. He fought everything; he was quoted in the papers and was always battling. When the Gaming Control Board banned him from one casino job, he would get another that didn't require a license. Then they would cite him again. But he fought it all the way.

Lefty had a fascinating background. He grew up in Chicago, and the resume that law enforcement put together alleged that he eventually ran one of the biggest illegal bookmaking operations in the country for the Outfit. That's apparently where he got to know Tony Spilotro. There were also allegations that he used bribes to fix sporting events. None of this was ever proven. In fact, the only conviction he had was a guilty plea to a minor gambling charge in Florida, where he moved his operation in the 1960s.

Shortly after arriving in Miami, he was subpoenaed to testify before a U.S. Senate subcommittee investigation of gambling and organized crime. I think he invoked the Fifth Amendment thirty-seven times and never answered a relevant question. His name also surfaced in point-shaving scandals amid allegations that he bribed college basketball players. But again, none of this was proven.

He came to Las Vegas in the late 1960s, apparently to avoid the intense law enforcement scrutiny he was getting in Florida. His association with Spilotro and his reputation in the gambling underworld were what attracted the feds and the gambling regulators to him. They wanted him out of the casino industry.

He basically told them to go fuck themselves and fought them all the way.

He started his own television show. He would go on TV and blast the gaming regulators who were after him. It was a horrible show, but everyone watched it. People would run home on Saturday night so they could see what he was going to say next, and then everyone talked about it at work on Monday. He had major entertainers on the show, such as Sinatra and O.J. Simpson, as well as showgirls and bookmakers.

Rosenthal really understood sports betting, and he changed the way the sports books worked in Las Vegas. Before him, a bookie joint would be a hole-in-the-wall kind of place with a bunch of guys standing around with cigarettes in their mouths. He made it comfortable and plush, with big-screen television sets and all kinds of information available. All the races from all over the country, all the ball games were there for viewing.

He was really good at whatever he went into, and he was always a step ahead. Whether you liked him or not, he was a force to contend with. For instance, before the bombing, when he was in charge of entertainment at the Stardust, he booked Siegfried and Roy.

Unlike Tony Spilotro, who never tried to be anything other than a street guy, Lefty considered himself a sophisticate. He always wore tailored clothes. It wouldn't be the latest fashion, but it was what he liked. Always light colors. He was very much into himself; he couldn't walk past a mirror without stopping to check out his appearance.

We used to meet on a daily basis because he had a lot of serious issues. They were trying to ban him from the casinos even though he didn't have a serious criminal record. He worked for the Argent Corporation casinos (the feds would later charge that Argent was a front company for the mob). At different times he held posts at the Stardust, the Freemont, the Hacienda, and the Marina. Usually he'd take a job that did not require state licensing, something in entertainment or food. But whatever job he was assigned, the state would come in and demand that he get licensed. Sometimes they'd change the regulation because of him. It was a vendetta, and it wasn't based on anything he had done, but rather on who he was.

That's one of the problems I have always had with the Black Book and the approach that the regulators took. These holier-than-thou guys on the gaming board considered it guilt by association—guilty until proven innocent. I found that to be fundamentally unfair, but the courts upheld the regulators. I thought it was all bullshit.

Rosenthal and I would meet, sometimes at restaurants, but rarely in his office. He was concerned about bugs, and I didn't like speaking to him in that atmosphere. When we would meet at his home, invariably he would be wearing one of those Hugh Hefner–type bathrobes. His wife, Geri, who was the nicer of the two by far, waited on him hand and foot. He would demean and berate her, acting as if he were entitled to do this.

He was also a perfectionist, which I guess made him a good businessman, but he had a mean streak. At the casino, if he saw a cigarette butt on the floor, he would pick it up. Then he would find out who was supposed to be picking it up and have that person fired. Even the way he raised his kids was very demanding. He made sure they got up every morning at 4 A.M. to go to swimming lessons before school.

All these guys treated me well, but I learned a really important lesson when I first started representing Rosenthal. I was supposed to file something on a minor case, but the time had lapsed. I told him what had happened, and instead of berating me, he said, "As long as you tell me, it's okay. Just don't ever try to hide anything from me."

A judge once told me the same thing: "When a lawyer tries to hide a mistake, it grows."

It was a good lesson.

Rosenthal wasn't an intellectual, but he was innately smart. He always wanted to know what I was doing. And I can tell you, it wasn't a pleasant experience to be around him.

The car bombing only made things worse.

At the time, there was already a lot going on in the circles in which he and Tony Spilotro traveled. A year earlier, the cops and feds had made a big bust, bringing down several members of the so-called Hole-in-the-Wall Gang.

These were burglars who went about their business by cutting holes in the roofs or walls of establishments they had targeted.

Law enforcement believed these guys worked for Tony, and that some of the merchandise, particularly when there was a heist at a jewelry store, ended up for sale at The Gold Rush, a jewelry shop that Tony and his brother John had opened.

On the previous Fourth of July, 1981, the Hole-in-the-Wall Gang had targeted Bertha's Gifts and Home Furnishings. An informant had given up details about the planned heist, and the police and feds were waiting. Six members of the gang, including a former cop, were arrested.

One of the guys busted was Frank Cullotta, who the feds had identified as a "top associate and bodyguard" of Tony Spilotro, but I never believed that. I was having dinner with Tony once at Piero's, a nice Italian restaurant, and he pointed to Cullotta, who was sitting across the room with some other men.

"Never say anything around that guy," Tony said. It was clear he didn't trust him.

Cullotta, like Tony, had come to Las Vegas from Chicago. He had a pizza parlor called "The Upper Crust" and appeared to be one of those hangers-on types. I never liked him. Later Cullotta would claim that I had represented him, but that wasn't true.

I bumped into Cullotta once while he was on his way to court. His lawyer had an office in the same building, and they were coming down the stairs through our lobby. Cullotta asked me, "How do I look?"

I told him he should be wearing a tie because it was important to show respect for the court. He said he didn't have one, so we found one in the office. Then he said he didn't know how to tie a knot, so I showed him. In hindsight, I probably should have strangled him with it.

After the Bertha's bust, Cullotta cut a deal with the government. Among other things, he had been suspected of the murder of a guy named Sherwin "Jerry" Lisner. Lisner was found dead in the backyard pool of his Las Vegas home in 1979. He had been shot multiple times.

When Cullotta agreed to cooperate, he said he was the shooter in the Lisner hit, but claimed it was ordered by Tony. He also tied Tony to the infamous M&M murders in Chicago and said Tony was the brains behind the Hole-in-the-Wall Gang.

This was another example of law enforcement's willingness to deal with despicable people in order to make cases against individuals like Tony. Cullotta eventually admitted to being involved in four murders, yet the government was happy to use him as a witness and to vouch for his credibility in front of a jury. As far as I was concerned, he was a low-life. The FBI hated Cullotta when they were investigating him, but after he flipped, they fell in love with him. He was still the same rotten person he was when he was on the streets, but now he was their guy and could do no wrong.

He ended up getting eight years—not bad for four murders. And I think he actually spent little more than a year in jail. When he came out, he became this "Mafia expert" and gave talks and made appearances. It was as if he had become Professor Cullotta, which disgusted me.

Shortly after word got out that Cullotta had flipped, John Spilotro's home was shot up. Somebody sprayed his house with gunfire in a drive-by. No one was ever charged, but speculation is that some of the investigators who were working the Tony Spilotro case were behind it. They were "celebrating" Cullotta's decision.

That's not the way law enforcement is supposed to conduct its business.

But the mob also had changed. Cullotta was not the kind of guy who would have made it to the inner circle of any organized crime group twenty years earlier. The oath of omerta, the code of silence, meant something back then.

This is not to justify or defend the Mafia, but merely an attempt to explain it. Those so-called "men of honor" from the 1930s and 1940s were different than the wiseguys of the 1980s. Some of them—not all of them, but some—truly believed they were part of a special society. They lived by their own code. They were outlaws, but they had rules and—I know it sounds bizarre—ethics.

Cooperating with law enforcement was unheard-of. To them, the Mafia was a way of life. If someone was arrested and sent to prison, his family would be looked out for. When he finished his time and came home, there would be a job waiting for him. A lot of that had fallen by the wayside by the 1980s. For many of these guys, the Mafia wasn't a way of life, but a way to make money. And when they got jammed up and were looking at a prison sentence, omerta wasn't part of their mindset. Instead, they looked at it from a business perspective: how do I cut my losses?

Cooperating with law enforcement was the simple answer. And so in case after case in city after city, you saw the government making deals with murderers, extortionists, and drug dealers. Cullotta fit into that category.

So did Aladena "Jimmy the Weasel" Fratiano, another Mafia snitch who had the perfect nickname. I was with Tony in San Francisco a few years earlier when we crossed paths with Fratiano. We had gone up there for a grand jury appearance, and Fratiano was in the hallway of the courthouse when we got there, ready to testify against Tony.

Fratiano was a big-time Mafioso who had turned rat. He saw Tony and gave him the finger. Although he was surrounded by all his handlers, FBI agents, and prosecutors, Tony wanted to go after him. I think Tony would have ripped his head off. Fratiano was very smug. I looked at him, and the only thing I could think of was, "This guy's a mouse practicing to be a rat."

Fratiano was never able to hurt Tony with his testimony, but Cullotta was another story. The only thing he had to deal with was information about Tony Spilotro, and so he gave the feds what they wanted. I believe he made a lot of it up, but the FBI was only too happy to make a deal with this devil.

That was the background, the buzz, the tension in Las Vegas in October 1982 when Lefty Rosenthal's car was blown up.

The next time I saw Lefty, he was lying in his bed at home still trying to figure out who was behind it. He never said he thought it was Tony, but after that incident, he was a changed person. He wasn't as arrogant. I think it took him down a peg, humanized him, showed him his mortality. Shortly after that he went through a divorce proceeding. I couldn't get involved in that because I knew his wife Geri. I advised both of them, but I couldn't be the lawyer for either one of them.

I remember thinking that things were getting out of hand. To see something like this happen on the street was mind-boggling. I never thought Rosenthal would end up in that kind of spot. I had a lot of respect for his acumen as a gambler and for the way he ran a casino; he was great at that, perhaps one of the best. But you have to understand, he was not a lovable fellow.

Still, the car bombing showed that in the world in which he did business, somebody—maybe more than one person—considered him expendable.

Tony never said anything about the car bombing. I always look for the unusual: when somebody dies, I go to the funeral and look around for who isn't there. I thought it was very odd that Tony never brought up the bombing, and that we never had any type of discussion about it. He had no opinion, no speculation about who did it. I wouldn't bring it up because it wasn't my place. I was a "need-to-know" lawyer. If you have a criminal case, I want all the information available that will help me defend you. But if there's no case, I don't need to know what else is going on in your life.

I said there never were any bombings in Las Vegas, but that's not entirely true. There had been a couple, but it wasn't the soup of the day. In Las Vegas, the Chicago way of doing things—a .22 bullet to the head—was more common.

When I first got to Las Vegas, somebody was blown to smithereens in a parking lot at one of the casinos, but that was the exception. When the mob was in control, there really were few murders in town. The rule was, if they were going to kill you, they took you to Arizona or California. The idea was not to bring attention to the area. It was bad for business, and they didn't want to scare away the tourists. Kansas City was where there were bombings.

There was one funny bomb-plot story about Ash Resnick, a guy who was a casino executive at Caesars. Ash was a big guy who had played for the Boston Celtics when he was younger. He was very well liked, but he apparently had a problem with a guy named Chuckie Berns, one of the city's more notorious cat burglars. Berns spoke with a heavy Russian accent. He was picked up on a wiretap talking about blowing Ash up. When he was asked when he was going to do it, he said in that thick accent of his, "Boom, boom. Ash Vensday." Whoever was listening told Ash, and consequently, there was no boom boom.

At the time of the Lefty Rosenthal car bombing, I was representing members of four different crime families who were at odds with one another. I didn't realize this until I saw the movie

Casino. I just knew they paid me well and treated me great; I had no idea there were factions. If I had known all that was going on at the time, I would have charged a lot more money, and would have had my own private plane and an island in the Caribbean.

Every day was an eye-opener. People I thought were clowns or jokes were the ones making the skim work for the hidden owners in a half dozen casinos. I wasn't a big fan of Carl Thomas, but everybody seemed to love him. He was indicted with Nick Civella, the alleged mob boss, in Kansas City for skimming cash out of the Tropicana. I had met Thomas through Jay Sarno. Like so many of these casino guys, Carl was a gentleman's gentleman. He was very generous, and always polite. I thought he was a legitimate businessman. He owned a place called Slots-A-Fun on the Las Vegas Strip across from the Riviera and next door to Sarno's Circus-Circus. It was like a pinball arcade except it was full of slot machines. It was a joint where they offered customers hot dogs and beer in the hopes that the food would be enough to draw them in as they walked along the Strip.

While his business establishment wasn't anything like the city's gambling palaces, Thomas nevertheless was a mover and shaker in town. He wined and dined with all the important people. For twenty-three years he was part of the society—whatever that means—of Las Vegas. I had no idea of the role he was playing.

But he was picked up on a wiretap telling Civella and those guys in Kansas City how to work the skim. He went to great extremes to make sure he was not followed when he traveled to Kansas City. They would meet at this secret location and Nick apparently told Carl to take a train, a bus, or walk through the desert if he thought he was being followed. Carl always took a circuitous route to these meetings, which took place in the basement of the home of one of Civella's relatives. Unfortunately for

Thomas, Nick Civella, and several other fellows, the feds found out about the location and managed to have the room bugged. They got a complete discussion of the skimming operation on tape.

When I got a look at the transcripts of that conversation and the FBI affidavits, it was as if my world turned upside down. It was unreal. Things I had taken for granted weren't so. It was like Alice in Wonderland.

Joe Agosto was another person who got indicted in the Tropicana case. He had been represented by my law office in an immigration dispute before the U.S. Supreme Court. He spoke with a really thick Italian accent and wore a silly hat. I always thought of him as a go-fer, and not much else. It wasn't even clear that he was a citizen. There was a dispute over whether he was born here or in Italy. The story he told was that he was born here, and that his parents sent him to live with an aunt in Italy when he was a child. He came back and took over as the producer at the Folies Bergere at the Tropicana. I thought he was a clown; a chauffeur for some people. Turns out he was an inside man for the mob.

Civella was my client in the case. I had no idea he was involved with these casinos and the skims. I was representing him in cases in Kansas City, but I never knew he had relationships with the guys back here until the Tropicana indictment. I just knew him as someone who loved to come to Las Vegas. Even after they banned him, he used to sneak in wearing a disguise.

I realized that it was like a spider web: I was running from court to court representing my clients, attacking the wiretaps, fighting for their rights under the Fourth Amendment. Never once did I hear about a skim. I started reading this stuff, and my eyes were popping out of my head.

Civella's problem was that he liked to talk. And back in Kansas City, they had this mistaken belief that if they used their lawyer's office, it was sacrosanct; that there was no way the government could be listening. Nick and some of his guys would get on the phone in the lawyer's office and think they were immune from government wiretaps. That's how the Tropicana skimming case got made.

The bottom line is, if they weren't so greedy, they could still be running the casinos. In some of these cases, they were getting maybe $25,000 a month after they split it all up. It was insanity to risk what they had for that small amount of money. And the front people they had—such as Allen Glick with the Argent Corporation, or Mitzy Briggs, who was a wealthy heiress to the Wrigley family fortune in Chicago—were as welcome in the Las Vegas community as a rabbi or a priest would be.

Glick, it turned out, answered to Lefty Rosenthal. When this eventually came out it created problems, but I wasn't aware of it initially.

Spilotro was also named in the Tropicana indictment that came out in Kansas City, but I was able to get him severed from the case. Most of the other defendants, including Civella and Thomas, were convicted. There wasn't much you could do to defend them once the government played the tapes for the jury.

But Spilotro had more pressing problems at the time. Cullotta was singing up a storm for the government.

Tony was indicted in Chicago for the M&M murders. Cullotta said he helped Tony set up the hits, which occurred back in 1962. The victims were James Miragllia and Billy McCarthy, and as mentioned earlier, the M&M came from their last names. The allegation was that these two characters had robbed and murdered three people in an affluent Chicago suburb where a lot of guys from the Outfit lived. This was considered disrespectful, so Tony got the order to kill them. The murders were gruesome and included the use of a vise that caused the eye of one of the victims to pop out.

We went to Chicago to try the case. Tony had local counsel as well, and I was convinced to go along with a strategy that included a non-jury trial, so we'd be in front of a judge. They told me not to worry, but as the case drew to a close, I was very worried.

At the end of the trial I argued that the government had failed to prove its case and that the judge should throw out the charges and dismiss the indictment. He rejected my motion. Now I had no hope. Our closing arguments would be basically the same as my motion for dismissal. Tony and his co-counsel said not to worry.

After I made the same arguments, the judge took the case under advisement. A few days later, he came back with his verdict: not guilty. We beat the case and headed back to Las Vegas.

Several years later, the judge was indicted for taking bribes to fix criminal cases. The M&M murder case was not one of the cases listed in the criminal complaint against him, but I have always wondered about it.

Back in Las Vegas, we had to defend against the charges brought in the Hole-in-the-Wall Gang case. Again, Cullotta was the chief witness. In that case, we called a state court judge who testified that when he sentenced Cullotta on a burglary charge, the FBI—Yablonsky—had come to him begging for leniency. The judge said he went along, but he also said that at the time he had no idea Cullotta was a confessed murderer. The FBI had left that part out when they talked to the judge.

I also heard from another person who had been in jail with Cullotta. He said Cullotta had told him that he was making up most of what he was saying about Tony, but that that was what the FBI wanted to hear.

The prisoner was a guy named Frank Sweeney who apparently was in a protective custody wing of a prison in San Diego with Cullotta. Sweeney had also been a government witness in a murder case. Now he was telling me how Cullotta used to laugh about the FBI, calling them "stooges." He said Cullotta told him, "You've heard of the traveling circus? I'm the traveling perjurer." We used Sweeney to undermine Cullotta, and the prosecution in turn tried to discredit Sweeney, claiming he was unreliable and unstable.

I found that both hypocritical and typical. The government vouched for Sweeney when he was their witness in a murder case. But when he was saying something they didn't want to hear, then he was unreliable.

We were in the midst of the Hole-in-the-Wall trial when the judge heard that a couple of jurors had overheard a discussion that they shouldn't have been privy to. He reluctantly declared a mistrial. It was one thing after another.

Tony was also charged with the Lisner murder, and again Cullotta was his chief accuser. Tony was a fighter, and I was happy to represent him. I had gotten to know him very well over the years. To me, this mobster who supposedly had killed twenty-six people was a very caring person. When he was in my law office, he was always very courteous to the staff and the paralegals. They all liked Tony, and some of them loved him. He would bring trinkets from his jewelry store if it was someone's birthday or anniversary. He was not the kind of guy that I saw portrayed in the media; he was likable, and he had the ability to laugh at himself.

When he saw the caption in the Tropicana skimming case, and read the words "The United States versus Anthony Spilotro," he laughed.

"How fair is that?" he asked.

Even with all the trouble he was in, he could joke about the people who were trying to put him away for life. I wish every client I had had been like Tony. He came from the streets, and he knew who he was. He also listened to his lawyer.

Don't misunderstand me; he compensated me very well. My mother used to tell people, "Oscar's clients always take him to the best restaurants." But it was more than that. When I was out of town on a case, Tony would call Carolyn and ask if she or the kids needed anything. He was one of the first clients to do that, and I thought that was pretty extraordinary. And he had a great philosophy. He'd always say, "You can only eat one steak at a time." That was the difference between him and a guy like Steve Wynn or some of these other casino owners who think they have to conquer the world. Tony wasn't like that.

In many ways, Tony was a family guy. And I mean that in the true sense of the word "family." His father came to the United States from Bari, Italy, and ran a little restaurant in Chicago called "Patsy's." Mob boss Sam Giancana and some of the other big Outfit guys from back in the day, including Frank Nitti, used to be regular customers. I never met Tony's father, but I did meet his mother, Antoinette, who Tony doted over. He called her "Ma" and couldn't do enough for her. There were six brothers, Tony, Pat, Victor, Vince, John, and Michael.

John and Michael were the only ones I really got to know. John had a restaurant in Las Vegas and lived down the street from Tony. They both had beautiful homes in a nice residential area. Michael, the youngest brother, lived in Chicago. He also had a restaurant and like John, was very close to Tony.

Probably the most interesting of the brothers was Pat. He was a highly regarded dentist back in Chicago. He had eleven kids and was very well-educated. We had some great discussions when he would come out to visit. Pat was a bigger version of Tony. Of all the brothers, Pat and Tony looked the most alike. I remember sitting in a coffee shop with Pat at the Sahara early one morning. We're drinking coffee. Pat was having some breakfast, and, as usual, the discussion focused on the Black Book and how unconstitutional we both thought it was. I got up to go to the men's room and when I came back, Pat was gone.

It took me a few minutes, but I found out the Metropolitan Police had grabbed him. They had gotten a tip—I figure it was someone who worked in the place—that Tony Spilotro was in the restaurant. Since it was part of the casino and since Tony was in the Black Book, he wasn't permitted to be there.

Pat, to his credit, didn't say a word and let the whole thing play out. They questioned him in the security room of the casino and blew me off when I tried to tell them they were making a big mistake. They took Pat down to the Detention Center and told him he was going to be arrested. They were just about to book him when someone thought better of it. They finally established Pat's identity and let him go.

Unlike his brother Pat, Tony got his education on the streets. Short and stocky, but tough both mentally and physically, he already had a reputation as a wiseguy when he got to Las Vegas and became my client. By that point, if you believed the police and the FBI, he was a one-man crime wave and was behind almost every act of violence that occurred in the city.

Tony and I used to meet for dinner at Joe Pignatello's restaurant, Villa d'Este. Tony said that Joe had once been the chef for Giancanna back in Chicago. Tony loved a veal-and-peas dish that Joe used to make. One year during Christmas week we had dinner there with Sister Domenica, who had gained fame as "the singing nun." It was Tony, his wife Nancy, his son Vince, the good sister, and myself.

My wife says I'm wrong to say this, but if I had read the script for *Casino* before they made the movie, I would have told the writer, Nick Pileggi, and director Martin Scorsese that they had it wrong. They really didn't capture Tony's personality. Robert DeNiro was good as Lefty Rosenthal. However, Joe Pesci as Spilotro throws around words like "peckerwood" or "mullanyan," racial epithets that I never heard Tony use.

But I have to say that Pesci got Tony's look perfect. I played myself in the movie, and there was a scene where I was walking out of court with him. It was remarkable how much he resembled Tony: his mannerisms, his gait, the crook of his arm.

This is the kind of guy Tony was. We would be out of town for a trial, staying at the same hotel. I always got a room next to his. And in the morning, he would never wake me up. But he would start moving around his room and I would hear the clinking of coffee cups and breakfast plates. He was subtly letting me know he was awake.

All the times I was with him, I never saw any indication that he was using drugs, yet that's the way he was portrayed in the movie. Other clients would come to see me with their noses running, but I never saw that with Tony. And I never *dreamed* that he was having an affair with Geri Rosenthal.

The idea that Tony Spilotro and Lefty Rosenthal weren't getting along, or that Spilotro was sleeping with Rosenthal's wife, never occurred to me. I didn't have an inkling; both were my clients, and neither one ever said anything that indicated they were at odds.

My relationship with Rosenthal began to cool a little bit after the car explosion. I don't know if he thought Spilotro was behind it, but our relationship changed after that, maybe because he thought I was too close to Tony. I would hear that they continued to meet secretly, and Rosenthal never indicated to me that there was any problem.

It was hard for me to say what was going on because, as I stated earlier, I tried not to get involved in people's personal lives. I was the same way with my office staff. I would do anything for my staff, but I didn't get involved in their private business. That's just my personality.

I never felt endangered when I was around those guys. If anything, they protected me, and they would not allow me to get involved in their business activities because I was their lawyer. As I said, my wife, Carolyn, would always tell me, "Don't become your client." And I listened.

I was never worried about my personal safety. I was more concerned with the FBI trying to entrap or frame me. My clients viewed me as an asset, someone who they valued and someone whom they protected. They would never put me in any situation that might compromise my ability to defend them.

Lefty got out of Las Vegas shortly after the bombing. He took his kids and moved to the San Diego area. Later, he relocated to Florida, and I didn't have much contact with him after that.

While speculation put Tony behind the attempt on Lefty's life, I later heard that some investigators believed the car bomb was because the guys in Kansas City thought Rosenthal was cooperating with the FBI. In fact, there was a wiretap in which Nick Civella was on the phone with me asking about Rosenthal. This was when Lefty was making all those public statements and arguing with the gaming regulators and going on television.

"Is he crazy?" Civella asked me on the recording.

The feds took it to mean that Civella was asking me if Rosenthal was cooperating, but I don't represent rats.

I knew Rosenthal talked to guys on the Gaming Control Board, but to my knowledge, there was never any quid pro quo. Rosenthal just thought he was smarter than a lot of these guys, and sometimes I think he really believed he could convince them that he deserved to be licensed. He thought he had a relationship with some of them, but he was deluding himself. Newspaper guys and politicians weren't his friends, but he always thought he could beat the system. He didn't believe he was doing anything wrong, and he thought they owed him. He was indomitable, as far as his spirit was concerned. But he wouldn't listen; not to me, anyway.

He wasn't like a lot of the others who went before the board. He accused the regulators of being hypocrites, which they were. They were taking comps at the Stardust, getting rooms, seeing shows, and Rosenthal started blasting them. That's why Civella asked me if I thought he was crazy, and I said, "No."

In fact, I thought the things Lefty was saying, either before the Gaming Control Board or on his television show, were the truth. Now obviously, people in the underworld didn't like all that attention, all that publicity. I think that was where he had a problem. See, Rosenthal never thought he was mobbed up. He thought the authorities were abusing him. Although I have to say, if there was such a thing as being a "dry snitch," Lefty might have been that. You know, someone who talks to the authorities, but not because he has a deal or is an informant, but because he thinks he's smarter than them or just wants to establish some kind of relationship.

Despite his arrogance, sometimes I think Lefty just wanted to be liked. I don't think he ever gave authorities any damaging information. I think it was more about who he was talking to rather than what he said.

Look, I know that the guys I represented had some questionable dealings and associations. But I always thought my job was to be their lawyer, and to give them the same legal benefits any citizen deserved. There's no question that being a so-called mob lawyer gave me the opportunity to practice law at a very high level. Every day I would wake up to some monumental issue concerning wiretaps or the Rico law, or a search and seizure, or the Black Book. I had to perform at the peak of my ability, or my clients would have been gobbled up by the system.

Tony Spilotro is a prime example. He was never convicted, but they said he was the mob's guy in Chicago, and that he committed twenty-six murders. They were never able to prove that, so they labeled him. They called him a vicious Mafia killer and they went after him. I thought that was out of line; that they should make the case and prove the case. I was there to make sure they played by the rules. If that's being a mob lawyer, then that's what I was. I have no problem with that.

When Tony got killed, no one from the FBI ever asked me anything about it. Not that I would have told them anything, because I didn't know anything. But that's not the point. They didn't want to solve that case; they were just happy he was gone.

We were waiting to retry the Hole-in-the-Wall case when Tony went back to Chicago to see his brother, Michael. Michael was somewhat involved in Tony's business, and he also had a great little restaurant in Chicago called "Hoagies."

About a week after Tony left, I got a call from his wife Nancy telling me that she was worried. She hadn't heard from Tony in several days, and he and Michael were missing. The next thing I knew, their bodies were found in a cornfield in Indiana. They had been beaten and buried alive; just planted in the ground. Whatever happened to him had to be a surprise or an ambush. He was one tough fireplug, and he would have gone down swinging.

After he was murdered, I never heard from anybody other than the family. I had tried cases with Tony all over the country. We had appeared at grand juries in different jurisdictions, and had spent an inordinate amount of time together because he had so many outstanding issues. But nobody from law enforcement came to see me when he "went missing." I was even more shocked when no one, especially no one from the FBI, came to see me when his body was found. Did I know anything? Had I heard anything? Did Tony have any pressing problems? None of these questions were asked of me.

I came to the conclusion that they were happy to be rid of him. I didn't believe them when they said they were trying to solve the murder. After Tony was killed, the media coverage shifted. Tony wasn't the mob's guy in Vegas anymore; he was just a street punk. Now that he was gone, there was a media campaign to belittle him.

That's not who he was. I saw him as a human being, not some dime-store fictional character.

I went back to Chicago for the funeral, curious to see who would be in attendance. The FBI and the Chicago Police Department were there, taking notes and snapping pictures as they do at most "mob funerals." But the thing that struck me was that several of the so-called wiseguys who Tony was supposedly representing in Las Vegas weren't there. They saw no need to pay their final respects.

That said a lot to me about who was behind Tony's murder. A few years ago, there was a federal investigation in Chicago that included details about Tony's death and those who were behind it. The feds love to give sensational names to their investigations, and this one was called "Family Secrets."

Actually, it was a fairly accurate description. A mobster in Chicago became an informant and testified against dozens of members of the Outfit, including his own father and brother. That's how far the "men of honor" have fallen.

According to the informant, Tony and his brother were killed on the orders of James Marcello, one of the bosses back there. The Spilotro brothers were lured to a hunting lodge, beaten, tortured, and shot, and then buried in a cornfield.

I find it somewhat ironic that the government could only solve this case when a rat came forward.

At a trial in 2008, there was testimony that one of the Outfit's hitmen had boasted that he had orders to kill Tony, his brother Michael, and me. The hitman said he planned to use an Uzi sub-machine gun and take all three of us out.

By the time I heard about this, of course, I was mayor and no longer practicing criminal law. I always said I never worried about my own safety when I was representing mobsters, but maybe I should have.

CHAPTER 9
A VISIT TO THE MUSTANG RANCH

A month after Tony's body was found, and while I was still trying to make sense of it all, the House of Representatives in Washington handed up articles of impeachment against my good friend Harry Claiborne.

Harry was a federal judge who had been convicted in an income tax case. I represented him in that matter. After his conviction he was sentenced to jail, but he refused to resign as a judge. So congress moved to impeach.

Lawyers are supposed to remain above it all, detached, focused. But Tony and Harry were more than just clients; they were friends. And I took what happened to them personally. I never shied away from events surrounding either of them. My relationship with them was on a different level than most of my other clients. And just because they had been charged with a crime, I wasn't going to stop being their friend.

The interesting thing was that while they came from entirely different backgrounds, they shared some common traits. They were fearless, honorable to a fault with me, and neither one of them ever complained about the hand they were dealt. They were fighters; they believed in themselves and they never backed down.

The fact that one was an alleged gangster and the other was a lawyer and judge was of no consequence to me. I dealt with people as I found them, not as others might describe or label them.

The move to impeach Harry was, as far as I was concerned, the last act in a vindictive, personal witch hunt.

Harry was the best defense attorney in Las Vegas when I first came out here, and I was privileged to work on some cases with him. I learned a lot about the law and about people. Harry was genuine; there was no pretense about him. He was born and raised in Arkansas, and still had a bit of a Southern drawl. He also had that Southern way about him—never flustered, never seeming to be in a hurry, but sharp as a tack. He was a master at marshalling facts and distilling information, and was a great lawyer. He was my mentor. Later, when some people compared me to him, I was honored.

He also had a dry sense of humor and a quick wit that he used to great advantage in front of a jury. We were trying a drug case together up in Reno one time. We each had a client in the case who was a privileged hippie—that's the only way I can think to describe the two of them—who routinely had large quantities of marijuana flown in. The plane would land at a makeshift airfield in a dried-out lakebed outside of Reno. The area was called Grass Valley.

In this case, the plane had crashed, the drugs were discovered, and our clients were arrested. The sheriff who investigated the crash went into great detail for the jury about how and where all this had happened.

When Harry opened his cross-examination, he looked at the sheriff and said, "Can you tell me, sir, what was that valley called before the plane crash?" The jury loved it. We didn't win the case, but those kinds of things help establish a relationship with the jurors. In a criminal case, even having one juror sympathetic or empathetic can help. A hung jury is the next best thing to "not guilty."

Over the years, Harry's clients included Frank Sinatra when Sinatra was fighting with the gaming commission, Dean Martin, and Judy Garland. I think he even represented Bugsy Siegel back in the day. But during his career, Harry had rubbed some people the wrong way, particularly some people in law enforcement. And I think they set out to get him. Joseph Yablonsky, my FBI nemesis, was leading the pack.

Harry was well aware that he had been targeted. Even before he became a federal judge, he had developed a unique habit. He knew that in order to be charged with conspiracy, you had to agree with at least one other person to commit whatever the offense might be. So whenever he left a meeting, in addition to saying goodbye, he would add, "Count me out." He figured if anyone was secretly taping the meeting and trying to set him up, those words would indicate that he was not agreeing to whatever conspiracy might be alleged.

It was a hell of a way to have to live, and I think it was sad that someone of his stature and reputation had to protect himself that way. But I also knew that just because he might have been paranoid, it didn't mean the feds weren't out to get him.

I found this out firsthand when another attorney came to me with a story about Yablonsky. This lawyer had gotten himself jammed up with some gambling problems for which he might face criminal charges. He told me Yablonsky came to him with a proposition. The FBI wanted the lawyer to attempt to bribe Harry by offering him $50,000 to fix his case. And the feds wanted him to make the offer through me. They wanted to put me and Harry in the same "conspiracy." Instead, the lawyer told me what was going on. It just reinforced Harry's perception that they were out to get him.

And unfortunately, they did.

It's hard to know where to begin the Harry Claiborne story, but I think his problems started when he was appointed to the federal bench in 1978 by President Jimmy Carter. He was chosen to fill a vacancy on the District Court of Nevada. Two years later, he was chief judge, and he remained there until 1986, although his last year was spent in prison rather than on the bench.

I had tried some cases in front of Harry, and he was always fair. He understood the law, and he also understood the roles of the prosecution and the defense. Some prosecutors, who were used to judges being government proxies, didn't like that.

But Harry had problems with the feds even before he started to hear cases. His appointment raised eyebrows in law enforcement circles because of his lifestyle and his associations. Harry was a good friend of Benny Binion, a legendary casino owner with a checkered past. Binion had come to Las Vegas in the 1950s from Texas, where he had been involved in illegal gambling and had been the target of several murder investigations.

Harry never turned his back on his friends. Some people might consider them outlaws, but he didn't. And whether he was a lawyer or a federal judge, he was always going to be true to his beliefs.

He used to have lunch every day with Benny at the Horseshoe. Binion would have squirrel stew; you could see the squirrel's little buck teeth and shiny eyes in the bowl. Harry had ham hocks and lima beans. Every day it was the same. I would have lunch with them once in a while. I was always on a diet, and if I was splurging, I'd get a little olive oil on a pile of lettuce and tomatoes.

Harry would look at my plate and say, "Oscar, you keep eating like that and it's gonna make you impotent."

Harry loved the ladies, and went out with lots of pretty women. He was divorced, and he had an eye for the girls. He

On the gridiron at Haverford College. (Courtesy of Oscar Goodman)

Frank "Lefty" Rosenthal sits as Oscar goes over a chart at one of his many casino licensing hearings. (Courtesy of *Las Vegas Review-Journal,* reprinted with permission, photo by Jeff Scheid)

Oscar (third from left) and the rest of the defense team after a victory in one of the Philadelphia mob trials. (Courtesy of Oscar Goodman)

Left: Tony Spilotro and his defense counsel. (Courtesy *Las Vegas Sun*)

Below: Tony and Oscar arriving at a hearing. (Courtesy *Las Vegas Sun*)

Oscar celebrates daughter Cara's 13th birthday with friends Tony Spilotro, Chris Petti, and Joey Cusamano. (Photo by Cara Lee Goodman)

The infamous law enforcement chart that mocked Oscar and others outside the grand jury room. (Courtesy of Jonathan Ullman, CEO Mob Museum, photo by John Gurzinski)

Las Vegas Mayor Oscar B. Goodman in his office. (Courtesy of the LVCVA News Bureau, photo by Bob Brye)

Oscar and his good friend, Judge Harry Claiborne, in happier times. (Courtesy *Las Vegas Sun*)

Mayor Oscar Goodman throws out the first pitch during MLB Big League Weekend game at Cashman Center. Cubs VS White Sox. (Courtesy of the LVCVA News Bureau, photo by Brian Jones)

Muhammad Ali takes a shot from the mayor. (Courtesy of Oscar Goodman)

Our trip to London. (Courtesy of the LVCVA News Bureau, photo by Simon Wright)

Obama and Oscar. (Courtesy of AP Images)

Wax likeness and the Mayor himself at Madame Tussaud's Wax Museum. (Courtesy of the LVCVA News Bureau, photo by Bob Brye)

Oscar swears in Mayor-elect Carolyn G. Goodman at City Hall, July 2011. (Courtesy of the LVCVA News Bureau, photo by Darrin Bush)

Carolyn grabs Oscar's nose during a ceremony at the Oscar B. Goodman Tribute Plaza in Symphony Park. (Photo by Mona Shield Payne)

Oscar and friends at the opening of the Mob Museum. (Courtesy of the Mob Museum, photo by John Gurzinski)

Carolyn and Oscar recite "The Night Before Christmas" with the Las Vegas Philharmonic at the Smith Center for the Performing Arts. (Courtesy of the Smith Center for the Performing Arts, LVCVA News Bureau, photo by Brian Jones)

Goodman Dynasty: Oscar and Carolyn surrounded by their children, their children's spouses, and their grandchildren. (Photo by Carol Cali of The Meadows School)

also drank. The vetting process when he was nominated by Jimmy Carter was intense. Investigators went to prisons to interview former clients of Harry's and asked all kinds of questions about how he had represented them and how he had been paid. They were looking for ways to undermine the nomination. They weren't able to do that, but they didn't stop after he got on the bench. He became a target of federal law enforcement.

There was a private investigator, Eddie LaRue, who Claiborne had used when he was a defense attorney. LaRue was a character. In the television show *VEGA$*, the private investigator Dan Tanna, played by Robert Urich, was patterned after LaRue. LaRue wasn't as good looking as Urich; he was a former jockey, only about five-foot-two. He came from Kentucky and spoke with a twang. But he was just as resourceful as the Dan Tanna character Urich portrayed in the series.

Claiborne was very close to LaRue, and Eddie would often join Harry and Benny Binion for lunch. The feds came to believe that Harry had had an electronic listening device planted in a girlfriend's apartment because he thought she was seeing another man. Naturally, the feds figured LaRue had planted the bug. He got indicted and asked me to represent him. He said the feds were telling him that if he gave up Claiborne, they'd drop the charges against him.

Eddie wouldn't do it. "Fuck them," he said.

The case got moved from Las Vegas to Reno because of the publicity, and because it was decided that it would be unseemly for LaRue to be tried in the same federal courthouse in Las Vegas where Claiborne was sitting as a judge. Aldon Anderson, a judge from Salt Lake City, was brought in to hear the case. He was a staid, conservative man, the kind of person who would have taken issue with the mere fact that a federal judge like Claiborne would even associate with a guy like LaRue. So we had that problem. In addition, up until that time, a Las Vegas defendant with a Las Vegas defense attorney had never won a federal case in Reno.

We were staying at the Pioneer Hotel in downtown Reno and would walk back and forth to the courthouse each day. It was a beautiful, relaxing walk along the Truckee River. Eddie used to play a Keno card every evening at dinner, and every day he would fill it out in the shape of an extended middle finger. It kept us laughing. That was his response to the government's offer to cooperate and give up Harry.

We got lucky. Eddie didn't deny planting the bug, but said it was part of a case he was working on. He never gave up the particulars and never mentioned Claiborne. A key part of Eddie's defense was that he had been told by a lawyer that what he had done—planting an electronic listening device—was legal. Reliance on an attorney's advice, even if it's bad advice, is a defense. One of our arguments was that Eddie thought what he was doing was legal, even though it wasn't. The lawyer who had given Eddie that advice came forward and testified that he had, in fact, told Eddie he could do what he did and not be breaking the law.

Eddie also had a state supreme court justice as a character witness. We beat the case, and to this day, I'm convinced Eddie LaRue wasn't the target. The government wanted him to say that Claiborne ordered him to bug a girlfriend's home because he was jealous of other men, but Eddie wouldn't say it.

At the same time, we were pretty much convinced that the feds had planted a bug in Harry's office. We couldn't ever prove it, but LaRue was certain the FBI had been listening in on Claiborne's conversations. That's a pretty blatant violation of a lawyer's privacy, but that was the kind of stuff Harry had to deal with.

Here's another example. After he was nominated, Harry said he stopped drinking. He had conceded that he drank too much, but said that he was now on the wagon. When he went to the Horseshoe—he used to keep money in a safety deposit box at the casino—he'd order a non-alcoholic drink or a cup of coffee. Several times after he left, an FBI agent casually walked up to the bar, picked up Harry's glass, and smelled it to see if it had contained whiskey.

A lot of this goes back to Joseph Yablonsky. The FBI agent wanted another notch in his gun, and he didn't care how he got it.

The funny thing is, Harry was a damn good judge; tough but fair. I had plenty of appearances before him and he always gave me a fair trial, but I got no favors. He called things as he saw them. He was a lot better than some other judges I know who are still on the bench.

But the feds were determined to get Harry Claiborne, and they found a tool in Joe Conforte: liar, cheat, pimp, and whoremonger who would say whatever the feds wanted him to say.

In December 1983, I was trying a case in front of Judge Claiborne when word came that he had been indicted. The charges were bribery, fraud, and tax evasion. He immediately declared a mistrial in the case I had before him. He said he thought it would be inappropriate to continue because of the indictment. Then he asked me if I would be willing to represent him, and I said it would be a privilege.

The bribery charge was based on an allegation that Conforte made. Conforte and his wife Sally ran the Mustang Ranch, the famous brothel out in Storey County. A few years earlier, Conforte had been convicted of four counts of tax evasion. He owed $1.9 million, and he was looking at a minimum of five years in prison. Harry Claiborne had represented Conforte's wife Sally at the trial, and she had also been convicted. Their verdicts were on appeal to the Ninth Circuit.

After Harry was appointed to the federal bench, he asked me to do him a favor and represent Sally at her sentencing. Sally was nothing like her husband Joe. She was a madame, but not a whoremonger. She had a tough veneer, but underneath was a pretty nice lady. A couple of weeks before the sentencing hearing, I flew up to Reno to interview her. She sent a driver to pick me up at the airport and he took me out to the ranch. It was the first time I had ever been there, and to tell the truth, it wasn't what I expected. I went through the doorway and Sally was waiting for me. The first thing she did was introduce me to her girls.

It was a real smorgasbord. Something for everybody—fat, thin, short, tall, all shades and colors. Each girl was wearing a peignoir or a teddy. She asked each one to tell me whether they were happy there, and whether they were treated properly. They all had positive things to say. Then she took me on a tour of their rooms, which reminded me of a college dormitory.

There was also a pool area where some other girls were relaxing. From there I was escorted to the dining room, which was off-limits to customers. I was served a delicious gourmet meal.

"That's what the girls eat," Sally said proudly.

I happened to look out the window during the meal and saw the biggest snowflakes I had ever seen.

"I have to get back to Las Vegas," I said.

"No way you're flying out in this weather," Sally said.

Instead, her driver took us back to her home on Sullivan Lane in Reno. It was a huge, old home. She and Joe were estranged, and she was living by herself. At the time she was involved with the great Argentinian heavyweight, Oscar Bonavena. She showed me to my room, which was decorated in red and black. The first thing I did was call Carolyn.

"Sweetheart, I'm stuck in Reno in a snowstorm and won't be able to get home until tomorrow," I said.

"What hotel are you staying in and what's the phone number?" she asked, two questions that she always asked whenever I was out of town on business.

"I'm at Sally Conforte's home," I said.

She paused, then told me, "Be careful."

The next day I got a flight back to Las Vegas. I was catching a cold, and when I got home, I was sniffling. Carolyn just gave me a look that said, "How'd you catch that?"

The indictment against Judge Claiborne alleged that Joe Conforte had paid him a bribe to find out when the Appellate Court was going to render an opinion on his appeal of the tax conviction—and more important, what that opinion was going to be. If the court upheld the conviction, Conforte would know in advance and would take off. The Claiborne indictment also contained some income tax evasion charges, but the bribery issue went to the very heart of Harry's integrity.

The evidence also included a statement from now-Supreme Court Justice Anthony Kennedy, who was then on the Ninth Circuit. In a deposition I took of him, Kennedy said his clerk had told him that Harry Claiborne had called the office to ask when the decision in the Conforte case would be coming down. I was able to argue that even if true, the call asked "when," not "what." In other words, Harry wasn't asking what the decision would be, but merely when it was going to be announced. That's not especially uncommon or, I would argue, criminal.

Conforte was a weasel. He had fled to Brazil to avoid prison after the Ninth Circuit upheld his conviction. Then he called the prosecutors and said he could give them Claiborne's head on a silver platter. The government lawyers went down there with all kinds of promises to get him to come back. They told him all he had to do was testify against Judge Claiborne.

I looked forward to cross-examining him, but even at that, I had to concede that the five-year sentence that caused him to flee was extreme. I thought it was personal. Conforte had been convicted of failing to withhold wage taxes from the girls who worked for him at the Mustang Ranch. The judge who had sentenced him was a master bridge player, and so was Conforte. They played against each other in tournaments, and this judge was apparently livid that Conforte, whom he considered a "whoremaster," was taking part in these tournaments. So at sentencing, he hammered him.

Justice is supposed to be blind. In this case it wasn't. Conforte got more time than he probably deserved, but that doesn't excuse what he did. He tried to throw Harry Claiborne under the bus to get out from under his own problems. And the feds were only too happy to buy into the story he was selling. In fact, they went all the way to Brazil to get it. Only after the government made him all kinds of promises did he agree to come back.

Bill Raggio, a Reno attorney and Nevada's most powerful state senator, was my co-counsel on the case. Years before, when Bill was a district attorney, Conforte tried to set him up with an underage prostitute. Raggio didn't fall for the trap, and legend has it that after that, he personally participated in the burning down of one of Conforte's whorehouses. Raggio hated Conforte. He asked me for a favor: would I let him cross-examine Conforte? He then ripped Conforte apart on the witness stand.

Conforte testified that he had paid Claiborne $85,000 for the information from the Ninth Circuit. He described in great detail Harry's apartment, where he said he had gone to deliver the cash. He described the layout to a T. The problem was, he had it backwards.

I can only believe that the government had shown Conforte an apartment in the same complex where Harry lived, but it was a reverse layout. The rooms were opposite the rooms in Harry's residence, as if you were looking in a mirror. It just goes to show you what means the government will go to in order to get the end that they want.

It was a technique I was familiar with. The government gets its witness to testify, and ninety percent of what is said is the truth. The other ten percent is a lie, but the jury usually believes the lies as well as the truth, resulting in a conviction.

The trial went on for several weeks. Like the Eddie LaRue trial, it had been moved to Reno from Las Vegas. This time, a judge was brought in from Norfolk, Virginia, to preside over the case.

Judge Walter Hoffman looked like a side of beef. He was huge; half a cow at least. And by the middle of the afternoon, his mind would start to wander. After three o'clock, you never knew what was going to happen. It was very bizarre.

One of the reasons the case was moved to Reno was because of publicity. The *Las Vegas Sun,* a local newspaper, was a big supporter of Harry Claiborne. Hank Greenspun, the publisher, thought Harry was getting railroaded, and the paper said it continually in front page headlines. When the case moved to Reno, Greenspun sent newspaper racks up there and had them placed outside the courthouse entrances. So every morning as the jurors arrived, they would see copies of the *Las Vegas Sun* screaming its pro-Claiborne headlines. Judge Hoffman went nuts. He ordered the racks confiscated and had them put in jail. I swear to God—the racks were behind bars. We finally got them released, but this was the kind of stuff that was going on.

Most of my legal motions went nowhere.

"Denied," roared Hoffman. "Denied, denied, denied."

That's all I heard. But you win or lose a case with the jury, and I thought we had a shot.

Teddy Binion, Benny's son, came up to Reno with us, and we had dinner each night during the trial. Teddy was probably the smartest and most street-wise guy I ever met. He was kicked out of every school he ever attended, but he had great insights. He came to me one day and said, "You can win this case if you tell the truth."

"What do you mean?"

"The judge had a drinking problem and suffered blackouts," he said. "Look at the tax returns. Some of them are written in pencil; they make no sense. He wasn't trying to evade taxes. He was drunk when he filled out the forms. He probably had no idea what he was doing."

Teddy, like his father, was a good friend of Harry Claiborne's, and he thought Harry was getting a raw deal. A couple of years later, Teddy was found dead in the den of his home. It was a sensational case; his girlfriend and a male accomplice were charged with murder. The prosecution theorized that his death was made to look like a heroin overdose.

Teddy's girlfriend and her lover were tried and convicted of murder, but on appeal, that conviction was overturned. At the retrial they were acquitted.

I didn't think Harry would go for Teddy's "I was drunk" defense on the tax issues, so I didn't bring it up. But we still nearly beat all the charges. The jury deadlocked 11 to 1 in our favor on each count. We ended up with a mistrial, a hung jury.

Conforte was totally discredited. He looked like the scumbag that he was. I think even the feds realized it. Conforte got time served for the withholding tax evasion charge—what little time he had served in jail after they brought him back from Brazil. The reduction of his sentence was illegal. The government attorneys got a judge in Washington, D.C., to reduce the sentence years after it was imposed, when the time for reduction of sentences had to be within 120 days of the conviction. On top of that, his tax liability was reduced. That was his payoff from the government for ruining Harry Claiborne's life. The feds gave him the candy store and he gave them nothing from the witness stand.

After the trial, Conforte headed back to Brazil. I don't think he ever paid the taxes he owed. Occasionally I saw pictures of him with a big Cuban Cohiba in his mouth and what appeared to be several teenage girls with their arms around his fat, hairy stomach.

When the government moved to retry the case, they dropped the bribery charge. They weren't going to put Conforte on the stand again. So at Harry's new trial, there was the income tax issue and some minor ethics offenses. The prosecutor offered us a deal. If Harry would resign as judge, they'd drop the charges. But Harry wouldn't go for it.

"I'm right," he said.

I wanted to use the defense that Teddy Binion had suggested. The tax returns were ridiculously prepared, and an argument that Harry was impaired would have great jury appeal.

The government theory was that Harry lived high and that after he became a federal judge, he couldn't maintain that lifestyle on a salary of $78,000. But I knew him. He was frugal; he didn't have a fancy car, he drove a truck. He wore the same clothes all the time, and I never saw him in a new suit. He just lived the way he always had.

There was a check, a refund from an earlier tax return. It was more than $100,000, and Harry still hadn't cashed it. It was sitting in a drawer. This was somebody who didn't care about money, and who obviously wasn't paying attention to his tax preparer—who wasn't that good, by the way. Harry would provide his accountant with all his information, sometimes written in pencil and scrawled across sheets of paper. The accountant would fill out the forms based on that information and then Harry, who may have been drunk at the time (according to Teddy's theory), would sign his tax returns.

As someone who drinks a lot, I know how that can be. There are times where you might appear lucid and act in a manner that people around you would believe you were not inebriated, but the next day, you have no recollection of what you were doing.

But Harry was a proud man, and I wasn't sure he would allow us to use drunkenness as a defense. First he would have to admit that he had a problem. And I think if I had suggested that defense, he would have lost all confidence in me. It was very tough, because I had such great admiration and respect for him as a man and as a lawyer.

In the end, I decided not to broach the drunken defense. Harry was convicted of the tax offenses and sentenced to two years in prison. He never flinched and never complained. He believed he was right, but he accepted the verdict. In a lot of ways, he was like Spilotro and some of my other clients who didn't whine or complain.

Harry stayed out on bail while we appealed. We went in front of the Ninth Circuit in San Francisco. The group included Harry and me, Harry's law clerk and secretary, and Tom O'Donnell, the judge from the Crockett case. He was a good friend of Harry's and mine. We had dinner the night before at one of Harry's favorite restaurants and we talked about the appeal, the arguments I would make the next day, and how things looked. One of the things we discovered was that Harry had gotten mail that was intended for O'Donnell, and O'Donnell had gotten mail that was intended for Harry. The only thing we could figure is that the feds were monitoring their mail, opening their correspondences. Obviously one of the idiots had put the mail back in the wrong envelopes. So my take on that was that both judges had been targeted by the federal government, and Harry was the one they got.

We also spent time that night talking about old times, trying to keep things light.

We were going to meet for breakfast the next morning and then head over to court. I was drinking a cup of coffee when Harry walked into the restaurant and said that Tom O'Donnell wasn't feeling well. Harry planned to go with me to court, but now said he would meet me there after he checked on Tom.

When it was time to make our argument, Harry still hadn't shown up, so I asked the judges if they would take another case before ours. They graciously agreed, but eventually I had to make my arguments without Harry there. After the hearing I walked out in the hallway and there was Harry Claiborne, tears in his eyes. Tom O'Donnell had had a massive heart attack while he was taking a shower that morning.

Harry didn't want to tell me because he didn't want to upset me before the hearing. Now he was standing there in that hallway, his future on the line, but all he could do was cry over the death of his good friend.

Harry Claiborne and Tom O'Donnell were good judges and even better men.

We lost the appeal, and Harry ended up doing his time at the Maxwell Air Force base. That's where he was when the impeachment proceedings began. They brought him back East and kept him in the brig at Quantico, the Marine Base.

The first day he was brought into the Capitol for the Senate impeachment hearings, he was in shackles, shuffling in full-body chains and manacles. It was totally demeaning. I was able to get Senator Warren Rudman from New Hampshire to correct that. He told the marshals that this was not going to be tolerated.

But that was one of the few breaks we got from the Senate. We never really got a full hearing. The full Senate was supposed to read and review the transcript of proceedings, which were held before a committee of twelve senators. I'd wager that most of the senators hadn't read any of it. It was a rush to judgment. If the constitution wasn't broken that day, it surely was bent.

The senators just couldn't understand why Harry didn't resign. Several came to me, pleading with me to convince him to step down. If he had, I think the impeachment proceedings would have ended. But he was steadfast, so we had to go through it.

I wanted a full-blown trial in front of the entire Senate, to which we were constitutionally entitled. This was, after all, the first impeachment proceeding in fifty years. I had a witness list of nearly sixty people. But the Senate opted for a streamlined proceeding before the twelve-member committee. They permitted us to call a dozen witnesses. The hearing lasted seven days, and then the committee issued transcripts of the proceedings that the rest of the Senate was supposed to read before voting.

During the committee hearings, they would bring him from the brig to a safe house on Sundays to prepare. When he arrived, I'd ask him what he would like to eat. I told him I'd get him whatever he wanted. You'd think he'd ask for a steak or some other type of fancy meal. But no, he just wanted a hot dog with chili from the 7-Eleven, and he wanted to watch the football games on television.

I argued as best I could in front of the full Senate, but it was like arguing in front of a juror who was asleep. Most of the senators had already made up their minds. Al Gore was convinced that Claiborne was a bad person. I looked at the copy of the report on Barry Goldwater's desk. It looked like it hadn't been opened. I don't think there was anything I could have said that would have saved Harry.

The senate voted overwhelmingly in favor of three articles of impeachment. Harry Claiborne was found guilty of "high crimes and misdemeanors." He was stripped of his judgeship and sent back to finish his prison term.

Harry just sat there as the "guilty" votes were tabulated, one senator after another. We both knew what was happening. I looked out over that crowd of senators and saw that most hadn't even cracked the spine of the report they were supposed to read before voting.

As the vote was being taken, Harry wrote a note in red ink that he wanted me to give to Hank Greenspun of the *Las Vegas Sun*. After the hearing, I read the note to other reporters who came up to me. This was only the fifth time in all of our history that the Senate had voted articles of impeachment, and there was obviously a lot of media attention.

Here's what Harry wrote:

"A part of me died here today, not because of defeat, but because everything I believe in was assaulted beyond repair."

I look at it now, and I'm still shaken by the whole process. The investigation, the indictment, the trials, the impeachment. Harry Claiborne was a marvelous judge and an even better human being. But he was targeted by a venal group of individuals. The whole cast of characters—the FBI, the IRS, the Strike Force Attorneys, the trial judge, and most of the U.S. Senate—was not interested in justice.

Harry came back to Las Vegas after he finished his sentence, and the Nevada Supreme Court restored his law license. I think that says a lot about how they felt about what had happened. He was a lawyer again, but he was never the same. The impeachment had broken him. I think he was so disappointed in the system that he lost some of his love for the law.

In 2004, in the middle of a battle with cancer, Harry Claiborne killed himself. But as he said, a part of him had died long before that.

CHAPTER 10
IBM, NOT FBI

They say you can't go home again, but in the mid-1980s I got a chance to spend quite a bit of time in Philadelphia. The FBI had a major investigation into the crime family there, targeting mob boss Nicodemo "Little Nicky" Scarfo and most of his top associates.

Bobby Simone, Scarfo's lawyer, had recommended me to Leland Beloff, a city councilman who had gotten caught up in one of the many cases the feds had pending against the Scarfo organization. Beloff called me and I flew out to meet him. Once again, informants were the key. The mob rat I had mentioned earlier, Nicholas "Nicky the Crow" Caramandi, was the chief witness.

It was interesting to return to the city where I grew up and where my Dad had built his reputation as a lawyer. Some people still remembered him, and those who did always had nice things to say about him.

What they were saying about my client was another matter. Philadelphia had long had a reputation for political corruption. "Corrupt and contented" was a phrase coined back in 1904 by one of the muckraking journalists of the day, a man named Lincoln Steffens. He wrote an article for *McClure's Magazine* in which he said Philadelphia was one of the most corrupt, if not *the* most corrupt, city in the country.

Many were saying that still applied, although Steffens was writing about a Republican political machine. As a city councilman Beloff was part of the Democratic machine that controlled the city in the 1980s, and still does today.

Beloff was a millionaire. He had inherited a nursing home business that his father, a former Philadelphia judge, had founded. He was a handsome, well-spoken councilman whose district included part of South Philadelphia, which was the mob's nesting place, and an area along the Delaware River that had been targeted for redevelopment. For years the city had talked about Penns Landing, a location along the river that supposedly was the place where William Penn had landed when he came to Philadelphia.

Urban planners saw the riverfront as a natural location for a commercial, residential, and community development, something like the Inner Harbor in Baltimore or the South Street Seaport in New York. The city had finally gotten its act together and had tapped Willard Rouse, a nationally known developer, to spearhead the project.

According to a federal indictment, the mob jumped into the middle of the project through Beloff. A couple of city ordinances needed to be passed before the Penns Landing project could qualify for some federal aid programs. Several million dollars were at stake in terms of the federal funding, and many more millions when you considered the entire development plan. Beloff, as the councilman in whose district the project was located, could either hold up those ordinances or shepherd them through.

The feds said he cut a deal with the mob. Caramandi, a con artist, degenerate gambler, and overall low-life gangster, became the point man. He went to the Rouse people and told them he could hold up the ordinances or have them passed. What he wanted in exchange was $1 million.

It was a not-so-subtle mob shakedown. What Caramandi and his mob associates didn't figure on was Rouse. They were apparently used to dealing with corrupt politicians and corrupt businessmen. But Rouse, who wasn't from Philadelphia, went to the FBI. The feds got an undercover agent into the negotiations, posing as a Rouse project manager. He met with Caramandi, who repeated the demand, claiming that he had Beloff in his back pocket.

Scarfo, Caramandi, Beloff, and Bobby Rego, one of his council aides, were indicted. A short time later, Caramandi flipped and began cooperating, claiming he was convinced that Scarfo was going to have him killed for screwing up the shakedown. At around the same time, another member of the Scarfo organization, Thomas "Tommy Del" DelGiorno, cut a deal with the New Jersey State Police. Eventually DelGiorno was turned over to the feds.

These guys were murderers and had been targets of federal and state investigations, but now they were welcomed into the federal fold with open arms. Both were treated with kid gloves by their law enforcement handlers and by the judges who eventually sentenced them. They didn't spend time in prison, but rather in safe houses.

At one point, Caramandi was spotted by the mother of one of the defendants in the mob case. He was living in a condo in Ocean City, Maryland, a comfortable summer resort town, surrounded by a detail of FBI agents who rotated "duty shifts" at the seashore.

DelGiorno had an even better deal. Traditionally, the government rents a house in a safe location before relocating a witness and his family to that spot. DelGiorno got the okay to purchase a house in Virginia, where he and his family were moved while he was cooperating. The government then agreed to "rent" the house from him. He became both the proprietor who was renting to Uncle Sam, and the witness who was living in a safe house. All his family's needs were taken care of on taxpayer dollars, plus he was collecting rent from Uncle Sam.

In exchange, Caramandi and DelGiorno were "confessing" to all sorts of crimes—murders, assaults, and extortions—that stretched back for years in Philadelphia, Atlantic City, and Southern New Jersey.

That was the legal minefield I walked into when I was hired to represent Beloff. He was somewhat volatile, but was treated with a great deal of respect in the city. His constituents loved him. His aide, Bobby Rego, was a charming guy who lived in South Philadelphia and had grown up with some of the mobsters. And Lee's wife, Diane, was very nice. She was the better part of that duo.

We met for dinner one night at Bookbinders, a famous (now shuttered) Philadelphia landmark restaurant in the historic part of town. I was joined by Bobby Simone, who was representing Scarfo in the case, and Beloff and his wife. Beloff was under a lot of pressure at the time, and was a little paranoid. Plus we had a few drinks before and during dinner. All the while he kept looking across the room at another table where two men in suits were having a meal. They were dressed in conservative suits with white shirts and rep ties. As the night wore on, Beloff became convinced they were FBI agents who were there to keep tabs on him.

Bookbinder's was a great restaurant, and I was enjoying my meal and going over some preliminary details. All the while, Beloff kept looking at the two guys. Finally, as we were leaving, he flipped out, picked up a butter knife, and ran at them, screaming, "FBI motherfuckers!"

I don't know what he intended to do. We grabbed him, and the two guys in the business suits were shaking. After they got over their shock, they said, "We're not FBI. We're IBM."

That was my introduction to Leland Beloff and Philadelphia politics, circa 1987. We had a decent defense in the case and were able to beat up Caramandi pretty good on the witness stand. He looked like something out of central casting, wearing a leather jacket, a two-day beard, and had a gruff, heavily Philadelphia-accented voice. He also had a criminal record that went back decades. He was a scam artist with a conviction for passing counterfeit bills, and he was now admitting to being a hit man for the mob.

Another witness was a woman who was described as Beloff's girlfriend. That's always a ticklish situation, and as I said, I thought his wife Diane was a very nice lady. In another alleged extortion charge, the feds said Beloff had gotten his girlfriend a rent-free apartment in a building owned by a developer who needed city council approvals for another project.

The jury had only been out a couple of days when they sent a note saying they were deadlocked. The judge, John P. Fullam, a very dour man, immediately declared a mistrial. I think he knew the prosecution's case had gone badly, and in effect, he gave them a second chance. It was as if he was on a mission. I thought he was totally out of line, and I think if he had let the jury deliberate longer, we might have gotten acquittals.

Fullam either had a bug in the jury room or was listening through the wall, because I've never seen a mistrial declared without an instruction—they call it an Allen charge—asking the jury to go back and try again.

We tried the case a second time, but retrials are always bad for the defense. I like the spontaneity of a trial, but you tend to lose that the second time around. The prosecution knows what your game is and can bolster its case accordingly.

For example, in the second trial, Caramandi came in clean-shaven and wearing a jacket and tie, which de-emphasized his wiseguy look. The government also changed prosecutors. Edward S. G. Dennis, Jr., who was the United States Attorney for the Eastern District of Pennsylvania, handled the prosecution. This was highly unusual because Dennis was the boss. He had about 150 deputy and assistant U.S. attorneys who normally tried cases. But this time, Dennis brought the prestige of his position into the courtroom. This was the top law enforcement official in the city, and it had to have an impact on the jury.

Dennis did a very extraordinary thing that I had never seen before or since. He read his closing argument to the jury, and while he was reading it, he had it flashed on a screen on the wall, like a PowerPoint. I thought this gave added weight to what he was saying, and obviously the jury thought so, too.

Scarfo, Beloff, and Rego were convicted. Beloff got ten years, Rego got eight, and Scarfo got fourteen.

And that was just the start of Nicky Scarfo's problems.

We were constantly in court fighting pretrial battles and picking juries.

Jury selection is another interesting process. I know a lot of attorneys like to depend on "experts" who help analyze the questionnaires that potential jurors fill out and who try to develop insights into a juror's character based on how he or she answers questions posed during the selection process, which is called the *voir dire*, Latin for "to see and to say." I usually went with my own instincts.

It used to be that I would pick anyone who said they had a tattoo. That used to signify, at least in my mind, that the person was an individualist and a non-conformist. Today that's no longer the case. Tattoos are like fashion statements, and they don't tell us much about a person anymore.

I'm a Leo, born on July 26, and I would try to slip that fact into the question-and-answer sessions with possible jurors because I believe that you can sometimes make a connection that way; that a fellow Leo might be more sympathetic to the arguments of a lawyer who had the same birth sign. I would always try to keep naturalized citizens off the jury panel. I worried that they might be too gung-ho and rah-rah, and would accept anything the prosecution—the embodiment of the United States of America—might say. Another thing I tried to ask about was bumper stickers. You can sometimes get an idea of who a person is by the bumper sticker he or she has on the back of the car.

At the end of the day, jury selection is really a legal crapshoot. We had a lot of that when I was back in Philadelphia for those mob trials. Unfortunately, we didn't roll many sevens.

The FBI and the New Jersey and Pennsylvania State Police had been building cases against the Philadelphia mob for a number of years, and it all came to a head in the mid-1980s. Two murder cases were pending in Philadelphia's Common Pleas Court, and a drug case and a racketeering case were pending in federal court. Bobby Simone and I got along very well during the Rouse extortion trial, and he asked me to get involved in the other cases.

Scarfo's nephew, a handsome young man named Philip Leonetti, was a co-defendant in three of those cases, and Bobby asked me to represent him. He was an easygoing man who was thirty-six at the time. I met his mother Nancy, who was Scarfo's sister. She was very nice, and I felt sorry for Philip. I thought he had been targeted in part because of who the feds said his uncle was.

Scarfo was portrayed in government motions as a psychopath. The media, naturally, ate it all up. You would think this was the second coming of Al Capone or the Philadelphia version of *Murder, Inc.*

Several other alleged mob members were also charged, and it turned into a traveling circus. We just moved from courtroom to courtroom, defending these guys. Caramandi and DelGiorno were always the key witnesses. There were audio- and video-tapes, wiretaps, and other informants and alleged victims. It was a real onslaught, but we held our own.

Scarfo, Leonetti, and the others were charged with being involved in the distribution of millions of dollars of methamphetamine. Meth was a big drug on the streets of Philadelphia in the 1980s. But as we looked at the case, it was clear that the government had brought the wrong charge, and we were able to convince a federal jury of that.

One of the prosecutors, in very dramatic fashion, told the jury during his closing argument that if they came back with convictions, they would "effectively put an end to the mob in Philadelphia." It was typical government hyperbole, but the thing that struck me was that as he was saying this, these five hulking mobsters, guys with no necks, who had been attending the trial almost every day, stood up and walked out of the courtroom.

Clearly the mob still had a presence in Philadelphia, even with our clients in jail.

The evidence presented during the trial showed without much doubt that the Scarfo organization was shaking down drug dealers. The mob had what they called a "street tax," and any-one who was bringing P-2-P (the illegal chemical that you needed to make meth) into the city had to pay a tax of something like $2,000 a barrel to the Scarfo organization.

The evidence clearly showed that the drug dealers were making those payments to Scarfo and his crew. But that wasn't one of the charges in the case; there was no extortion count. The government really dropped the ball when they put this case together, and we made that point in our closing arguments. I told the jury that even if you accept the evidence that the defendants were collecting a street tax from these drug dealers, you have to find them not guilty because that wasn't what they were accused of.

Our clients were charged with running a drug organization, but there was no evidence to support that. They were clearly extorting drug dealers by forcing them to pay a street tax, but our clients were not part of a drug operation. There was no evidence linking them to the importation of the P-2-P, the manufacturing of the meth, or the sale and distribution of the product. In short, we argued, our clients were not drug dealers. They were shaking down drug dealers, but they were not dealing drugs themselves.

We won big-time; acquittals across the board. But no one went home. They were still being held without bail for the racketeering and murder cases.

The problem when a government launches a multi-pronged attack—and that's what it did against the Scarfo organization—is that the odds are stacked against the defense. We had to win every time, but the prosecution only had to win once. Scarfo was already doing fourteen years for the Penns Landing extortion, but he was facing much more time.

We beat a murder case in Common Pleas Court where Caramandi and DelGiorno were again key witnesses. It was during that case that authorities had to acknowledge that DelGiorno was provided with the services of a prostitute while in the custody of the New Jersey State Police.

DelGiorno had testified at a preliminary hearing against Scarfo and was being driven back to the safe house where he was living. He and his escorts stopped at a bar-restaurant in New Jersey for dinner and drinks, and apparently DelGiorno caught the eye of a working girl at the bar. The State Police looked the other way while he and the hooker got together. I thought that was demeaning. Think about it: law enforcement authorities, State Police detectives, standing around outside a hotel room while a mobster has sex with a hooker. Is that how low the government would stoop to bring down the mob?

During cross-examination, DelGiorno had to admit to it all. And one of the defense attorneys asked him, "Is this what you call doing hard time?" Since this was a Common Pleas Court jury, it was comprised entirely of Philadelphia residents, unlike the federal cases that draw from a pool that stretches out into the wealthy and more conservative suburbs. Several of the jurors got a big kick out of that comment, and I think it helped us. We won that case as well: not guilty across the board. And that night we partied. I was staying at the Four Seasons Hotel, and the defense team and lots of supporters and family members headed over to the hotel lounge, which wasn't far from the courthouse.

Scarfo, Leonetti, and the other defendants, of course, went back to jail since they were still being held without bail. The party got pretty raucous; in fact, they moved us to a special room. People were downing $50 shots of Louis XIV cognac, and $100-a-bottle Taittinger champagne was flowing freely. At the end of the night, the bar bill was something like $16,000.

Scarfo's son, Nicky Jr., who was in his early twenties at the time, came up to me and said he couldn't cover the bill. I liked Nicky Jr.; he was always polite and went out of his way to help my mother when she was with us at dinner after court. He'd hold the door open for her, take her arm and guide her up and down steps or through a doorway. He always called her "Mrs. Good-man," and would help her order off the menu, suggesting what was good and what she might like. After dinner, he would drive her back to the condo where she lived and make sure she got in safely. He behaved like a true gentleman, and I always appreci-ated that. So when he asked if I would put the hotel bill for the party on one of my credit cards, I agreed. In exchange, he said he would give me his Dad's Rolls Royce, a cream-colored, vintage

1973 model. Obviously the father wasn't going to need the Rolls for the next fourteen years, so I agreed to the deal.

I had no idea what I was getting myself into. For the next eight years, I had to battle the federal government over the gift. They seized the car before I could take possession, arguing that it was forfeiture for Scarfo's crimes. During the long legal battle, another federal judge ruled that I should have known that the car, which Scarfo purchased for $25,000 in Florida, was the fruit of his ill-gotten income. That was a dangerous precedent for any criminal defense attorney. If we are going to be required to assess and determine where our client's fees originated, the entire system of justice could come undone. Those accused of serious crimes could be denied the right to the best defense available.

I fought legal battles up and down the federal judicial system over the Rolls Royce, and finally won. The car was mine. However, during all those years, the feds had parked it in some outdoor facility where it had been exposed to all kinds of weather. It was a rusted, worthless shell by the time I got legal possession, so I left it where it was.

Looking back on it now, it cost me the $16,000 bar bill and more than five times that in legal fees. But I'd do it all again. Well, maybe not all of it. I'd fight the same legal battle over the same legal issue. However, I might think twice about covering the cost of a Philadelphia victory party with my credit card.

Two more cases played out in Philadelphia with the same cast of characters, and this time the defense went down. It was the government onslaught that Tony Spilotro used to joke about. The United States versus Nicodemo Scarfo et al was a legal avalanche that eventually we couldn't win.

The RICO case ended with all sixteen defendants, including Scarfo and Leonetti, being convicted. A second murder case in Common Pleas Court, in which Leonetti was not a defendant, resulted in more convictions (although that case was later overturned on appeal).

Here's the way the law is stacked against defendants in RICO cases. You know that murder case that we won in Common Pleas Court? The federal government was permitted under the law to attach that same murder as a predicate act in the RICO trial. A racketeering case is built around a series of connected crimes. These are called predicate acts. In the Scarfo case there were nine murders, four attempted murders, and dozens of gambling, loansharking, and extortion allegations. Each was a predicate act in the indictment. To be convicted of racketeering, a jury has to find that the prosecution has proven at least two of the predicate acts. In some cases, there are dozens. That's how the government stacks the deck.

In this instance, it was even more troubling. While Scarfo, Leonetti, and their co-defendants were acquitted in Common Pleas Court of one of those murders, they were convicted of the same murder as a racketeering act in the RICO trial. That sounds like double jeopardy to me, but the courts have ruled otherwise. That's the kind of unlevel playing field defense attorneys have to deal with.

Scarfo got fifty-five years for the RICO conviction, and that sentence was to run consecutive to the fourteen he got in the extortion case. So he was looking at sixty-nine years in the federal can. It was tantamount to a life sentence, and he is still in jail. Leonetti got forty-five years, which shocked me because I thought the evidence against him was weak. Despite all the tapes and all the informant testimony, there wasn't much hard evidence linking him to the crimes. He never said very much to anyone. They called him "Crazy Phil," a nickname he hated, and the government alleged he was involved in ten murders, but I didn't see him as a violent gangster, and I didn't think the prosecution had proven its case. Even during the trials, he never said much, although I still can remember him whispering to me whenever one of those informants was testifying. I had never heard the expression before, but he called each one of them "lying motherless motherfuckers."

I guess it was a Philadelphia thing.

But so was cooperating. The Philadelphia mob has spawned more cooperating witnesses than any other crime family in America. Some people jokingly refer to them as the South Philadelphia Boys Choir. To my amazement, Leonetti joined the choir shortly after he was sentenced. He turned into a rat and became a government witness in cases up and down the East Coast. Many in law enforcement circles say that he was the reason Salvatore "Sammy the Bull" Gravano turned. Leonetti was ready to testify about Gravano's involvement in a mob murder in Philadelphia.

I couldn't believe it when I heard that Leonetti had flipped. I really thought we had a chance on appeal to overturn his convictions. But I was informed that he was replacing me with another attorney, one who worked out his cooperating agreement. I couldn't believe that a guy with his reputation, a guy I had thought was like Tony Spilotro, would become a rat. I couldn't believe he was such a weakling. The first time he faced any kind of adversity, he turned on his family. And I don't mean crime family; he turned on his own uncle, his mother's brother, the man who had raised him after his father left. As far as I was concerned, the government made a deal with the devil.

They said Leonetti had committed ten murders. After testifying at a number of trials, he went in for a sentence reduction hearing. Instead of forty-five years, his sentence was reduced to five years, five months, and five days, which was the time he had served when the hearing was held. He walked out of the court-room and into the Witness Protection Program. Five years for ten murders? Not a bad deal.

I love Philadelphia. It's a great city. And going back there to try all those cases was a wonderful experience. I only wished my father had still been alive so that he could have come to court and watch me practice law. I think he would have been proud of me, and that makes me feel good.

The only sour taste I have from the whole experience was Leonetti. I don't represent rats, and I think he's a liar. I know he lied about me after he began cooperating, claiming that he had paid me thousands of dollars in cash and implying that I had taken the money under the table and had not declared it as income. Any payment I ever received for those Philadelphia trials came in the form of a check written by Bobby Simone, Scarfo's lawyer.

Don't get me wrong—I was paid well. And while we're on the subject, let me point out that I always charged a flat fee. I'd quote a price to a client based on what I thought was involved, how much time, how much research, how complicated the issues in the case were. Other lawyers might charge by the hour, but that wasn't the way I did it.

It usually worked out fine. If, for some reason, a case settled quickly or a trial took less time and effort than I had anticipated, I made out really well. On the other hand, I once quoted a client a fee for what I thought was going to be a six-week trial. I hadn't factored in that this was one of the judge's first cases. He was a "virgin" and was feeling his way along. The trial lasted six months.

I never gave a fee back if a case wrapped up quickly, and in this instance, I never asked for more money. I just had to take my losses. That's the economics of practicing criminal law. Overall I did very well and, as a result, my family and I lived very well.

I was a high-profile criminal defense attorney, a go-to guy in a world that people wrote books and movies about. It was a heady experience and I loved almost every minute of it. The strategy, the battles, the clash of wit—all were an adrenaline rush. I loved being center stage and that's what a courtroom was. The stakes were high, and that made it all the more exciting.

One of the greatest thrills in the world is, after a long, contentious case, to hear a jury say those two lovely words, "Not guilty." As a defense attorney, it's a euphoric experience. Almost as good as sex.

But at the same time, I don't want to glamorize organized crime figures. The criminal underworld can be a dark, uncaring, and inhumane place. Some of my clients lived and died there. But when I could, I tried to look at my clients from a different perspective.

First, under the law they were entitled to legal representation, and I was going to give them that. Second—and not everyone might agree with this—they lived by a certain morality that you and I might not be a part of. But I respected the fact that they had a code.

That was never made clearer to me than when I headed to Boston to represent Vinny Ferrara in a big mob case up there. Vinny was the antithesis of Phil Leonetti.

In 1990, Vinny was indicted along with six other reputed members of the Patriarca Crime Family, including Raymond Patriarca, Jr., and J. R. Russo. The charges included murder and extortion. One key piece of evidence was an FBI tape of a mob-making ceremony in a home in Medford, Massachusetts.

A classic line from Vinny was picked up on that tape. After the induction ceremony had ended and the guests were heading home, he said, "Only the ghost knows what really took place here today."

The ghost and the FBI, it turned out.

Vinny, who was nicknamed "The Animal," hired me to represent him. I also helped out J. R. Russo, who was acting as his own attorney. I liked both those guys because they were genuine. They didn't pretend to be anything other than what they were, and they lived by the code.

Vinny was a graduate of Boston College and had a degree in accounting. He certainly was no fool, and he had a presence about him. When he walked into a room, people knew he was there, and they waited to see what he had to say. He was like the E. F. Hutton of the underworld. He also was charming, and we shared an interest in sports.

I didn't know much about the Boston mob other than the name Whitey Bulger, the Irish-American gangster on whom the Jack Nicholson character is based in the movie *The Departed*.

The making ceremony tape was a classic; the FBI must have had an orgasm when they heard it. I can just imagine the looks on the agents' faces while they were sitting in a van down the street listening in. The ceremony had taken place in the house of the aunt of a Boston mobster. The feds had gotten a tip and had the place wired for sound. They apparently got it all, even the preliminary stages where mobsters were arranging seats and planning the menu. It sounded like the Paris Peace Talks; everyone had to be seated in just the right spot. Then they discussed what kind of wine and what the temperature should be on the pots of gravy (tomato sauce) for the pasta.

Finally there was the induction ceremony itself. There was a gun and a knife and a holy card that each proposed mob member had to hold in his hands while it was set on fire. While it was burning in his cupped hands, he had to swear allegiance to the family, promising to burn in hell like the holy card if he betrayed the family's trust. He was then told that he had to come whenever he was called, even if he was at his own mother's deathbed. This new family he was joining, this crime family, came before everything else.

Pretrial, I had a discussion with Vinny and J. R. about that tape. I said we could probably try to work around it, but the thing that would hurt us the most if the tape was played for a jury was the line about leaving your mother's deathbed. Jurors would find that repulsive, and they wouldn't understand it.

Vinny looked at J. R. and said, "Next time, let's leave that part out."

He was a very candid fella and, like Tony Spilotro, he was a realist. There were thirty-five counts in the racketeering case; just about everything you could think of. One of the key charges was the murder of a guy named Jimmy Limoli. Vinny kept telling me, in that thick Boston accent, that he had nothing to do with the Limoli hit.

"Oscah," he'd say, "we may have done this and we may have done that, but Oscah, I didn't kill Jimmy Limoli. I would nevah kill Jimmy."

The pretrial discovery evidence indicated that the government had a statement from another mob informant claiming that he saw Vinny order another mobster to kill Limoli. Vinny insisted that wasn't true.

We were fortunate that the case was in front of U.S. District Court Judge Mark L. Wolf, probably one of the smartest and fairest judges before whom I've practiced. During pretrial hearings, the judge demonstrated that he was a caring individual who recognized that while the defendants were portrayed as mobsters by the prosecution, they were also American citizens who were entitled to fair treatment.

There was an issue about transportation to and from court. The judge made sure the prison transport vans were safe, and the defendants, in handcuffs and ankle shackles, were not bouncing around in the back of some tin can on wheels. In fact, he rode in the back of one of the vans himself to determine what the ride was like. Extraordinary!

At another point, one of Vinny's co-defendants complained that they weren't being served "live" food. None of us knew what he was talking about (this was before I had moved my mother to Las Vegas, where she, too, made the same argument). But he explained that the potatoes were powdered and the vegetables were canned and chemically preserved. The judge helped straighten that out.

A few weeks before we were to go to trial, I got a call from the judge's office. It was Martin Luther King weekend, and he said if we were going to work out a plea, it had to be now. If not, the trial would move forward. I flew out to Boston and convinced Vinny to take a plea. The statement of the cooperating witness putting him in the murder and the mob induction tape were just too strong. He was forty-five, and he was looking at a life sentence if convicted. The prosecution was offering twenty-two years in a plea deal. Vinny thought long and hard, and finally told me to make the deal, but to make sure that he couldn't be charged in any other jurisdiction for the murder or any of the other offenses. We worked out a global plea that guaranteed that Vinny wouldn't face any related charges in state court.

The federal prosecutors I had to deal with were exceptionally arrogant. When I first got involved in the case, they went out of their way to extol the power of that making ceremony tape while mocking me. They asked me what I was going to do now, since in almost every mob case I had been involved in, I would attack government witnesses who claimed to have been formally inducted into the Mafia. With the tape, they said, there was no way

I could raise that argument. They were right about that; I just didn't like their smug attitude. Now getting Vinny and his co-defendants to plead guilty only made them worse.

At sentencing, they looked like cats licking their paws after catching the mice. Both Vinny and J.R. were told that if they admitted they were members of the Mafia, they might get a year or two knocked off their sentences. Neither would do it; they stood firm, and they each got an extra year. But that's the code they lived by. You have to respect that. I left Boston feeling as if I had saved Vinny's life. At least he had a chance to come home from prison. He thanked me, never complained, and went off to a maximum security prison to serve his time.

We stayed in touch. Years later, after I had become mayor and was no longer actively practicing law, there was a hearing in another case up in Boston. Information came out that the witness who had implicated Vinny in the Jimmy Limoli murder had recanted that statement. The prosecution knew about that when we were about to go to trial, but had never told the judge or the defense.

What's more, a police detective testified that the witness had been told he'd get a break if he helped the feds get Vinny. The detective said he took both the first statement from the witness, in which he implicated Vinny, and the second statement, in which he recanted. The detective said he turned both those statements over to the prosecution. We never heard about the recantation.

When Judge Wolf heard about this, he ordered a new hearing and established that the prosecutor, Assistant U.S. Attorney Jeffrey Auerhahn, had altered the witness statement and had never turned over potentially exculpatory evidence to the defense.

Vinny applied for a new trial. He was represented by my former law partner, David Chesnoff, and by Marty Weinberg, who had a practice in Boston. Their legal argument was that had Vinny known about conflicting witness statements, he never would have pleaded guilty to the murder charge. Had I known, I never would have recommended that he take the plea deal. I filed an affidavit supporting Vinny's application, stating that had I known about the recantation, I never would have allowed my client to plead to the murder.

Judge Wolf directed the Massachusetts Bar Association to take up the issue and consider sanctions against Auerhahn for violating a basic tenet of the criminal law practice and procedure. The prosecution has to turn over all evidence to the defense; it's part of due process.

Instead of a new trial, Judge Wolf reduced Vinny's sentence to seventeen years. It was a long time, but it allowed him to come home. Nothing ever happened to Auerhahn, which, if you've been paying attention to my story, shouldn't surprise you. Everyone is equal under the law—except federal prosecutors, who play by their own rules.

PART THREE
CITY HALL

CHAPTER 11
FROM MOB LAWYER TO MAYOR

For decades, the mob cases in Philadelphia and Boston kept me busy and kept my name in front of the media. But my job was becoming very repetitive. Now it seemed with every new case, one of the first questions I was beginning to ask was how much could I charge. Could I get more for this case than the last one? Sure, I was making plenty of money and probably could have just put things on cruise control and continued for another ten or twenty years, but that didn't appeal to me. I wasn't feeling satisfied.

My wife Carolyn was busy with the Meadows, the school she had founded. It was the first pre-K-through-12 non-profit, non-denominational college preparatory school in Nevada. Our kids were educated and making it on their own.

And here I was, going to work every day and doing the things I always did. I realized I didn't like this person I was becoming. I didn't like who I saw in the mirror. This wasn't the reason I became a lawyer. This wasn't what the law was about. Most important, it wasn't who I wanted to be.

It's a funny thing when you say it out loud, but I always liked myself. I always liked who I was and what I was doing. It wasn't just the mob cases and all the attention. I enjoyed that; don't get me wrong. I've said this before, but I really felt what I was doing had a purpose. It was something good.

They called me a mob lawyer or the mob's mouthpiece, but I wore that with pride because I knew what the stakes were and what I was fighting for. It's why I became a lawyer. But I started to feel as if I had done everything I could do as a lawyer. I had represented high-profile mobsters, a federal judge in an impeachment hearing before the United States Congress, and a drug dealer accused of assassinating a federal judge. I had spent years running around the country. A prosecutor once said you could drop Oscar from a plane anywhere in the country, and he'd say the same thing and do the same thing, no matter where you put him.

There was some truth to that; maybe I was getting bored. There was a void in my life, and the law wasn't filling it. It wasn't the "jealous mistress" that Justice Holmes had said it would be. I had lost the joy of practicing law, of doing something important, of accomplishing something that I knew was good, and now was mostly doing it for the money.

I would think back and remember better times, like a day back in the early 1990s when a young woman showed up at my law office. My secretary said she had come in without an appointment, but really needed to see a lawyer. She wanted to talk about a civil suit. I said that's not the kind of case I handle, but my secretary said, "You'd better see this lady."

Her name was Jo Ann Allison. She came with her son Tommy, who was about five years old. He was in a wheelchair. He was blind, spastic, deaf, and mentally retarded. It's sad to say, but he was a vegetable. Yet I could see how his mother loved him and how she was caring for him. It broke my heart.

She told me her son had contracted encephalitis when he was 17 months old, after being given the compulsory vaccination for measles, mumps, and rubella. The drug, MMRII, was manufactured by Merck. She wanted to sue—she told me that a lawyer down the street thought he could probably get her $5,000. I said I didn't do that kind of work.

I looked at that little boy and thought that $5,000 wasn't going to do him or his mother any good. She was on welfare and didn't know what else to do. My heart went out to her. I knew, and I knew she knew, that her son was never going to get any better. But she loved him. To me, she was like an angel. It was remarkable to see someone who can care for and love a child in that condition.

So I said, "Let me do some research." I ended up filing a lawsuit against Merck under the product liability law, arguing that Merck had not given the parent adequate warning about the potential dangers, and that the parent's decision to have her child vaccinated was made without full knowledge of the risks.

Merck had a team of high-priced lawyers, and they were ready to fight the case. At a pre-trial conference, the judge put a zero value on my claim. There was no way Merck could be liable, the judge said, since the vaccine was recommended by the health department. Children had to be vaccinated. The judge issued a summary judgment in Merck's favor, throwing out our claim.

I appealed and ended up taking the case all the way to the Nevada Supreme Court. And in the end, we won. Here's part of what the high court said in a decision, Allison versus Merck, that has become one of the standards in product liability law:

> We conclude that Merck may be liable to Thomas Allison by reason of its strict liability as manufacturer if Thomas can prove that the vaccine in question is the cause of his disabilities. In addition, we conclude that Merck may be liable to Thomas and Ms. Allison for failing to provide a proper warning regarding the vaccine. Accordingly, we reverse the summary judgment in favor of

Merck and remand to the trial court for a trial on Thomas' strict liability claim and on Thomas' and Ms. Allison's failure-to-warn claims.

The lawyers for Merck knew they could be in real trouble if we went in front of a jury with Tommy propped up in his wheelchair. He was a special little fellow, and they knew there was nothing they could say or do in court that would be as powerful as the image of that little boy. After that, we worked out a multimillion dollar settlement.

Under the terms of the settlement agreement, I'm prohibited from saying how much, but Jo Ann Allison was able to care for her son for the rest of his life without any worries. Tommy eventually passed away, and I spoke at his funeral. That case was one of the most satisfying in my career. It's what the law is really all about.

The settlement gave me a lot of satisfaction. It wasn't the kind of case where you went out and partied in celebration, but it was the kind of case where I knew I had done something good. Justice had been served, and to me, that was what being a lawyer was all about. I smile even now when I think about it, and I shake my head when I remember how Jo Ann Allison told me another lawyer said he "might" be able to get her $5,000.

Those were the kind of people and circumstances I was thinking about when I decided to run for mayor. I could probably have continued practicing law and made even more money, but I wasn't enjoying it anymore. I needed a new challenge. I needed to look in the mirror and like who I saw.

It wasn't about the type of clients I had or the criminal law I was practicing. I had just reached a point where I had done everything a criminal defense attorney could do. I'd had a rich and rewarding career as a lawyer, but I wasn't getting the same satisfaction out of what I was doing. And I didn't want to be the kind of lawyer who evaluated every case based on how big a fee he could charge. That wasn't what I was about when I started practicing law, and it wasn't what I wanted to become.

Toward the end of 1998, I took the family on a cruise and told them I was thinking of running for mayor. The kids all voted against it. I think they were worried about the things that would be said about me, since they knew how the media treated me. They had grown up hearing and reading about their father, "the mob mouthpiece," and had heard the snide remarks about how my law office was the "house that crime built." In addition, they thought there was no way I was going to win.

"Dad, you've got more baggage than a skycap at the airport," they said.

But it was something I wanted to try. I had never even been to City Hall; I had no idea what a mayor did. But I loved the city, and I needed a new challenge. I had accomplished everything possible as a defense attorney, and I was tired of a lot of it. So I appreciated my kids' concern, but I was convinced, from the very beginning, that I would win. Again, it was one of those things where I thought I could "will" it to happen. You know, like the Chagra case. I shouldn't have won that, or the Spilotro cases. No way could I keep him out of jail all those years—but I did.

In March of 1999, on the last day of the filing period, I announced that I was running for mayor. I had a press conference on a Friday in the lobby of my law office. I was holding a copy of the Constitution. I said that I wanted to lead the city into the next millennium, that I loved the city, and would be honored to work to improve it. That weekend, the *Las Vegas Review Journal*'s editorial headline blared, "Anybody but Oscar for Mayor."

My platform was straightforward. I told people that the greatest thing I had going for me was my intellect. I said if you want someone who is smart and who will keep the interests of the city in the forefront and keep the city moving forward, I'm your man.

When I walked around the city as a candidate, I saw things differently and noticed things that I never saw before. Downtown was a mess, which became a key issue for me. Something had to be done, and that became part of my platform.

"The whole downtown area stinks," I would say as I campaigned. "You've got a Neanderthal type of operation there. People have to realize that Las Vegas is the entertainment capital of the world. Unless we maintain and improve the downtown, it's going to be like the core of an apple rotting from within." I said we had to do something about it or we would lose the apple, and then maybe the whole barrel.

Part of my pitch was also to sell myself, who I was, and how I conducted myself. I've always had an ego, I've always been good at what I do, and I've always thought I was the best. I would joke and say, "I realize nobody's right all the time . . . I just can't remember when I've been wrong."

"When people come to Las Vegas, they come to see glamour and glitz," I said during my campaign speeches. "I'm the man for that. I'm not going to be one of those boring politicians. If that's who you want, don't vote for me." I was bringing some of the same attitude to the campaign that I brought to the courtroom. And I think it worked.

Elections in Las Vegas are set up in two rounds. The first round is an open field; as many candidates as file are on the ballot. I think we had nearly a dozen candidates. Jay Bingham, a former county commissioner who was very prominent in the Mormon Church, was the favorite. Shortly after I filed, he dropped out. The story was that he had a heart problem, but the rumor was that he feared mob retaliation if he ran against me.

What can I tell you? People are funny. The ironic thing was many of my former clients and guys I had gotten to know while representing mobsters shied away from me after I announced that I was running. In fact, there were guys who stopped talking to me for the next twelve years. I couldn't understand it; it was as though an iron door had been pulled shut. After I left office, one of them explained it to me.

"We didn't want to cause you any embarrassment," he said. "We knew you were taking heat, and we didn't want to add to that fire. We had too much respect for you."

Mob guys understood better than the public. They knew I was going to be fair and honest, the same as I had been when I represented them, and they had a tacit agreement amongst themselves not to put me in a sensitive spot.

With Bingham out of the race, Arnie Adamson, a sitting councilman, became the favorite. The odds makers made a "line" with me being a 17-to-1 underdog.

I went up to San Francisco shortly after I announced my candidacy to visit my daughter Cara, who had gone to Stanford and was working as a consultatnt in San Francisco. While I was there, the *San Francisco Chronicle* had an editorial urging Las Vegas voters to reject me, calling me "the barrister to butchers." It was nuts! San Francisco was in the midst of a big financial crisis at the time, and they had a major problem with the homeless that was getting national attention. Yet its paper was worried about who was running for mayor in Las Vegas.

As you can imagine, I was the outlaw candidate, but I didn't mind. I raised about $900,000 for my campaign. I got no help from the casinos—zero. I had no idea how to run a campaign, and even less of an idea how City Hall worked. But I was convinced I was going to win.

Carolyn was unbelievable. She was out there every day, knocking on doors. We went from neighborhood to neighborhood, talking to people. One day we were up in the Summerlin section, which was populated with wealthy, older, mostly retired residents. You couldn't go up there in the morning because they were all out playing tennis or golf or walking their dog. And you couldn't go too late at night because they'd be in bed.

I knocked on one door, and this nice elderly lady smiled and invited me in. She called out to her husband, "It's the mob lawyer."

I sat in her kitchen and she served me chocolate chip cookies and milk. I don't think I'd had a glass of milk in forty years. Now that was campaigning.

We eventually put a staff together, and they came up with an absolutely awesome idea. They decided to "humanize" me in order to counteract the negative stuff some of my opponents were putting out. Nobody said it directly, but the buzz was that if Oscar got elected, the mob would take over City Hall.

Our campaign emphasized "the five best things in Oscar Goodman's life." It offered snapshot descriptions of my wife and our children, and said I never missed a soccer game. I didn't do any formal polling, but every Saturday and Sunday I went down to the Costco store and talked to people. I kept on doing that after I was elected. You got a real sense of what people thought, and I knew I was going to do well.

In order to win in the first round, you have to get 50 percent of the vote, plus one. On election night, I was close. At one point I had 51 percent, but the final count gave me 49 percent, so there was a runoff. Arnie Adamson was the second highest vote-getter, so he and I squared off in the runoff.

Now there were going to be some debates. I knew I was good on my feet, but I also had a temper. What might work in court wasn't necessarily good in a political debate. Adamson had started to run a negative campaign with ads sprinkled with allusions to what I supposedly represented—hypodermic needles, money bags, guns. I was livid. Carolyn knew that I wanted to strangle Adamson; that I wanted to put my hand down his throat and pull out his innards. She tried to calm me.

"Say something nice about him," she said.

"Nice?" I said.

"Yes," she said. "Say he has a nice wife."

As the first debate was approaching, I got word that the Police Protective Association, the police union, was going to send someone in to bait me. They saw me as the anti-Christ; it was like I had 6-6-6 tattooed on my forehead.

The night before the debate, my son Ross, who was a captain in the Marines, called. He said he was just checking in and wanted to say "hi," but I knew he was concerned. I told him about the debate and what was planned, and he came up with a strategy.

"You've got to use a pre-emptive strike," he said.

I had no idea what he was talking about.

"Whadda ya mean?" I said.

"Come out of the box first. Take the initiative. Don't let them raise the issues. You raise them before they can."

This made a lot of sense. If it was good enough for the Marines, it was good enough for me. At the debate, one of the first people to ask a question was a former reporter who I had thought was a friend. He came up to the podium, and very smugly he asked me, "When's the last time you were in City Hall?"

And then he started to walk away.

"Hey, wait a second, buddy," I said. "Don't you walk away. Come back here. I'll answer your question."

Then I delivered my pre-emptive strike.

"I've never been to City Hall, okay. The first time will be when I'm elected. And I know there have been questions about my drinking. Let me tell all of you, I drink in excess, sometimes a bottle of gin a night. And something else: I'm a degenerate gambler. If there's a cockroach running around out there, I'll bet on whether he goes right or left. I've represented bad guys, but the last time I checked, they were entitled to representation under our Constitution . . ."

I went on like that for about five minutes. The people in the audience loved it. And after that, there was nothing negative my opponent could say about me. I said it all first, and I took the sting out.

I won the election in what they called a landslide. I got sixty-four percent of the vote.

I got a call from President Clinton congratulating me on being elected to lead the fastest developing city in the country. Five minutes later I got a call from Manny Baker, the heroin kingpin, who also wanted to congratulate me. Bill Clinton and Manny Baker—that about summed it all up for me.

In the next two elections, I got over 80 percent of the vote. I spent twelve years in office, and it changed my life. It freed me, and I loved it.

When I was practicing law, every day, every hour, I was on guard. I had to be circumspect, and careful about what I said and to whom I said it. It got to the point where the only person I knew I could trust was my wife. After I heard myself on wiretaps, it got even worse. If you've never experienced that, you really can't appreciate what it does to you. You never feel secure after that; it's like a home invasion. You really do feel violated.

As mayor, I never worried about any of that. I talked to everyone. I rediscovered the value of social intercourse. I had press conferences every week and I let it all hang out. I'd stand there nude if I thought it was necessary. I was a great believer in open government, and that was the way I approached the job.

My perception of being mayor, of course, was not the reality. I had thoughts of Boss Tweed, Old Man Daley in Chicago, or Richardson Dilworth in Philadelphia. These were mayors who were in charge.

I soon discovered that I was just one member of a five-member (and eventually seven-member) city council. My vote counted for no more than any other council member. So I had to learn to count to four to operate effectively in the political world. But the biggest thing I had going for me was that I didn't need the job.

Don't misunderstand me—I loved the job. But I wasn't concerned about the politics of being an elected official. I wasn't worried about a political career. I ran for mayor because I wanted to do something for a city that I loved. That was the only reason I was there, and it made me more powerful. I was immune to lots of the petty nonsense that comes with any elected office. I said what I thought, and I did what needed to be done.

I never turned down a speaking engagement unless it conflicted with some other commitment that had already been scheduled. I was accessible twenty-four–seven. It was a part-time job that I worked at full-time.

Once a month we scheduled "coffee with the mayor," moving around the different wards of the city. People would be lined up outside the shops. They'd come with ideas and suggestions. I'd have staff people with me, and we'd take notes. We listened to everyone and heard about everything, from local zoning issues to the legalization of medical marijuana. It was a great way to find out what was going on in my city. You can't hole up in an office and expect to be a leader. If you're going to represent the people, you've got to get out and talk to the people.

That's what government is about. It's not about getting re-elected; it's about serving the common good.

As time went on, we also started a monthly "martinis with the mayor," which were meetings in local bars. They were my favorites. People usually left those sessions feeling very good about themselves.

It was during one of those martini nights that the thought occurred to me that bartenders and waitresses were great ambassadors for the city. They were the ones who were meeting tourists and visitors every day. So we started a monthly program where we would honor one of them in recognition for the way they treated people. I'd give them a key to the city during a presentation ceremony. It was a great way to show how we appreciated people who, day in and day out, made Las Vegas what it was. I also realized that I enjoyed making people happy.

To me, the most important part of being mayor was being a leader. As mayor, your goal should be to make the city a better place, a place where people enjoy their lives and are able to thrive. You're a cheerleader as much as anything, and you set the tone.

Becoming mayor was one of the best things that ever happened to me.

I started to dream again, and I had all these ideas about making the city a better place. I wasn't sure how I was going to accomplish it all, but I knew what I wanted to get done, and that I was going to work hard to get it.

It was a wonderful feeling. And in the morning, when I woke up, I liked who I saw in the mirror.

CHAPTER 12
BITTEN BY THE BUG

When I was thinking about running for mayor, I was invited by Steve Wynn to fly to Biloxi, Mississippi, for the opening of his new casino, the Beau Rivage. Wynn's an interesting guy. He's accomplished a lot, but like so many others, he's mostly interested in what works for him. I guess in that sense, he's no different than any businessman.

We flew down on a private jet. There was a group of wealthy Las Vegas residents on the plane, and I saw it as a chance to float my ideas. I had a captive audience, and I took advantage of the opportunity. I went up and down the aisle seeing if these people would support me, and I got really good feedback.

Wynn especially liked my ideas for downtown. He had sold his downtown property, the Golden Nugget, when he began to develop beautiful sites on the Las Vegas strip, including the Mirage, Treasure Island, and the Bellagio. But he told me that he would be supportive of me if I were elected mayor. Those were the kinds of commitments I was looking for. I knew I needed major support if I was going to do anything about turning the inner city area around.

He told me if I were elected, he would help me redevelop the urban core. Having him committed was huge. Frank Luntz, the great pollster, was retained by Wynn to ascertain what the community was lacking and whether the taxpaying citizens would be supportive. He determined that the two things Las Vegas needed were a first-class performing arts center and an arena. Wynn said he would be a moving force behind those projects.

As soon as I got elected, Wynn went south on me. He said he wanted nothing to do with downtown. When I confronted him, he told me, "Your downtown is never going to come back, and I'm not going to build down there."

The same thing happened with Michael Gaughan, whose father Jackie had been a founder of some of the great downtown "joints" like the Union Plaza, the El Cortez, and the Las Vegas Club. Michael was a great operator. When I approached him for a contribution, he was very generous, but he said downtown was dead. He wanted no part of it because it was never going to be successful. Instead he went out, way south of the Las Vegas strip. He also bet me that I wouldn't be elected. He still owes me a dinner, thirteen years later.

It was a rude awakening for me, but it made me even more determined. As a lawyer I had traveled all over the country. I had seen cities like Newark, Philadelphia, and San Diego attempting to fight urban blight.

I've seen places in those cities and elsewhere that looked like war zones. We had the same thing downtown: boarded-up storefronts, empty buildings, vacant lots covered with trash. I knew I had to do something about it. San Diego created the Gas Lamp District in what was once one of the worst sections of town, and I wanted to use that as a model.

I remember being in San Diego before the redevelopment. A friend had a law office in the area, and when I went there, there were tiny bugs everywhere. They had been attracted by the urine. At night, the street people used his doorway as a bathroom. There were hookers all over the place chasing the sailors. These were hookers, not call girls. There were drug dealers and drug users, filthy dirty strung-out people, holding out their hand for change. It wasn't the image of a vibrant city, by any means.

Today, it's a different place. They've built a brand-new convention center and a baseball stadium. I said to myself, this is what has to happen in Las Vegas. I wasn't inventing the wheel; I didn't have some revolutionary idea. I just knew that we had to make this happen.

The battle was fought on so many different levels. I learned a lot about urban planning and redevelopment, but what served me best was common sense and not being afraid to say what I thought. That's the way I approached the job. I've said this before, but it's worth repeating. I was a better mayor because I had no idea what the job was supposed to be. I didn't have preconceived ideas about how the office functioned; I just felt that my job was to lead the city and to hopefully make it better. That's what Doug Selby, who became city manager shortly after I took office, told me. A mayor, he said, was supposed to be the face of the city—its cheerleader—and his job was to leave the city a better place than when he found it.

I also believed that people had to do what I told them to do. And while that wasn't the case, it didn't stop me from trying. Part of my attitude was political naiveté, and part of it was ego. I was never in doubt, and I know that bothered some people. It still does. But it's who I am.

And let me clear something up right now. There is absolutely no truth to the rumor that every morning Carolyn gets up, comes around to my side of the bed, and begins applauding in order to get me going. I'm self-motivated. Even without her, I hear the applause in my head.

I had played myself in the movie *Casino* while I was still actively practicing law. As I mentioned earlier, the film was written by Nicholas Pileggi, directed by Martin Scorsese, and starred Robert

DeNiro, Joe Pesci, and Sharon Stone. They played characters based on people I had represented: Lefty Rosenthal, Tony Spilotro, and Geri Rosenthal.

Being involved in the movie was a fabulous experience, hobnobbing with all the stars and with Scorsese. I never saw anyone who was more a seeker of perfection than he was. He'd do a scene over and over and over until he had it just the way he wanted it. Naturally, he went way over budget, but he was a genius.

DeNiro was quiet, a decent fellow. He made me feel very comfortable on the set. I clowned around with Pesci and Don Rickles and Tommy Smothers. And Sharon Stone was just a sweetheart, nothing like the characters she plays. She's more the girl next door.

During the filming, we had them over to the house for dinner. Steve Wynn, who was then a neighbor of mine, threw a tantrum when he wasn't invited. He had his wife call us, and we finally let him come. Carolyn cooked, and after dinner, Sharon Stone and Elaine Wynn helped wash the dishes. Unbelievable. I loved the whole experience, but I don't think I brought a lot to the big screen. After the movie came out, I got a call from my mother, who was still living back in Philadelphia.

"I saw your movie," she said.

"What did you think?" I asked.

"It's a good thing you're a lawyer."

It didn't matter. I had been bitten by the bug, and I wanted to do it again. Once I was elected mayor, I saw a way to stardom. One of the first things I did after being sworn in on June 28, 1999, was head over to the city permit department. I told the woman in charge that I was the new mayor and I had a directive for her. From now on, anyone who came in for a permit to film a movie in Las Vegas had to agree to give me a part in the film.

"You can't do this," she said.

"Yes I can," I said. "I'm the mayor."

A couple of weeks went by. One day my receptionist came into my office very excited and whispered, "Jackie Chan and Bret Ratner are waiting to see you."

Perfect, I thought.

"Send the gentlemen in," I told her.

They came in and didn't know where to begin. Ratner seemed very flustered.

"We can't believe what we were just told," he said. "For us to get a permit to film *Rush Hour Two*, you have to get a part?"

"Absolutely correct," I said.

It was a great part. It was filmed at the Desert Inn before it was imploded. The casino had been decked out in an Asian motif. Jackie Chan, Chris Tucker, and Alan King were in the scene with me.

I couldn't wait for the movie to come out, but my scene got left on the cutting room floor! I was livid. I got Chan and Ratner on the phone.

"Do you know who I am?" I screamed. "As long as I'm mayor, you'll never make *Rush Hour Three* in Las Vegas."

They were so scared of my ranting they restored my scene to the DVD edition.

The next movie was the sequel to *Ocean's Eleven*. There was a great fight scene at the MGM. Steven Soderberg on the camera. Wayne Newton, Danny Gans, Seigfried and Roy, Angie Dickinson, and me.

Again, cutting room floor!

I went to the city attorney, a guy named Brad Jerbic.

"A fraud is being perpetrated on the City of Las Vegas," I said. "These producers come in, promise to give me a part, get the permits, and I end up cut from the film."

"Mr. Mayor," Jerbic said, "what would you want me to do?"

"We need an airtight contract," I said. "If we give them a

permit, and I'm not in the film, I want to be able to go to court and enjoin them from showing the movie."

"You can't do that," he said.

"Yes I can. I'm the mayor."

The next movie was a film called *Angel Blade*, not exactly an Academy Award nominee. I had them sign an agreement guaranteeing that my part would not be cut. It was a cameo appearance, an Alfred Hitchcock moment. I played the mayor. They told me *Angel Blade* was going to be an "exotic" thriller. Turns out it's an erotic thriller. And I am in it.

I did a little better on the small screen. I became friends with Anthony Zuiker, the creator of the *CSI* television series. He's an amazing guy, and he's actually from Las Vegas. When he was attending UNLV, he used to work as a conductor on one of the trams that ferried people from one casino to the other. He came up with that great idea for a dramatic series, and it has changed the way lawyers try cases, especially prosecutors.

Before *CSI,* most people had no idea how evidence was gathered or how important forensics could be to a case. Now, jurors come into a trial expecting it. It puts an added burden on the prosecution, the same way the old Perry Mason shows had jurors expecting dramatic confessions and neatly wrapped up evidence, adding pressure to the defense. *CSI* created the same kind of anticipation, and it also made jurors more cognizant of modern science and technology. In that respect, it worked both ways. If the prosecution didn't have DNA evidence, for example, or blood tracings or fingerprints, then it was harder to convince a jury. But if the prosecution did have those things, then the defense was hard-pressed to refute and counteract. And it all came from a television series.

I appeared on *CSI* three times, and each time I was treated like a king—first class hotel, great cuisine, and my own trailer on the set. I've done scenes with Ted Danson and Paul Guilfoyle, and two wonderful actresses, Ann Margaret and Frances Foster—all really nice people. My problem was that I had trouble remembering my lines.

In court, I could make a six-hour closing argument without any notes and never stutter or stumble. But put me in front of a movie or television camera, and I can't find the words. It might go back to my childhood. I took piano lessons, and I distinctly remember a day when I was supposed to give a recital for my family, my mother, father, aunts, uncles, cousins. My piece was a cacophonous one by Béla Bartók, the great Hungarian composer. I sat down at the piano and my mind went totally blank. I couldn't play a note. I ran out of the house that day thinking, "I hope I get hit by a truck." I was just despondent. Since that time, I can't memorize lines.

When we filmed *Casino*, I drove Scorsese nuts. We were doing this scene based on actual events where Lefty is challenging Harry Reid during an appearance in front of the Gaming Control Board. But I kept screwing up my lines.

Finally, Scorsese—perhaps the greatest director in American cinema—couldn't take it anymore. He said to me, "Oscar, just do it the way you would do it in real life."

I stopped worrying about the lines, and it worked. But the next time you watch the movie, check out the scene. You'll notice the other actors don't have a clue; they had no idea where I was going.

I was on another *CSI* set one time with the great actor Laurence Fishburne, and I told him I felt like an idiot because I needed cue cards. He said, "Oscar, don't feel bad. Marlon Brando uses them, too."

That puts me in pretty good company. And truthfully, over time, I think I've gotten better. I really do enjoy acting. It can be both an exhilarating and a humbling experience. I finally felt comfortable as an actor on the last episode I did on *CSI*, a show called "Maid Man."

Dustin Lee Abraham, who had been with the show since its inception, wrote a part especially for me. It's funny how things connect. Dustin had worked with my daughter Cara during summer breaks at a Banana Republic store when they both were in college. Cara spoke Spanish and became one of the best salespeople on the staff. She dealt with the Mexican tourists who were in Las Vegas and went to the mall to shop. I'm not sure what Dustin's job was at the store, but if I remember correctly, he also had another job, collecting for a bookmaker. Those would be the kinds of experiences that would help any scriptwriter. I knew from the criminal cases I had handled that you can't make the stuff up any better than it is.

Dustin wrote a part where I got shot at the Mob Museum during an opening night party. Martha Coolidge, a wonderful director, was in charge of the episode. She gave me two pieces of direction that I like to think made me a better actor. The first thing she told me was to slow down and to speak slowly. I think I was rushing to get through my lines because I was worried about messing them up. I knew I had a problem memorizing, and I just wanted to get the lines over with. She told me to relax, slow down, and be natural.

She also gave me perspective.

"What are you going to do next?" she asked as we were shooting a scene.

"I'm going over to the X," I said.

"What's the X?" she asked.

I said, "You know, the X mark taped on the floor where I'm supposed to stand for the next scene. I'm going over to the X."

"No you're not," she said.

I looked puzzled. I didn't know what she meant.

"You're not going over to the X," she said. "You're going to see your client in jail."

And it hit me. It seems simple, but I had gotten so caught up in the process that I had lost the meaning. I've been a "method actor" ever since. And I've stopped worrying about the X. I've also developed a greater appreciation for actors and their craft. Sometimes we lose sight of that, because they make it look so easy that you don't even know they're acting.

I worked with James Caan when I did a spot on *Las Vegas,* the television series that ran from 2003 to 2008. He was the star of the show. I knew him before that, of course. He had that great part playing Sonny Corleone in *The Godfather*, and was just a genuinely good guy. I first met him out at Dean Shendal's ranch in the Las Vegas valley.

Dean was one of my favorite people: handsome, rugged, what you pictured when you thought about Las Vegas and the American West in the old days. He had come here from St. Louis and started working in casinos, but also had his own ranch where he roped and rode.

When I was still actively practicing law, I helped Dean with a problem. He had been indicted in federal court for possessing a silencer. The judge who was to hear the case had come out from Los Angeles. Before the trial was to start, he called me in and asked how I intended to offer a defense.

"He had the silencer, didn't he?" the judge asked.

I told the judge what I intended to argue. "Dean is a duck hunter," I said. "But he's not a very good shot. He needed the silencer so he wouldn't scare the ducks away."

The judge laughed, and I was able to work out a deal where Dean pleaded guilty and was given unsupervised probation.

Dean and I became good friends, and on weekends I would take my children out to the ranch, where they would ride ponies or swim in Dean's pool. Ralph Lamb, the sheriff, would be out there with show biz people and local folks, just regular guys. It was a great time. James Caan was always there, and we became good friends. When I shot the episode for the television series, he let me use his "star" trailer. I had a scene with Mollie Sims and Josh Duhamel, two other stars of the show. In the scene I had to drink a boilermaker, a shot of whiskey in a mug of beer. Given my background and experience, it wasn't really acting. I nailed it.

I had a part in another show with Tom Selleck, who is as suave and as professional as it gets. We were in Los Angeles doing a breakfast scene early in the day. When I finished, I got up and started to leave the set.

"Where are you going?" he asked.

"I'm finished," I said. "I'm going back to Las Vegas."

He looked disappointed.

"That's rude," he said, looking me right in the eye. "The cast was here while you were acting. The least you could do is show them the same courtesy. Stay until they complete the scene."

I did, and I've never thought about leaving early again. It was a great lesson, not only about acting, but about life. Movies and dealing with celebrities were the fun part of being mayor. But I also had some serious business I needed to take care of.

CHAPTER 13

A RIVER IN
THE DESERT

eing mayor was a part-time job, and it paid $48,000. But as
I said, I turned it into a full-time position. I worked at it
every day; ten, sometimes twelve hours a day, seven days a
week. And I loved every minute of it. But like anything else, there
was a learning curve.

There was one adjustment that I had to make immediately.

While there were plenty of perks associated with being mayor
and I was happy to avail myself of most of them, it wasn't the
same as when I was a defense attorney. As mayor, I was an
elected official, so I had to be cognizant of my role and of "public
perception." When I was actively practicing law, if someone
wanted to buy me dinner or give me tickets to a ball game or a
concert, I would gladly accept. Gifts and favors came with the
turf. The Chagra brothers gave me a pair of gorgeous leather
cowboy boots made by Lucchesi. Tony Spilotro gave me a set of
ivory Chinese statues. Other appreciative clients showered me
with gifts like Cuban cigars and Crystal champagne.

The most unusual gift I ever received came from Natale "Big
Chris" Richichi, John Gotti's consigliere, and Charlie "The
Moose" Panarella, two mob figures I had represented. They were
funny guys. I don't think I ever laughed as much as I did when I
was around them.

I was in Palm Beach once with Big Chris getting ready for a trial in which he was charged with extortion. We were staying at the Chesterfield Hotel. They have a great bar there, the Leopard. We were having drinks one night and Chris, who was in his late seventies, couldn't stop looking at the cocktail waitress. He was a loyal husband and family man, but he loved women with long legs. And this waitress had the longest legs in the world—at least it seemed that way to us after we'd had a few drinks.

After she brought another round of drinks over, Chris had this big smile on his face and he said to me, "Oscar, do you know what osso bucco means?"

I said, "Yeah, it's veal in a shank sauce, right?"

He had this twinkle in his eye.

"Nope," he said. "It means hard bone."

Then he started laughing and he couldn't stop. He kept looking at the waitress and shaking his head.

"Osso bucco," he said again and again.

Chris got convicted of extortion and racketeering in that case, which involved payoffs from a "gentleman's club" in Florida, in which he supposedly had an interest. After the verdict I asked the judge to allow him to remain free on bail pending an appeal. I cited his deteriorating health as one reason. But the judge wouldn't hear it. He ordered him remanded immediately to prison.

I had to go back to the hotel where we were staying and collect his belongings—his clothes, his shaving gear, some family photos, even an extra set of false teeth that he had on his nightstand. Those are the kinds of things the public doesn't know anything about. They see the headline and hear the prosecutor describing this Mafia figure. To me, Chris was a kind and funny old man. I'm picking up his false teeth in his hotel room so that I can give them to his family, and the thought that he's some kind of racketeer is the furthest thing from my mind.

Chris eventually got sentenced to six years in that case. He never made it home. He died in prison in January 2001. I was the mayor by that point and I took some criticism for it, but I went to his funeral. He was a friend. It was the right thing to do.

It was the same way with Charlie Panarella. I had represented him in a number of cases, and you couldn't find a more thankful client. The feds, of course, had a different view of him. His reputation in the underworld was steeped in violence. It was said that he once forced one of his victims to eat his own testicles before he killed him.

That piece of underworld folklore took on added meaning when The Moose and Big Chris gave me a plaque with two steel balls mounted on it. I hung that plaque over the door in my law office. It was a daily reminder of what they thought of me, and what I needed to battle the federal government.

Once I was elected, of course, I had to be more circumspect about gifts and favors. In the political world, the concept of influence peddling can quickly turn into a criminal offense. I was always conscious of that.

I had been in office for a few weeks when I was running late for an appointment. I pulled my car out of the neighborhood, the Scotch Eighties, where we live. The way the roads are set up, I wasn't able to make a left-hand turn. But I was late and there wasn't anyone coming the other way, so I made what I still believe to this day was a U-turn, not a left turn.

Seconds later, I heard a siren and saw a police motorcycle in my rearview mirror. I pulled over.

The officer walked up to the car. I rolled down my window. He recognized me.

"Oh, my God," he said.

"No, just the mayor," I replied.

He wasn't sure what he should do, but I told him to just write me a ticket. I paid my fine and spent five hours in traffic school for some remedial driver's ed. I was the mayor, and if anything, I had to bend over backwards to follow the rules. If I had been practicing law, I probably would have either tried to talk my way out of a ticket or tried to get the ticket fixed once it was issued.

That's one way my approach to things changed after I was elected.

Another thing I had to adjust to was the "celebrity" of the job. I've always enjoyed the spotlight; there's great ego gratification that comes with being center stage. I had that as a criminal defense attorney representing high-profile clients in high-profile cases. And I had it again as mayor of a great city. But there also can be petty aggravations that as an elected official you just can't dismiss or ignore.

During my tenure, a couple of gadflies tried to raise ethics questions about the way I did business. I don't want to bore you with all the details here, but one issue had to do with my son Ross's involvement in a start-up company called iPolitix. I encouraged some people to touch base with him at a cocktail party. I got nothing out of it, but the issue got traction in the media, as they say, and I had to defend myself before the city's Ethics Commission. I won on every issue but one, and had originally intended to let it go at that. But Carolyn, whose advice I almost always follow, said I had to challenge the one negative ruling.

"The only things we leave our children are their educations and their good names," she said.

I appealed the one negative ruling and won a reversal in state court. Then the Ethics Commission, much to my surprise, appealed that decision to the Nevada Supreme Court. I had to hire lawyers to represent me through all of this, and we eventually prevailed.

Carolyn was right, of course. She usually is.

There was another situation, however, where I needed no encouragement to legally defend myself. I was just beginning my second term in office when James McManus, a professional poker player, wrote a book that included anecdotal stories about Las Vegas.

In one chapter, he wrote that local "lore" had it that I was sitting at a table with Benny Binion and Jimmy Chagra in the Horse Shoe Casino when the assassination of Judge Wood was planned. Now, I'm a man of some principle, but I also have a tough skin. I was used to less than flattering things being written about me.

The mob could afford to hire the best lawyers in the country and they chose me, so I wore the badge "mob lawyer" with honor. But this McManus had crossed the line; what he wrote was not only untrue, but it was libelous. I can't think of anything more damaging you could say about an individual.

I don't know what he or his publisher, Farrar, Straus and Giroux, thought they were doing or how they thought couching this nonsense as "lore" would protect them. There was no truth whatsoever to the allegation.

I went bonkers when I read it and contacted Tony Glassman, a friend and lawyer. He represented me, and we had the situation rectified in ten days. They put a full-page retraction and apology to me in the Book Review section of the Sunday *New York Times*. They also agreed that the lines would be eliminated from any further editions of the book, and I received a big check.

I thought it was absolutely cavalier that someone thought they could just throw that kind of gossip out there and think they could get away with it. My reputation as a mob lawyer was one thing, but my integrity and my good name are another matter.

These were the kind of things I had to deal with after becoming mayor. Looking back on it now, I wouldn't have done anything differently. Some people try to call attention to themselves by challenging and criticizing in the public forum. I was an easy target in that respect, and I guess the gadflies also benefited from the fact that I didn't suffer fools gladly.

There was a situation at a city council meeting where one of these attention-seekers referred to the showgirls that I traveled around with during promotions as "bimbos." These women worked hard at what they did, and the city benefited from the attention that their presence generated. They were a symbol of Las Vegas. So when this idiot took a public shot at them, I had to say something.

"Look, buddy," I told him. "You can say whatever you want about me, but don't malign those ladies. Okay? Now sit down. I've had it with you."

He wouldn't let it go, and eventually I had him ejected from the council meeting.

There were a few other ethics issues and occasionally there were whispering campaigns and snide comments about the awarding of city contracts, the allegation being that I had favored someone who I knew or who had done something for me.

At one point I tried to make my position clear, although I'm not sure any of my political opponents cared about what I said or what the real issue was.

"I want to do business with people that I know, rather than people that I don't know," I said during one news conference, explaining that when everything else was equal in terms of a bid or a contract, I'd favor someone with whom I'd had a relationship. "If you know somebody and they're honorable and you have done business with them before, they get the best of it."

That wasn't exactly a revolutionary statement. It was, I thought, a frank description of the way government and politics have always worked.

There was a mayor back in my old hometown of Philadelphia, John Street, who said pretty much the same thing when he was challenged about non-bid contracts and businesses that the city awarded to his friends and political associates.

I may be paraphrasing here, but in essence, Mayor Street said, "Who would you expect me to favor, my enemies?"

Street was an aggressive mayor who rubbed a lot of people the wrong way. The FBI, in fact, planted a bug in his office, but the investigation never went anywhere. I don't know that much about him or his politics, but in my opinion, he will always be highly rated.

A few years after I was in office, I got a call one night from my cousin Paul Brazina back in Philadelphia. My mother had been rushed to the hospital and was on a gurney in the hospital hallway waiting for a room. Thank God the medical problem didn't turn out to be that serious, but at the time we had no way of knowing. I told Paul I'd be on the next plane to Philadelphia. I also called Mayor Street. I had been to a Conference of Mayors meeting and had a list of the home numbers of all the mayors in the country. It was two o'clock in the morning my time, which meant I was calling him at 5 A.M.

He picked up the phone and couldn't have been more helpful. I told him of my plight, and he said not to worry. He would take care of it. When I arrived at the Philadelphia airport that rainy day, there was a police escort waiting for me. I was driven to the hospital with the sirens wailing and the lights flashing.

When I got there, my mother was in a private room and was being treated like the Queen of England. As I said, Mayor Street had quite a few critics during his two terms in office, but with me he's always going to be aces. When you're an elected official, you don't forget your friends. And you don't forget those who go out of their way to help you. John Street went above and beyond.

You also don't forget those who fail to deliver what they've promised. In those instances, I found it especially rewarding to succeed in spite of them.

I was still obsessed with the idea of revitalizing downtown, particularly the area east of the railroad tracks, and even after Wynn, Gaughan, and some other early supporters backed away, I pushed forward. The city's inner core is separated by railroad tracks. The west side was basically an old railroad yard that had sat fallow for more than a quarter of a century. The east side had Fremont Street and what was left of a financial district. It had no energy and it bred lethargy.

Part of my thought process was preserving the city's history. Las Vegas hadn't done much of that; implosion was the first thought when it came to redevelopment. Blow up the old buildings and put up new ones. That's how we lost classic casino-hotels like the Dunes, the Stardust, the Sands, the Hacienda, the Landmark, and the Desert Inn. When I took office, the old post office and courthouse building, where I had tried my first federal case, were sitting empty down the street from City Hall. It was a great old structure, and I didn't want to see it go. I figured it could be a cornerstone for the downtown revitalization, and eventually it was.

But first I had to build my river. Las Vegas is in the middle of the world's driest desert, so you don't need to tell people how important water is. But water is also symbolic; it's nurturing, replenishing, and a source of life and of energy. I decided the way to get life back to the downtown area was to build a river, so I got the city engineers involved.

There was a vacant piece of city-owned land between Fourth Street and Las Vegas Boulevard near the new federal courthouse and an abandoned former elementary school that had been a police substation. That was where I wanted my river, and the engineers made it happen. Now, "river" may be a bit of an exaggeration. "Man-made rivulet" is probably more accurate. The water is re-circulated, cascading along a culvert that is about three feet wide. But the area along both banks has been cleaned up, and there are plants and trees and benches where people can sit and relax, eat their lunch, read the paper. A plaque on an adjoining wall calls it "Oscar's River." I wanted it to be a place that had life. What I had in mind for the old police substation and the area around it was to convert it into an agora. The ancient Greeks used to have open spaces in the middle of the city that would serve as meeting places for citizens. I pictured Plato and Socrates meeting and talking with people, debating, philosophizing.

They were more than just places; they were a way of life, a way to communicate, to interact. The great European cities have something similar with their piazzas. I think people who live in cities hunger for that kind of connection. You just have to provide them with the opportunity. My river and the agora were steps in that direction.

The Greeks surrounded their agoras with public buildings, temples and commercial enterprises, shops and stores. Go to Vegas today, and I think you'll appreciate what I'm talking about. The old courthouse, which I got the federal government to sell to the city for a dollar, is now the Mob Museum. Actually it's called the National Museum of Organized Crime and Law Enforcement. Talk about taking heat: the pundits came out in full force when I began promoting the idea. "What's Goodman doing, building a monument to himself?" they asked. "He's glorifying his old killer clients."

Then the Italian-Americans weighed in. They were certain that I was going to vilify them. I faced a lynch-mob-like crowd in a packed room at the Justinian Club and tried to assure them that they had no fear of defamation.

"The mob I was thinking of being featured in the museum," I told them, "came from Bugsy Siegel, Meyer Lansky, Mo Dalitz,

Gus Greenbaum, Frank Rosenthal, and Oscar Goodman. It was the Jewish mob, and if this museum turns out the way I think it will, you'll be begging me to let some Italians in."

I was joking, of course, but it didn't do much to assuage their feelings. I pulled a brilliant move, though, which cooled off all the naysayers. I was able to persuade Ellen Knowlton, who had just retired from the FBI, to become chairperson of the museum board. She went back to the Hoover Building in Washington, D.C., and convinced the folks back there that this was a worthwhile project. As a result, we're able to display legitimate law enforcement memorabilia along with organized crime artifacts. We've got state-of-the-art lie-detector equipment, and we've got the barber chair where Albert Anastasia was killed. And we have the wall from the St. Valentine's Day Massacre, bullet holes and all.

We interviewed several individuals looking for the right person to "program" the museum. One of the candidates was Dennis Barrie, who came highly recommended. He had developed the Spy Museum in Washington, D.C., and the Rock and Roll Hall of Fame Museum in Cleveland. But for some reason, after interviewing him, I wasn't impressed. I told Betty Fretwell, the City Manager who was also part of the process, of my concerns.

A few nights later I was channel surfing on TV. I usually watch television at night, primarily to follow a game or two where I might have a bet on the line. I came across a courtroom scene in a movie. It was called *Dirty Pictures,* and was based on actual events. James Wood, whom I had met during the filming of *Casino*, starred as a Cincinnati art museum director who was being criminally tried because he would not remove a controversial exhibition that featured photographs by Robert Mapplethorpe. Several of the photographs were sexually explicit and depicted nude children or sexual acts, including one of a man ramming his fist up another man's anus.

The strain on the museum director, as portrayed by Wood, was overwhelming. You could see and feel what he was going through. He was defending art, and it cost him, among other things, his reputation and his marriage. I thought the movie was awesome. The museum director was the prototypical defender of the First Amendment. When I saw the credits at the conclusion of the film, I read that James Wood was portraying Dennis Barrie.

I reached for the phone and called him.

"You know, Mister Barrie, I was tepid about you," I said. "Now you're my hero. You are our man."

I said the job was his, and he hasn't disappointed.

When we had the grand opening of the Mob Museum, I got a call from Vinny Ferrara, my former client from Boston. He was in town with his soon-to-be bride, attending a boxing match. It had been a long time since I'd seen him, and I was genuinely happy he had been released from prison. We exchanged pleasantries, and he asked if he could attend the museum opening. I said sure. During opening ceremonies, Carolyn and I and Ellen were seated near the ribbon, which had been placed in front of the door. I looked out and there was Vinny in the crowd. Once the ribbon was cut and the festivities started, I lost sight of him. About an hour went by. There were interviews and photographs and lots of media. Then I saw Vinny come out of the building.

"How did you like it, Vin?" I asked.

"Oscah," he said in that thick North End Boston accent. "It was great. But I'm pissed at you, Oscah."

"Why?" I asked, since it's not good having Vinny unhappy.

"Because my picture isn't in it."

Be assured, Vinny, your picture is now prominently displayed.

*　　*　　*

The museum has made a big difference to the city's revitalization, but so have many of the other downtown developments. One of the first new buildings to go up was a modern bank building. The bank had been proposed, but then there was talk that it was going to be scuttled. I convinced the developer to stay in town and to build as originally planned.

We made the agora a cultural center, and it's now a place where we have poetry readings, plays, and intimate concerts. It's an intellectual marketplace where they give music lessons to youngsters. I walk by and I hear music wafting out onto the street. People sit by the urban river or in the park nearby, and they see children walking by with violin cases. I joke about that, comparing it to the old Las Vegas. Anytime I'm having a discussion about what's happened, I'll say, "This is not the first time violin cases have been seen on the streets, but this time the cases contain violins."

I'm really proud of what we have down there, what we've been able to accomplish, and what might still be to come. But it took some doing, and at first I didn't think it was going to be possible.

The river was a small step and it brought unexpected controversy. We got that little park together. I saw it as an oasis in the middle of a lot of rubble. But before you knew it, it was overrun by homeless people. This was part of the problem with the downtown area.

"What's this homeless crap?" I asked publicly. "They're ruining everything."

I understand the homeless problem, and I think government has an obligation to address it. Many homeless people have chronic mental problems. Ronald Reagan didn't do anyone any good when he cut back on funding that resulted in the closing of centers that were set up to address the issue. People poured out onto the streets, and many of them don't want to be anywhere else.

All cities have the problem. In Las Vegas, it's a little different than, say, New York or Philadelphia or Chicago, because it's always warm here. When people sleep on benches or in parks overnight, they're not going to get frostbite. Nobody's going to freeze to death. So we have to deal with it. If a homeless person has a mental problem, if a homeless person is someone who's come back from overseas where he or she has served their country and now can't take care of themselves, then the government has a moral obligation and should step in.

But there's another segment of homeless who are able-bodied and of sound mind, but who just don't want to conform to any kind of societal norms. They won't use the social service centers available to them, like Catholic Charities, the Salvation Army, or the Mission, because when they use those facilities they have to leave their drugs and booze behind. I have no use for those people, and I said as much. They don't want to work and take care of themselves. They'd rather stand on the corner all day with their hands out, almost daring people driving by in cars to hit them. I have no tolerance for them. "I'd like to run them out of town and all the way to the Pacific Ocean," I said during one press conference.

The media went nuts. It attracted national attention, and after that I got voted the "meanest mayor in America" by some homeless advocacy groups. I didn't care. I thought I was right, and I was going to speak my mind. I wasn't elected to get reelected; I was elected to lead the city. This situation with the homeless was a problem, and we were going to fix it.

Look, if you see somebody standing on a corner in an Army fatigue jacket and scarf in 115-degree desert heat, you know that person has a problem. We have to do something. I'm just saying not all homeless people are the same. And as a government, we have to recognize the differences. That's part of dealing with the problem.

I had another idea that added to the firestorm. There was an abandoned prison not too far outside of town on the way to the California border. I suggested that it be converted into a large shelter for the homeless. Take down the bars to the cells, and it's not a prison; it's just a building. You'd have a heated, air-conditioned commissary and a medical facility there. The idea lasted two seconds. The headline in the local paper, front page, above the fold:

MAYOR GOODMAN WANTS TO SEND HOMELESS TO PRISON

Those were the kinds of things I had to deal with. Part of the problem with the media is that they jump for the headline without presenting the issue. Sometimes the press would rather have people shouting at one another instead of discussing and debating in a civilized manner and coming up with a solution or a compromise in order to get something done for the common good. I saw it during my twelve years as mayor, and I think we all see it on a broader scale in the national discourse. Or should I say, lack of discourse.

I had a chance to let the local newspaper know how I felt about its policies after I had been in office about a year. The *Review Journal,* the paper who ran the editorial "Anyone but Oscar for Mayor," had an annual contest where their readers voted for "the best" and "the worst" in Las Vegas. The voting covered all kinds of topics, the best and worst places to eat, to drink, and so on. And they held a banquet where the results were announced.

I got a call inviting me to the event. I had a policy never to decline an invitation to a public event unless I had a scheduling conflict. So I said I'd attend, even though I believed I would be recognized as the "worst elected official."

The banquet was at the MGM Grand. All the men were decked out in tuxedoes and the women in evening gowns. I sat by myself, drinking a martini. I hadn't bothered to ask Carolyn to join me because I felt nothing good was going to take place. I didn't like the people who were attending; they thought they were big shots. It just wasn't my kind of crowd.

The event went on and on, boring as all get-out. And then I heard someone say, "Best Elected Official . . . Oscar Goodman." I was floored. I took my drink in hand and climbed the stairs to the stage and looked out over a very surprised group of people. More surprised than I was, I guess. This was my chance to even the score. My acceptance speech, as best I can remember, went something like this: "Ladies and Gentlemen, tonight I am the happiest mayor in the world. This past year everything has been perfect for me with one exception. When I was elected, I had two small puppies at home. One passed away, and now I only have one puppy in the house. As a result, I don't know what to do with the other half of the newspaper."

Dead silence. No one knew what to do.

I raised my drink in a toast and walked off the stage. It felt great.

Then I went back to working on redeveloping the inner city.

I have a tendency to think out loud. It's not carelessness on my part; it's part of my Socratic training as a lawyer. You postulate an issue and look at it from all sides. You have to recognize that it may not be all black and white. Everything has a tinge of gray.

Another example: if you want a job in Las Vegas, you have to have a work card. When I took office, it was standard for the police to deny anyone with a criminal record the right to work in the city. Criminal record? Work card denied. I called the cop who was in charge and said I wanted that to stop. I told him my philosophy. Las Vegas has always been a place for second chances; look at some of the Founding Fathers. If a business is willing to hire someone who has a criminal record—if the business owner is aware of this and still wants to give that person a chance—then the city shouldn't stand in the way.

We got more people working that way. It was just the right thing to do.

But I was frustrated. I was six months into my first term and other than building the river, I hadn't done much to get downtown moving. I wanted a Renaissance, but I was worried it was all going down the toilet. The thought occurred to me that I might spend the next three and a half years fighting a losing battle.

At about that time Dan Van Epp, the head of the Hughes Corporation, stopped by my office. He had opposed my election, but now he said he'd had a change of heart. He saw what I was trying to do and he wanted to help. I told him my ideas and my frustration, and he set up a meeting with one of the urban redevelopment experts who worked for the Rouse Company, which was a major player in urban renewal. The company had done projects like the Baltimore Inner Harbor, New York's Seaport, and the rebuilding of the North End in Boston, including Faneuil Hall. I needed a 101 course in revitalizing a city, and this expert could give it to me.

We sat in my office for an hour and I unloaded. I poured my heart out, told him all of my plans and dreams and what I wanted to do for downtown. He listened, and then he said it couldn't happen.

"You can't do it," he said. "You don't have any land."

When I went home that night, I was distraught. Three and a half more years of this stupid job, I thought. But then I realized that there was land available. There was an old railroad site, about 235 acres, sitting vacant right in the middle of the area where I wanted to rebuild downtown.

The prior administration had used—or perhaps "abused" is the better word—eminent domain to benefit private developers. I had made a commitment not to do that. There was no way my administration was going to use the power of the city to take land from one private property owner and give it to another so that he could profit.

But this was different. The land I had my eye on was owned by the Union Pacific Railroad. I called them up and asked about buying the property. They said no way, it's not for sale. But they said that they didn't own all of the parcel; Lehman Brothers had sixty-one acres. Some time ago, there had been talk about building a football stadium there. It never happened, and the New York investment group had foreclosed on a loan and was now holding the property.

I went to New York and had a meeting with Lehman Brothers. They wanted $33 million, which the city didn't have. But we had something else—vacant land in a technology park in an affluent section of the city. We worked out a trade.

The result was the beginning of the Renaissance.

Today, downtown Las Vegas is alive with shops and stores on the east side of the tracks. On the west side we have a brand-new cultural and performing arts center, a brain institute, a premium outlet mall, and a major furniture showroom. There is a great diversity of small shops, stores, restaurants, and bars. We've used tax abatements, a concept I learned about on the job. You give businesses a tax break when they come in, and they promise to put a part of that break back into their business. It's a win-win. Not every voter understands the concept of redevelopment and incentivizing. I had to fight some battles, but I knew I was right. We waived liquor license fees to attract taverns with entertainment components. We rebated taxes for infrastructure improvements. We became reasonable with permitting approvals. In short, we made it easier for a businessman to do business in the city.

When people go to the new Smith Center for the Performing Arts, as they did recently, to see a production of *Billy Elliot, the Musical* or to hear Itzhak Perlman, the violin virtuoso, they say, "Thank you, Mister Mayor, this is wonderful." They're not thinking about the tax abatements or the other city expenditures that were used to create the vitality. They don't care how it was funded; they're just enjoying themselves and their city.

That's what I wanted to do as mayor.

When we first got the ball rolling, Donald Trump came into town for a meeting. I had met Trump before. The first time was at a party given for a casino executive at the Hilton. We also got together once when Carolyn and I were in New York. Trump invited us to stop by his office.

We were ushered in and he was on the phone. He motioned for us to sit down. He was talking to Harvey Weinstein about his reality show, *The Apprentice*. Coincidentally, the night before, the popular television series *CSI* had aired an episode in which I had made an appearance.

Once Trump got off the phone, we started babbling to each other about how great those two shows were. When we left, Carolyn just shook her head.

"I never saw two bigger egos in one room at the same time," she said.

Trump came to Las Vegas and made a pitch about developing our site. He and I walked the sixty-one acres that the city had purchased from Lehman Brothers. He immediately understood its potential and was interested, but he wanted to develop the entire site himself. I was familiar with his product: sleek, modern, and, in my opinion, utilitarian. I wanted eclectic architecture. Not one style, but many styles, a conglomerate of many interesting and unique buildings. Trump did give me a perspective that has served me well. He said, "Don't look at the railroad tracks as an impediment. Treat them as though they were a river."

When you do that, you sort of like the tracks.

It was rewarding and exciting to watch it all take shape. Once we had the land and developers started to show interest, things took off. It helped, I think, that I was the mayor. I'm not being cocky when I say that, but realistic. If a podiatrist (and I like podiatrists since I have sore feet) had been elected mayor and tried to do these things, maybe he would have succeeded; maybe not. I think I was able to make it happen because of the attention I got. All the national publications wanted to do stories about the "mob lawyer who became the mayor." And whenever I was interviewed, I talked about my vision, about how I wanted to create a jewel in the desert; how the downtown I envisioned was going to be the heart and soul of the city.

There was a story in the *New York Times*, Sunday edition, front page. Then we got a cover story in *U.S. News and World Report*. Then the *Los Angeles Times* called. They wanted to do a piece about the jewel in the desert. We got a mall developer to build not in the suburbs, but downtown. People said I was nuts; malls weren't for downtown. But whenever I was asked, I would say, "It's the best dollar-per-square-foot-producing mall in America."

Actually, I made that up. But it got repeated and took on a truth of its own. I was the mayor, and I could say whatever I wanted.

There's nothing like a "Not guilty" jury verdict in a tough case. As I said earlier, when it comes to personal satisfaction, it's almost orgasmic. But when I look back now on what I accomplished as mayor, it's a different kind of feeling. It's lasting satisfaction, knowing you've made a contribution that will be there for a very long time.

Bricks and mortar and a feeling of community—that's what was built, and that's what kept me going. I woke up every morning and couldn't wait to get down to City Hall. It was like I was playing Monopoly, but with real money and actual real estate. It was a great feeling.

I have a friend, Larry Ruvo, whose father Lou had passed away from Alzheimer's disease. Larry runs one of the largest liquor distributorships in America. He wanted to keep his father's memory alive and do something about this horrible disease. As a favor to me, he agreed to develop his dream project as the cornerstone of Symphony Park.

The result is the Lou Ruvo Center for Brain Health, a first-class brain institute staffed by researchers and clinicians from the Cleveland Clinic. Think about it: the gambling capital of the world could be the place where a cure for Alzheimer's and other neurodegenerative diseases is discovered.

The futuristic building that houses the brain center was designed by the brilliant architect Frank Gehry. Frank was a real curmudgeon and wasn't that enthused when he was first approached about designing the brain institute. He was an imposing figure, with a craggy face and a shock of white hair. Larry Ruvo, Don Van Epp, and I met with him at his studio in Los Angeles to try to convince him to take on the project. It was a fascinating place. He had a group of young architects working for him, and you could see he enjoyed the creative process and the interaction. You could almost feel the creative juices flowing.

At the time, he was working on the design for a basketball arena in Brooklyn for the New Jersey Nets, who were about to move there. I thought it was ingenious. Television screens everywhere, special effects, lighting, surround sound. It would have made attending the game an experience, but the owners of the team decided that it would have detracted from the game itself, so they opted not to go with the idea.

We talked about a lot of things, and I told him about my "brand" and about the showgirls and the martinis, and how that was now one of the symbols of the city. He seemed intrigued. We were able to convince him to fly back with us on Larry's private jet. I arranged for him to meet my showgirls, we had a toast, and he agreed to take on the project.

And once he made his mind up—Katy, bar the door. The titanium building really can't be described. You have to see it. Critics said it was a depiction of the brain, or half of the brain. The truth is, after Frank told Larry and me that he would be the architect for the project, he picked up a piece of crepe paper, squeezed it in his hand, and threw it out onto a table. That shape and form is exactly the shape and form of the brain center.

The Smith Center was designed by David Schwarz, who did the Bass Center in Fort Worth. The World Market Center was created by Jon Jerde, who created the Bellagio. All of these fantastic buildings are thriving in Symphony Park.

You fight little battles and big battles, and you never give up. That was the approach I took when I was a defense attorney, and it was the approach I took when I was mayor.

I got the homeless out of the area by getting the health department involved. People sleeping on benches or pitching tents in the park and along my river created health hazards for everyone. It was obvious that they had to go. We moved them out, which the social service groups had been trying to do for years. I don't know where they went, but they're not causing the problems they used to. It hasn't made me popular with certain folks, but I don't care.

When I was mayor, every year I would go down to the Catholic Charities dinner to serve the homeless at Thanksgiving and again at Christmas. I would help serve the meals, and whenever the sponsors asked me to say a few words, I would get booed. Believe me, it didn't humble me, and it didn't bother me either.

Homelessness is a complicated problem for which there are no simple solutions. But a city can't give up its public space to a group of derelicts who know better. Not all of the homeless are disabled, mentally or physically. Some of them are out there making a good buck panhandling. Las Vegas is a unique place in so many ways, and the homeless take advantage of that. Gamblers are superstitious. They figure if they give a guy on the corner five bucks, they'll get it back tenfold at the craps table.

I don't think we should give them two bucks. I think the ones who need help, who are disabled mentally or physically or both, should get food, shelter, health care, a warm shower, and counseling. That's the obligation of government, to care for the needy and helpless.

And as for those who are just too lazy or too shiftless or who just don't want to work, I really don't care what happens to them. I just want them to stay out of our parks and away from my river.

CHAPTER 14
PROBLEMS WITH THE PRESIDENT

I've never been a big fan of President Obama. I think he's like most politicians; he talks a better game than he plays, and he says what he thinks people want to hear.

But the thing that really set me off was when he started using Las Vegas as a whipping boy for the country's economic troubles. I was chairing a meeting of the Las Vegas Convention and Visitors Authority in February 2009 when a reporter asked me if I had heard the news. The president was telling corporations not to go to Las Vegas, and not to take their corporate jets on junkets to the Super Bowl.

"You're nuts," I said. "He would never do anything like that. You must have heard it wrong."

After we got through the meeting's agenda, I asked people in the audience if they'd heard any federally elected official saying anything about trips to Las Vegas. No one had, so I thought it was just bad information. But at the end of the meeting, another reporter approached me with a transcript of what Obama had said. The president was at a town hall meeting in Indiana discussing the Wall Street bailout and got a big round of applause by using Las Vegas and the Super Bowl as whipping boys. He said the corporations that got a bailout should be more judicious with their money. Now, there was nothing wrong with saying that. But then he added that they shouldn't go to Las Vegas for their conventions or take their private jets to the Super Bowl. I'm reading this, and my eyes are popping out of my head.

"God damn it, he owes us an apology," I said.

And that was the beginning of my falling out with the president of the United States. Of course, Carolyn wasn't surprised. A few years earlier we had gone to Washington when I was being courted to run for the U.S. Senate. We went around and met a lot of the senators, and she remembered what it was like when Obama and I met.

"It was two ships passing in the night," she said. "Neither one of you was listening to what the other was saying."

But I didn't have any ill will toward him. In fact, I admired his youthful political acumen. When he was running I was chosen to moderate a debate in Las Vegas during the Democratic primary. He, John Edwards, and Hillary Clinton were involved. I had met Senator Clinton before. She was very bright and personable. She knew who I was by reputation, and we always had a good repartee whenever we were in each other's company. I had never met John Edwards, but he was very cordial.

And Obama remembered me from the trip to Washington a few years earlier. The first thing he said to me after we shook hands was, "How's that beautiful blonde wife of yours, Carolyn?"

I was impressed. He remembered the name, the blonde hair. Really extraordinary when you think of all the people he comes in contact with. So he got some political points from me that night.

He's a great orator; I'll give him that. He has a melodious voice, good expression, good movement. But get him off the monitors, and it's like a screw is loose. He says things without thinking of the repercussions.

We didn't have much contact after he was elected, but when he made that statement, I demanded an apology.

I wrote him a letter. I guess it wouldn't be fair to say I *demanded* an apology, but I said I thought we were entitled to some type of statement from him saying that Las Vegas was a good place to come for a convention.

I never heard a word. And in the meantime, we were losing convention business. A few days after he made that statement, Goldman Sachs, one of the Wall Street firms he was talking about, canceled a convention at Mandalay Bay, a big casino-hotel in town. They paid a $600,000 cancellation fee and instead went to San Francisco, where it's more expensive and where there's nothing to do except look at that stupid bridge. State Farm Insurance did the same thing, and I think we lost 1,100 beds. Heads in beds—that's how you measure the tourism business. It's the life-blood of the city. This was serious; I think we lost over 340 bookings. Was it all because of the president? I can't say. But what he said certainly added fuel to the fire.

A few months later, Obama was supposed to come out for a fundraiser on the Thursday after Memorial Day. I was invited to meet him at the airport. As mayor, I was supposed to welcome the president to the city. I didn't want to do it.

"I'm not going," I said to Carolyn.

"You have to go," she said. "Decency requires it. He's the president. When someone comes to your home, you have to greet them."

I said no, I wasn't going to do it. But I thought about what she said, and I decided I probably should. About that time we got a call from the White House.

"Mayor, we expect you to be at the airport," this official said.

I didn't like his attitude.

"I'm not coming," I said.

"What's the problem?" he asked.

"The president hurt my city, and he hasn't done anything to rectify it."

He asked for more details, and I told him. He said someone would get back to me. On Memorial Day, I went to the cemetery where there's the annual commemoration for those who made the ultimate sacrifice for our country. By 11:30 that morning, I was home sitting in the backyard relaxing. I had made myself a big martini, and I was planning to just enjoy a quiet afternoon. I was sitting in my favorite chair, looking at my koi fish and the fountain, feeling no pain. And the phone rang.

I rushed back in the house and picked it up on the third ring.

It was Rahm Emanuel, the president's chief of staff, although he introduced himself as "Congressman Emanuel."

It's amazing how fast you can sober up.

"I heard you have a problem with the president," he said.

"You bet I do," I said. "He was completely out of line and he hurt our community."

"What will it take for you to meet him at the airport?"

I said I wanted an apology, that I wanted him to say something like, "Las Vegas is a great place to do business and have fun." He said he could take care of that with the speechwriters. I took him at his word and when the president arrived, I was there at the airport to greet him, to welcome him to Las Vegas.

The first thing he said to me was, "I hear you're telling everyone I caused you to lose sixty percent of your business. What would happen if I said it's a great place to visit?"

"I'd tell everybody you got us back eighty percent of our business," I said. "I've got no problem with that."

There was a picture in the paper the next day of him and me talking at the airport. We don't really look like friends. The next day when he gave his speech to Nevadans, the only thing he said was, "It's nice to be in Las Vegas."

That was it. From where I stood, that wasn't a retraction. He didn't do what he or his chief of staff said he would do to right the wrong. I'm not someone who believes in letting bygones be bygones. I was angry, and I wasn't going to forget.

It's funny. These guys are politicians. They give their word, and they don't think they have to keep it. I represented people who the government said were vicious, terrible individuals; Mafia bosses, killers, gangsters. When they gave me their word, I could take it to the bank.

Who's more honorable?

But that's not the end of the story. About a year later, he did it again. He was speaking at some town meeting in New Hampshire. The topic was government spending and the tight economy. And here's part of what he said:

"Responsible families don't do their budgets the way the federal government does, right? When times are tough, you tighten your belts. You don't go buying a boat when you can barely pay your mortgage. You don't blow a bunch of cash on Vegas when you're trying to save for college. You prioritize. You make tough choices. It's time your government did the same."

I've got no problem with the point he made. Government has to be more responsible about the way it spends money. But why Vegas again? He had to throw us under the bus a second time.

I was livid. So were a lot of others. Harry Reid, one of our senators, demanded an apology, and got one of sorts. I've had my moments with Reid, especially when he was part of the Gaming Commission and putting my clients in the Black Book. But this time he did the right thing. He put out a statement chastising the president and warning him to "lay off Las Vegas and stop making it the poster child for where people shouldn't be spending their money."

The president responded to him, maybe because he was a senator, saying that his comments were not meant to be "anything negative about Las Vegas," adding that "there is no place better to have fun than Vegas, one of our country's great desti-nations."

To me it sounded like the part of the speech he forgot to give a year earlier. Those were the kind of lines I thought Rahm Emanuel was going to get a speechwriter to give Obama. But I was past the point of being placated. I was interviewed and I let it all come out. Today you can still find the video online.

"He has a real psychological hang-up about the entertain-ment capital of the world," I said. "An apology won't be accept-able this time. I don't know where his vendetta comes from, but we're not going to let him make his bones by lambasting Las Vegas.

"He didn't learn his lesson the first time, but when he hurt our economy by his ill-conceived rhetoric, we didn't think it would happen again. But now that it has, I want to assure you, when he comes back, I'll do everything I can to give him the boot back to Washington and visit his failures back there.

"I gotta tell you this, and everybody says I shouldn't say it, but I gotta tell you the way it is. This president is a real slow learner."

And the next time the president came to Las Vegas, I was not at the airport to greet him.

Those comments made me a hero in town with most people, but apparently they struck a nerve with some African-Americans. A group of black clergymen demanded I apologize. They said "giving the boot" had some kind of racial connotation. I said I wasn't going to apologize because I hadn't said or done anything wrong.

Louis Farrakhan gave a speech at Howard University where he referred to me as the "little Jewish mayor" and said I had snubbed the president because he was black. Farrakhan is a racist pig. I despise everything he stands for. What I said had nothing to do with race. I didn't care if the president was black, white, green, or had polka dots. Twice he said things that hurt my city, and I wasn't going to keep my mouth shut about it.

I don't know of any other mayor who stood up to a president like that. He really soured me on politics and politicians, the way he handled the whole exchange. It's so easy to just say, "I'm sorry. I made a mistake."

What's so hard about that? That's the problem with politicians. Consider Sanford from South Carolina and the woman in Argentina. Clinton and his "I did not have sex with that woman." Tell the truth and admit you made a mistake. The public is understanding—at least that's been my experience.

The racism charge was just something drummed up by people who use it at every turn to call attention to themselves. It was an economic issue, not a racial issue. That's another one of the problems we have in this country. You may disagree with what I say, but don't try to make what I say something that it isn't. You want to debate me on an issue, fine. Let's go. I don't care what color you are.

I think about that Rodney King question, "Can't we all just get along?"

Maybe we can't. I look at what's going on in Washington today, and I'm disgusted. One of the reasons I decided not to run for the U.S. Senate was the thought of trying to deal with that. I've talked to a lot of senators. They say things have changed, and not for the better.

There's no discourse, no compromise, no debate. It's all personal now, and they really don't like one another. That's the situation we have, and it's remarkable that they function at all.

As an elected official, I always took my position on any issue seriously. That's what I was elected to do. But once in awhile, you have to take a step back, look around, and realize what life is all about. And hopefully, when you do that, you stop taking yourself too seriously.

✶ ✶ ✶

I have licensed my persona for a restaurant in Las Vegas now, "Oscar's Beef, Booze, and Broads," and during last year's presidential campaign we had two special drinks on the menu. We had the "No Bama" in honor of President Obama. It was a complicated mixed drink: two ounces of Jefferson's 10-year-old straight rye whiskey, one and a half ounces of Canton ginger liqueur, a half ounce of Sombra, three-fourths of an ounce of lemon juice, and three-fourths of an ounce of simple syrup.

And then we had the "Romney" for Mitt Romney: tap water over ice.

After the election we discontinued the presidential drinks and started to feature "The Oscar"—four and a quarter ounces of Bombay Sapphire Gin, one jalapeno pepper, and a splash of olive juice over ice.

It's all about choices . . . and not taking yourself too seriously.

CHAPTER 15

FUN IN THE
PLAYBOY SUITE

One of the things I enjoyed about being mayor was having a platform to talk about and advocate for the things I thought were important. My battles over the homeless issue were one example. I'm proud of what we accomplished, and I think we've begun to address that problem in a sensible and honest way. I said what I thought, and I backed it up with action.

I took the same approach with another type of urban blight—graffiti. I don't see it as art; I don't see any Picassos out there. And I especially don't see any justification in defacing public property and calling it self-expression.

We have one of the ugliest highway systems in the country in Las Vegas. There are these concrete ribbons everywhere, a spaghetti bowl of intersections and overlapping roadways devoid of any touch of humanity. There was no landscaping and few public areas. After I was elected, I wanted to change that. We started a highway beautification project, and one of the things I was most proud of was a sculpture of a giant desert tortoise that was the centerpiece for one of the landscaping projects.

A couple of days after the tortoise was unveiled, I got a call from someone down at the highway maintenance office.

"You're not going to like this," he said. "Someone graffitied your tortoise."

I was livid, and I didn't try to hide that fact. I went on television and I said, "If we catch the person who marred my tortoise, I'm advocating that we chop his thumb off. And I think we should do it on TV."

Another media frenzy ensued, worse in some ways than the dispute over the homeless. Now I wasn't just the meanest mayor in America; I was a despot and a dictator who was advocating the maiming of graffiti artists, although I hesitate to use the word "artist" in describing these vandals.

An *Associated Press* article moved over the wires and, I assume, throughout the world. I was described as suggesting that graffiti artists have their "thumbs cut off on television." It also made reference to my comment about how the French used to have public beheadings of people who committed heinous crimes and to how I had gone on about public whippings and canings, suggesting that I thought those also should be brought back as punishments.

I had said a lot of that, but I was merely trying to make a point. Public floggings should only be permissible, I said, after someone had had a fair trial.

Sometimes I wonder if the American public is paying attention, or if the media is just trying to stir the pot. Satire used to be an accepted device to make a point, state a position, generate discussion. When Jonathan Swift wrote that the Irish could deal with the famine by eating their children, he wasn't advocating cannibalism. When he wrote that "a young, healthy child well nursed is at a year old a most delicious, nourishing and wholesome food, whether stewed, roasted baked or boiled," he wasn't providing a recipe. He was making a point.

There were times when I felt like screaming. I wasn't proposing that we cut off anyone's thumb. But I was trying to call attention to the tremendous cost, both in cleaning up the mess and in terms of a community's identity that graffiti creates.

That was one point I wanted to make. This so-called "art" costs taxpayers money and defaces the city. Another point was that the law should be a deterrent. Cutting off a thumb or resorting to caning were both hyperbolic expressions meant to underscore problems that need to be addressed. I also suggested that anyone convicted of spraying graffiti on public property should be put in a stockade that I wanted to have built on Fremont Street. I said that the offender could be put in the dock, and the public could come by and throw paint at him or her. A public embarrassment for the offender? Perhaps, but apt punishment for the offense.

They eventually caught the kid who sprayed graffiti on my tortoise, and part of his punishment was a requirement that he had to come to my office and apologize. I had been given a gift during one of my trips, a machete. I put it on my desk and when the kid walked in, that was the first thing he saw. He stammered and couldn't stop staring at the machete. I let him ponder the situation for a few seconds before I asked him if he had anything to say.

"I'm sorry," he said. "I'm sorry . . . I'll . . . I'll never do it again."

I wasn't going to forgive him, so I just told him he could go. But from the look on his face, I believed him when he said he wouldn't do it again.

The bottom line, though, is that in the aftermath of the "cut off their thumbs" controversy, the city started an anti-graffiti campaign aimed at making the public aware of the problems and the costs. And the police set up a squad that began to focus on graffiti "artists" and vandalism.

Like the homeless situation, there is no simple solution. But to ignore it or to somehow justify it as self-expression is ridiculous. You want to express yourself with spray paint? Do it on a canvas. Or ask your parents if they'll let you "tag" the walls of the home they own. See how that works. But know this: if you spray paint public property, there will be a price to be paid.

The media firestorm over my position on graffiti was, in the end, a benefit. It helped focus attention on the problem. And while some pundits may not have appreciated the satirical nature of what I was saying, at least they got my words right.

That wasn't always the case.

I was on a radio show and the issue of prostitution came up. I stated my position, but I said that as mayor, I would be bound by the wishes of the public, and that it was an issue the electorate and elected officials would have to decide.

The headline that followed was

GOODMAN WANTS TO LEGALIZE PROSTITUTION FOR LAS VEGAS

That's not what I said, but it didn't matter; it made for a great headline. I got into a similar dispute with Bob Herbert, a columnist for the *New York Times*.

He came into town to write about women being abused and the rampant prostitution in the city. I think he had the story written before he got here; it was going to be a hit piece filled with negativity. But he called up and asked if he could speak with me. I said sure. I've never been shy and this was, after all, the *New York Times*.

I told him that the question of legalizing prostitution was an issue worth discussing. I said there were two sides to every story, and I recognized that there were those who believed all prostitution debased women, and there were those who opposed it on religious or moral grounds. I understand that, I said. But I also said that smart people shouldn't be afraid to have a discussion. I wasn't advocating it, but I said I could see a time when a red light district might be worth having downtown, and that it could be a great boost to the economy.

The column he wrote made me sound like a misogynist. He either didn't understand the points I was making, or had simply decided that what I said didn't fit with the piece he wanted to write.

So much for the "paper of record."

I don't want to come across as someone who was a total political novice when I took office. True, I had never been elected to anything, but I had a pretty good idea of how the game was played, even though I had never set foot in the mayor's office at City Hall.

One of the first things I did was hire a guy named Bill Cassidy as a special assistant. I figured it would create the right "atmosphere" I needed to deal with the city council and the other politicos who were waiting for me to fail.

I had met Cassidy when I was defending a client in a drug case in Oklahoma. He was an investigator for the lawyer who represented my client's brother. To describe Cassidy as a "character" doesn't even begin to tell the story. He was slim, mustachioed, always wore sunglasses, and walked with a slouch reminiscent of Groucho Marx. I don't think City Hall had ever seen the likes of him. He wore a Colombo-type trench coat and a Fedora, even in the Las Vegas heat. And I was pretty sure, as were most of the other people he came in contact with, that he was carrying.

When I saw a problem coming with one of the councilmen, I sent Cassidy down the hall. The problem tended to go away.

Everyone was cautious around Cassidy. Many were clearly afraid of him. I knew him to be a very bright guy and figured his presence would help ease my way into the arena that was Las Vegas government and politics. His resume was unbelievable. He had handled security for the Dalai Lama, and for Imelda Marcos and her husband, the president of the Philippines. He had been involved in covert ops for the CIA, and had been in Laos to help recover the remains of U.S. pilots whose planes had gone down there during the Vietnamese War. The Laotians were selling body parts as souvenirs, a practice he helped put an end to. He spoke Vietnamese and Tibetan, neither of which meant much in City Hall. But his mere presence gave me a leg up. Later he had some personal problems and I had to let him go, but he was definitely an asset when I started out in office. I guess I was just used to being around guys who gave off an aura and who had an attitude. But that never changed the way I went about my business.

My approach was always to tell the truth. From time to time, it's gotten me in trouble, but I still think it's the best policy. I was invited to speak to a fourth grade class at an elementary school as part of a literacy program, and I read a book to the children. It was a funny story about the three pigs and the wolf, told from the wolf's perspective. I enjoyed it, and afterward I took some questions from the students.

One boy raised his hand right away.

"If you could only have one thing, what would you want with you on a desert island in the middle of the ocean?"

I didn't hesitate.

"A bottle of gin," I said.

They had no idea what a bottle of gin was. I took several other questions, said goodbye, and headed back to City Hall. As I was leaving, the principal said she, the teachers, and the students really enjoyed my visit.

By the time I got back to the office, the phones were ringing off the hook. Reporters from newspapers, television, and radio were calling.

"How could you tell fourth graders to drink gin?" they wanted to know.

Again, it was a question of taking some information and getting it twisted so that it would make a better story. I don't know who turned me in. There were some other politicians and elected officials at the school that morning, and I think one of them called the media. So now I had to deal with another controversy.

I decided the best way to address it was head-on.

"I gave an honest answer," I said. "I'm the George Washington of mayors."

Not everyone was happy with the answer, but a few days later I was speaking at a Rotary Club luncheon and one of the cocktail waitresses came up to me and said she appreciated my honesty. Then she laughed. She said if someone had asked her husband that question, he would have said "porn."

I think people want their elected officials to be honest. They can see through the bullshit. The problem with politicians today is they're so worried about getting re-elected that they focus more on polls and worry more about public perception than about doing their job.

I loved being mayor. And I loved the fact that people liked me. For years when I was a defense attorney, I lived in a cocoon. Part of it was the nature of my job and the people I had to deal with. Not only was the job time-consuming, but I had to worry about law enforcement trying to entrap me, so I became ultra-cautious and maybe a little paranoid. But paranoia doesn't mean you aren't being targeted.

When I was involved in criminal defense, I would wake up, go to my office, go to court, go home, have a martini and dinner, and go to bed. Then I'd get up the next day and start it all over again. If I had a case out of town, I'd fly out on a Sunday night and wouldn't be back until Friday evening. I talked to my clients, I dealt with judges and prosecutors, and I spent lots of time in my hotel room prepping for the next day's court session.

I'd have dinner in my room or in the hotel restaurant, and then I'd have a martini or two at the hotel bar. It was a regimented existence based partly on the nature of my job, which I took very seriously, and partly on my distrust of the way law enforcement played the game. I was an advocate for some high-profile criminals and, as a result, I became a target.

Being mayor was an entirely different experience. For the first time in almost thirty years, I was able to interact with everyone and anyone. I could say and do what I wanted. If I made a mistake—and as much as it pains me to admit it, occasionally I did—it could be corrected. If you make a mistake in a criminal trial, your client ends up in prison. You usually don't get a "do-over." But in politics and government, you always have a second chance, and sometimes a third chance. It's a work in progress.

I really came to enjoy that. And let's be honest, I also enjoyed the public adulation. There were times when I'd feel like a rock star. I'd show up at a casino or a local restaurant and people would come up to shake my hand, to get a picture taken with me, to ask for my autograph. I billed myself as the "happiest mayor in the universe," and while that was a branding device, it also was true. The attention was like a narcotic. I was on a high and always wanted more. Anybody who says they don't enjoy that is lying.

We made fake casino chips with my caricature on them inscribed with the words "Happiest Mayor of the Greatest City in the World." I would give those out wherever I went. During my three terms in office, I think there were more than twenty bobblehead dolls made in my likeness. There was the pinstriped suit and baseball bat. Another was a pinstriped suit and a martini. You can also see me in tennis togs and in a hula skirt, among other things.

All the attention was remarkable, and I loved it.

Gin and martinis are important to me; I don't try to hide that. And a few years after I became mayor, I was able to parlay it into a windfall. I was asked to be the spokesperson/pitchman for Bombay Sapphire gin. My friends Larry Ruvo and Michael Severino set it up, and I jumped at the chance.

The deal included a payment of $100,000. I donated half to the Meadows School that Carolyn had founded, and the other half I gave to a program set up to combat alcoholism among the homeless. I'm still out there pitching for Bombay, although I haven't brought the topic up with any other fourth graders recently.

But I do try to mention gin or a martini in any adult conversation I'm having. It's my way of being a good representative for Bombay Sapphire. I did just that while I was in Washington, D.C., at a U.S. Conference of Mayors' gathering, and was asked to go on a radio talk show with Mayor Pat McCrory of Charlotte, North Carolina, who is now the governor.

The topic of the conference was a plan by the federal government to designate Yucca Mountain, which was located about ninety miles from Las Vegas, as a nuclear waste site. I opposed the plan, and eventually fought it and won. Even when I stopped actively practicing criminal law, it seemed like I was still battling the federal government at every turn. They wanted to dump nuclear waste at the site and they offered no safety guarantees— at least none that satisfied me. They also planned to transport this stuff virtually through the city of Las Vegas. I said I would lay down on the railroad tracks or the highway to block any train or truck that was moving nuclear waste through our city. It was another example of the feds trying to do whatever they wanted to whomever they wanted. This time it wasn't a criminal matter, although you could argue, and I certainly did, that what they planned was criminal, not to mention potentially life-threatening and environmentally devastating.

So we were on the radio talking about that topic, but somehow the conversation drifted. I had been on the Atkins diet at the time, and I started to rave about how effective it was. I ended by saying, "It's the only diet I've ever been on that allows me to drink a quart of gin a night."

The next day, when I got back to Las Vegas, there was a huge basket stuffed with Atkins food products and diet books, and a note from Dr. Atkins thanking me for the nice things I had said about his no-carb diet. I got on the phone and called the doctor to thank him in return for the basket of goodies. We talked for awhile and then he said, "Where in the world did you get the idea that you could drink a bottle of gin a night?"

I told him I had read that in the back of his book. "It says that gin has just a trace of carbs," I told him, quoting from his own work.

He laughed and said the next edition would have an asterisk next to that with an Oscar Goodman disclaimer.

Those were just some of the perks that came with being mayor. In fact, "perks" is probably not the right word. These were really opportunities, rather than the gratuities I used to get as a criminal defense attorney. But as mayor, I was happy to take advantage of them.

I also tried to establish my own sense of Las Vegas history.

Steve Sebelius, a Las Vegas political pundit, accused me of creating the founding date of the City of Las Vegas on May 15, 1905 so I could be assured that the city centennial would take place while I was in office. He insisted the real date was in 1911 when the city was officially incorporated. I told him to go jump in the lake, and we celebrated the centennial in 2005.

Another opportunity—and this was the greatest one yet—was a chance to do a photo shoot for *Playboy*. I'm not much of a photographer, but I jumped at the chance when they asked me to be the first elected official to work as a "guest" photographer. They told me no other politician would think of doing it.

"That's for me," I said.

The shoot was to take place in the "Playboy Suite" of the Palms Casino-Hotel. You can imagine what the room looked like; a huge bed, lots of mirrors, and this big picture of Hugh Hefner on the wall behind the headboard. I got there early, and the staff could see I was a little nervous. You see, I knew I would have to answer to a higher authority—my wife.

There was a whole crew in the room and then in walked Irina Voronina, the Russian model who was the playmate for January 2001. Blonde hair, blue eyes, in perfect shape. Not a blemish on her body—just gorgeous. She was wearing a red satin robe.

The crew was making small talk, trying to get me to relax. Someone poured me a martini. Irina and I chatted, and I tried to focus on her face and have a discussion. I relaxed a little. I can do this, I thought. Just aim and shoot. Out came the cameras, and off came her robe. Then very slowly she took off her bra and then her panties. I figured she did this slowly so as not to shock me and cause my heart to burst through my chest.

I was determined to make this work and not to take any pictures that would embarrass my family. Then I looked up and saw Hefner staring at me. I don't know why, but I couldn't focus. His portrait was distracting. They hung some of Irina's undergarments over the picture, but that didn't do any good. So we took Hef's picture down off the wall and put it in the closet.

After that, I was fine. The shoot went off without a hitch, and I got some nice pictures. Before we left, we took Hefner's portrait out of the closet and put it back up on the wall behind the bed.

When I got home that night, Carolyn greeted me with a kiss, handed me a martini, and said one of the misanthropic pundits from the local media had called her and asked, "What do you think of your husband taking pictures of a naked lady?"

Carolyn is sharp. She was ready.

"All I can tell you is that Oscar came home with a smile on his face," she told the reporter.

Later I got invited to the fiftieth anniversary party of *Playboy* at Hefner's mansion. It was awesome; game rooms, tennis courts, a zoo, and a stunning pool area that included a patio, a grotto, a sauna, and a bathhouse. The event was packed. Hollywood movie stars, athletes, movers and shakers, all in various stages of undress.

Hef took the stage and made a speech. Then he said, "I want you all to meet my good friend Oscar Goodman. Oscar's the guy who put me back in the closet."

Being mayor wasn't all fun and games, of course. But I also enjoyed the battles that came with being in office. I like to say that my twelve years were "Biblical"—there was feast and there was famine. The economy played a big part in that. Las Vegas always is at risk when there is a downturn, and the horror of September 11, 2001, was also a factor.

I had always been a staunch supporter of organized labor, and the unions in turn had largely supported me politically. I refused to attend the grand opening of the Hofbräuhaus, a massive restaurant and beer hall that opened in 2004. Both the Jewish Defense League and the Carpenter's Union were picketing the place—the JDL because Hitler had begun planning the Third Reich at a meeting in the original Hofbräuhaus in Germany, and the Carpenters Union because of some labor issues in the construction of the place.

I honored the union's line and wouldn't attend the grand opening.

In another instance, the Culinary Union, which has more than 70,000 members in our city, had thrown up an invisible picket line around Sheldon Adelson's Venetian Hotel. The Jewish Federation wanted to hold a fundraiser there with me as the honoree. I refused to cross the picket line (even though, because it was "invisible," there were actually no union members marching with picket signs). They moved the event to another hotel. That resulted in bad blood between Adelson and me, but I hope that time has begun to heal it.

I believed in what unions stood for, or at least in what they used to stand for: protecting the worker and making sure he or she got a fair deal in exchange for an honest day's work. I'm not so sure that's the case anymore. I think unions have become vehicles for their leadership to wield power and leverage deals for their own benefit, rather than for their membership.

I clashed with the Culinary Union over development plans for downtown. Specifically, we went to war over a proposal to build a new city hall. The union packed a city council meeting at which this project was being discussed. I looked out and saw this sea of red-shirted union members. I'm not sure they knew why they were there, but their leadership had called them out.

We intended to use city redevelopment funds to pay for the cost of the next city hall. It was a crucial part of the downtown revitalization. Redevelopment funds were also crucial to other projects that were planned for that area. But the union, or at least its pseudo-intellectual leaders, decided to rail against the proposal, arguing that taxpayers would foot the bill for these projects. That wasn't the case, but that didn't stop the union leadership from calling the plan "financially irresponsible" and claiming that taxpayers would be "on the hook" if the plan went forward.

The union decided to petition for an "initiative," which would have put the plan up for a public vote. This not only jeopardized the new City Hall plan, but all the projects for downtown. If every one of them had to be decided by a public vote, we'd never be able to move forward. The easiest way to get a "no" vote is to claim that whatever is planned is going to increase taxes. The claim doesn't have to be true to be effective. That's what we had to deal with.

I spoke out against the initiative and the union. "They're evil," I said of the proponents of the initiative. "There's no question in my mind that the leadership of the Culinary Union is using this as leverage. They're trying to blackmail the city. They want us to guarantee them jobs in all this new development. This has nothing to do with a new City Hall."

Right after that, Carolyn's and my cars were vandalized. Two large boulders that decorated our front lawn next to our carport were heaved through the back windows of our cars. We had the windows repaired, and two days later the boulders were thrown through the windows again. They were so big it would have taken more than one person to lift and throw them.

After a court fight and a lawsuit, the union backed away from its plan for an initiative. But the whole process soured me on organized labor. This redevelopment project was going to create new jobs and generate new taxes for the city. Why would an organization that represents workers—any kind of workers—oppose something like that when the economy was tanking and people were losing jobs? I just didn't get it.

Today I question whether unions have outlived their usefulness. Many are now tools of their leaders, a few self-aggrandizing jerks who make decisions without consulting the rank-and-file.

When they are doing what they're supposed to do, unions help advance the public good. But today, unions, and particularly those leading unions, have lost touch with reality.

I came up against the unions again when they represented the city workers. It was another battle that we fought and won, but the fact that we had to fight at all is what bothered me. We were in tough economic times—not just Las Vegas, but the whole country. We can argue forever about how we got there and who was to blame, but part of being a leader is to address the problem. When something goes wrong, you can either try to fix it, or look for somebody to blame. Playing the blame game may be good politics, but it's not good government.

I told the unions that we had to make cuts. If the unions were willing to make concessions—we were looking for something like an eight percent cut in wages and/or benefits—then I would guarantee that there would be no layoffs. This wasn't a complicated issue, and I figured the union membership would go along. You take a cut to save your brother and sister union members' jobs.

It's about sacrifice, another concept that seems to have gotten lost in the world of politics and government today. The union rejected my offer. I called them "selfish" and they called me a bully. I said I intended to fire everyone and then rehire based on the economic realities we were facing. This created panic, not only with the workers, but with the city attorney, who told me if I did that we'd spend the next twenty years fighting all the lawsuits that would be filed and that would bankrupt the city.

So I backed off, not because I thought I was wrong, but because the city attorney's legal position may have had some merit. The only other option was layoffs, and I said that's what we would have to do. The economy, the numbers, just didn't add up. There had to be some cuts. The workers understood this, and they knew I meant business.

Eventually the union came to the table, and we worked out a deal that saved everyone's job. But the entire experience reinforced my thoughts about organized labor. Union leaders don't really represent workers anymore, they just use them as leverage. They're like politicians; their only goal is to stay in office. They care more about their salaries and benefits than they do about the wages and jobs of their members.

You would think someone in a leadership role in organized labor would wake up and address that problem before it's too late. Look around: governors in Wisconsin and New Jersey have developed huge followings in part by bashing unions as unreasonable and unrealistic. It's a message that resonates with taxpayers, particularly taxpayers who have lost their jobs or had their wages cut. That's reality, and elected officials and union leaders need to recognize it.

CHAPTER 16

TO ROME,
WITH SHOWGIRLS

accomplished a lot of the things I set out to do when I became mayor, but one of the things I wasn't able to get was a professional sports team. It's a battle that I'm still fighting.

If Las Vegas is going to be a world-class city, and I think it should be, then we need a professional team. It's not about helping the economy. There's no guarantee that a team will attract more visitors, generate more tourist dollars, create jobs and employment. Maybe it would, maybe it wouldn't. But what a team will do is add to our sense of identity, and that can't be measured in dollars. It's an intangible, but one that I'm willing to fight for.

As I've said before, I'm a degenerate gambler. I have been all my life. I'll bet on anything, anytime, anywhere. I grew up playing sports and following sports, so I guess it was natural that I liked to bet on sports. I don't see anything wrong with it. I'm not influencing the outcome of a game, and I understand that over the long haul, I'm not going to win. That's the bottom line. I know that going in, but I still love to bet. Maybe I'll figure out a winning system; it's every gambler's hope.

It's amazing when you look at some of the professional odds makers and bettors I've represented: guys like Bob Martin and Frank Rosenthal and Billy Walters. They were genius-like in their ability to set a line. That's what it's all about. The bookie lives on that line, whether he's a guy working a bar in Chicago, a school yard in Philadelphia, or behind the counter at one of the sports books in the casinos here in Las Vegas. He's going to make $10 on every $100 bet if the line is set right and the bets are balanced. Out of balance is a different story, but on most days he's going to win more than he's going to lose. I should know; I've been on the other end enough times. Even still, it's in my blood.

I played poker all through college, and I was lucky that Carolyn liked to play, too. During a break while I was in law school, we went down to Atlantic City. I was clerking in the district attorney's office at the time, and one of the assistant district attorneys invited us down for a weekend. His family had a house there. There were several couples; most of the guys were lawyers in the office, and I was excited to have been invited. We started playing poker one night and I made up this stupid rule that only a winner could call the night over.

Carolyn went to bed. We kept playing and I kept losing. It got to the point where I knew I wouldn't have the money to pay the others when it came time to cash out. Luckily Carolyn came back down in her robe and pajamas, saw what a schmuck I was, and got back in the game. She got us even before the night ended.

But there's a difference between how I gamble and what a gambling addict goes through. I'm not "sick"; I don't risk the kind of money that would hurt my family or destroy my life.

This gambling compulsion—and how it can destroy you—was made clear to me shortly after a phone call I got one time from Robin Moore, the bestselling author. I had read several of his books, *The Green Berets, The French Connection, The Happy*

Hooker. He said he was working on a new book about a fellow named Joe Henry Hodges, a brilliant guy who ruined his life gambling. Hodges was well educated, had a lovely wife and two wonderful children, and at one time was the city attorney of Irving, Texas. But he was a compulsive gambler.

He'd say to his wife, "I'm going down to the Piggly Wiggly to buy a carton of milk" and disappear for three days on a gambling bender. He risked and lost it all; he had bad checks all over the Southwest. He got arrested by the FBI at LaGuardia Airport in New York and was brought back to Las Vegas to face charges that could have resulted in a long prison sentence.

Robin Moore asked me to represent Hodges, and I got him released on $100,000 bail. Moore managed to raise the money. Working on that case, I found out how really sick a compulsive gambler is. I had a medical expert testify on Hodges' behalf. We had to fight several cases, including one in Houston where the prosecutor wanted to send him to jail for life.

Basically my medical expert said that while Hodges realized what he was doing was wrong, he rationalized his actions and came to believe they were acceptable. The doctor used a lot of medical terms and jargon, but the thing I remember best was his comparison to sex. He said a compulsive gambler is like an erect penis during sex—you just can't stop it.

I was able to keep Hodges out of jail, but he lost everything: his wife, his family, his home, and his friends. You might think he had learned his lesson, but I'll bet against that.

Not everyone who bets is like Hodges. A lot of people are like me; they like to bet, and they do it within their means. That desire has created a multi-million dollar industry.

Look at the statistics. The Super Bowl is a great example. The amount of money bet on that one game is staggering. In Nevada, where's it's legal, casinos take about $90 million in action.

Internet gambling sites, according to some studies, do about $2 billion more. And the illegal bookies pull in about $3 billion. That's more than $5 billion bet on one game.

The thing that the do-gooders fail to acknowledge is that it's in everyone's interest to keep that game and all games on the up-and-up. That's why I have a problem with the heads of most of the professional sports leagues who won't even consider allowing a franchise in Las Vegas. Betting is a business, and it only functions when the customers think they have a fair shot. We have to build a world-class arena and then take our shot.

I think I've already laid the groundwork. One of the first things I did after I was elected was to go back to New York and meet with the commissioners of the NHL and the NBA.

Gary Bettman was very pleasant, and said as far as he was concerned, Las Vegas would be a great site, but the NHL wasn't expanding and none of the franchises were interested in relocating. I took him at his word. I believe he meant what he said. To me, the most important part of what he said was that he thought Las Vegas would be great. Unlike the commissioners of the other sports, he didn't say no. So getting a professional hockey team was, however remote, a possibility.

David Stern with the NBA was another story. I always had a lot of respect for him as a commissioner. But when I went to his office, it was like I was the enemy. And his position was "over my dead body" would the NBA ever put a team in Las Vegas.

"I'm never going to allow a franchise in a city where bets are made," he said. "As long as I'm commissioner, there's no way in the world that's going to happen."

I thought he was ridiculous for saying that. Talk to anyone in the business—and I've represented more than my share of those types of "businessmen"—and it's obvious there are bets taken in every city where the NBA has a franchise. The only difference between those cities and Las Vegas is that the bets outside of Vegas are taken illegally. I'll wager that there were more bets taken in Madison Square Garden—at least when the Knicks were good—than all the books in Las Vegas.

Has it hurt the integrity of the game? I think the brand of basketball, the school yard, individual style of play, has hurt the game of professional basketball more than any bookie taking a bet. But that's just my view as a fan of the game.

Lebron James and Kobe Bryant may be super talents, but I'll take Elgin Baylor and Oscar Robertson and the style of the game they played over what you see today. Give me Bob Cousy over Allen Iverson. You want Shaquille O'Neal? Fine, I'll take Bill Russell.

But those weren't the kinds of things Stern and I talked about. This was before the problem with Tim Donaghy, the NBA referee who was accused of influencing the outcome of games to win bets. That was an in-house NBA problem. How's that for integrity?

I told Stern that his position was draconian and that it made no sense. I argued that the Las Vegas race and sports books have more supervision than any other venue where bets are legal, and that there has never been an incident of cheating. He didn't want to hear it. When I left his office, I have to say I wasn't surprised by his reaction. But I was demoralized anyway because he didn't offer any hope. He was adamant; no way.

But I kept pushing for us to build a first-class arena, and the word started to spread that Las Vegas was going to get an NBA franchise.

Stern called me on the phone. "Didn't you hear what I said?" he asked. "Under no circumstances are you going to get a franchise."

But I noticed something in his voice. I could almost hear a smile over the phone. And I knew that some other people in his office were not as adamant, so I thought we might have a shot.

Around that time our Convention Authority got involved in a sponsorship deal with the NBA over "NBA Euro." This was a plan to create interest on an international level for NBA basketball. And as the chairman of the Convention Authority, I got to go on a trip with Stern and some other NBA officials. We visited three cities: Rome, Barcelona, and Paris. Not a bad junket, as far as junkets go. I love those cities, but we did the trip in five days—five brutal days. We were constantly moving.

The stop in Rome was the greatest. It's amazing what you can do in one day. Rossi Ralenkotter, the president of the Las Vegas Convention and Visitors Authority and a very good guy, led the entourage to the Vatican. I had been there before, so I passed. I decided it would be a chance to get in some shopping. I called Carolyn at home and asked if there was anything special I could treat her to while I was in the Eternal City.

Without missing a beat, she described a purse made by Prada. I left the hotel and ventured onto the streets of Rome in search of the Prada bag. I had taken Latin in school, but other than "amo, amas, amat," I didn't remember very much.

I managed to ask some folks along the way where the Prada shop was, and after several twists and turns, I found myself at the top of the Spanish Steps, one of the truly glorious spots in the city. Prada was on the piazza at the bottom of the steps. The 138 steps descend in stages, but there are no railings. I wear glasses with ground-in bifocals, and I have a devil of a time going down stairs, especially when there are no railings. But being the loving husband that I am, I soldiered on and began my descent.

It's a tradition in Rome for young people to gather at the Spanish Steps, and thankfully they were sitting all over the place. So as I began to walk down, I reached out and touched their heads for balance. One-hundred and thirty-eight heads; that's how I got down these famous steps.

When I got to the Prada store in the piazza, I was able to describe the bag. They had it in stock and I bought it. I just knew that when I got home to Las Vegas and told Carolyn of my heroic flight down the Spanish Steps in order to make the purchase, she would love me more than ever.

That's the image I had in my mind as I walked out of the store. Then I realized that I had no idea where my hotel was, the name of which had escaped me. I panicked. I had a cell phone that didn't work in Rome, and even if it did, I wouldn't know who to call or what to say. I broke into a cold sweat. After walking around in circles for about five minutes, I heard someone call my name.

"Mayor Goodman, Mayor Goodman."

I turned and saw a woman beckoning me over.

"I'm Bill Russell's wife," she said.

"I'm lost," I replied.

We shared a cab to the hotel where she and Bill, the great Boston Celtics center, were staying. I was never so thankful to be recognized.

That night, Rossi and I, along with Julian Dugas, who was the Convention Authority's sports guru, and Vince Alberta, a public affairs man, were supposed to present the key to the city of Las Vegas to the mayor of Rome, Walter Veltroni, at the arena before a basketball game. But Mayor Veltroni had left a message at our hotel that because of a transportation and media strike, we should go to his City Hall office instead, where the ceremony would take place. I thought there might be a problem since I was traveling with the showgirls, Porsha and Jen. Would they be allowed in City Hall in their suggestive outfits? I called the mayor, and without hesitation, he said that absolutely they would be welcome.

This didn't surprise me. By this point, the brand—me, the showgirls, and my martini—had been well established. We had come a long way from that first night back in Cashman Field when I "threw" that first pitch.

The showgirls and I had probably made several hundred appearances by that point. And every time we did, people would flock to us. They wanted their pictures taken with us. They wanted autographs. The martini was part of the routine, and after I signed that deal with Bombay Sapphire, it expanded as well. They gave me a watch that only had the number five on it. All around the face there were fives. No other number. Five o'clock was the traditional "cocktail hour."

If we were at an event at 7 A.M., I'd be holding a martini and I'd wave my watch and say, "It's five o'clock somewhere. Drink up!"

When we arrived at Mayor Veltroni's office, he introduced us to his wife and daughters. They weren't interested in the mayor of Las Vegas—they were there for the showgirls, captivated by their class and charm. As the girls were socializing, Mayor Veltroni invited me out onto the balcony. He pointed and said, "There is the Palatine Hill where Romulus and Remus were born."

It was an awesome sight.

"And Mayor Goodman," he said, "there's the Forum where public speeches and gladiator matches took place in the presence of Rome's great men."

Then he said, "Look just beneath this balcony where we're standing. There stood Julius Caesar."

What could I say?

"Mayor Veltroni," I said, "when you come to Las Vegas to visit me and we both look out the window from my office at City Hall, I'll show you U.S. Route 95 and Interstate 15."

Today, if Rome's mayor visited the new City Hall, he would see from the mayor's balcony the Cleveland Clinic Lou Ruvo Center for Brain Health, the Smith Center, the Premium Outlets, and the World Market Center.

After the basketball game that night, the Las Vegas contingent went to the best restaurant I have ever been to in my life. We drank wine and toasted the guests who were there. I handed out "good luck mayor chips" with caricatures of my likeness that described me as the "Happiest Mayor in the Universe."

We danced like Zorba the Greek. We were served sea bass the size of small whales, and it was delicious. I'd recommend the food and ambience to kings and queens.

Several years later, I told a Las Vegas reporter who was traveling to Rome that the restaurant was a "must" visit. When she returned, she called me. I asked whether the place was as great as I had remembered.

"It was closed down," she said. "Apparently it had been the front for a heroin smuggling operation. They were hiding narcotics in fish bellies that they brought into Rome."

Maybe that's why the sea bass tasted so good!

During that five-day trip, we visited arenas in each of the cities and watched basketball games. The commissioner and his right-hand man, Adam Silver, were always sitting in front of me, and we got along well. I think it helped that they got a kick out of the showgirls. Whenever I travel for the city, two beautiful showgirls are part of my entourage. At each game, I was taking bets. I was just fooling around with the other people on the trip, but I became their bookie. Stern seemed to like my *schtick,* and our relationship improved. That might explain how Las Vegas was chosen as the site for the NBA All-Star game. It was the first time the game was played in a city that didn't have an NBA team, so I took that as a good sign. It also was the first time the game was played on a college campus, at the Thomas and Mack Center at the University of Nevada, Las Vegas.

When I heard we had gotten approval to host the game, I thought a miracle had taken place. And I wanted everything to work out. We were to have the game in 2007, and the site was chosen a couple of years in advance. Houston had the game in 2006, so I made a point of going there to check things out. I remember being at the airport in Las Vegas leaving for Houston. I'm standing there and I see all these working girls, call girls, high-priced hookers, waiting for the same plane. I struck up a conversation and asked a couple of them what they were doing.

"Are you going to the game?" I said.

They laughed.

"No Oscar, we're going to party."

I got a bang out of that, but I think it said a lot about the All-Star Weekend. Talk to people in law enforcement, and they'll tell you the NBA All-Star Weekend is unlike any other professional all-star venue. Instead, it's a weekend party that brings together celebrities, "gangstas," and athletes. Drug dealers from cities throughout the country show up with their entourage, take up a suite of hotel rooms, and party all weekend. I didn't know this at the time, so when we were about to host the game, I went to all the casino executives and said we want to put on a full-court press. This was our chance to show off the city and make our pitch for a franchise.

During that weekend, I met with Commissioner Stern. He sat across from me in my City Hall office, and we were talking about a lot of different things. His son was working for the governor of Montana. We talked about family and kids and what it was like living in New York and in Las Vegas; just a friendly, general conversation. After an hour, he got to the point.

"Okay Oscar," he said in his charming manner. "You win. The ball's in your court. I won't stand in the way of you getting a franchise if you build a first class arena and if you're able to convince the owners."

I was doing a jig; this was a major movement on his part.

As a concession to Stern, I had gotten the casinos to take the game off the board in the betting parlors, so there would be no action on the all-star game. It was a big concession, but the casinos went along. Everyone was on board.

"We'll do whatever we have to do," the casino executives told me.

I felt good they had that much confidence in me. This was great. We did everything we could. But sometimes the best plans don't give you the best results.

The weekend turned into a disaster.

It was President's Day Weekend. There was a huge convention for men's apparel companies in town, and it also was a great celebration of the Chinese New Year.

A group of thugs came up from Southern California for the game. They ransacked rooms, stiffed waitresses, and scared people. When the weekend ended, those same casino owners told me, "Forget about it. There's no way we want a franchise if this is what comes with it."

Even though it was a big setback, I knew that over time, I'd be able to convince the casino owners that the All-Star Game Weekend was an aberration. Having a team doesn't mean that each of the forty-one home games would be like that game. I took their complaints with a grain of salt. I've since had discussions with the owners of several franchises, and none of them seem to have a problem with a team out here.

We have to get the arena built, of course, and the economy will have something to do with that. But I think it's just a matter of time. I believe Las Vegas will eventually get an NBA franchise. It's no longer a question of if, but merely when.

Bud Selig, the baseball commissioner, has told me not to talk to any team about relocating. And the NFL is completely unreasonable. Its commissioners, Paul Tagliabue and then Roger Goodell, took the same position; they didn't want to hear about it.

The NFL is the biggest hypocrite in all of this. Football generates more gambling than any other sport. They put out the injury report on Thursdays: who's unable to play, who's injured but likely to perform. They provide information about the weather forecast for game day. What do you think all that's about—do you think the NFL is just being fan-friendly? That information is for setting the line and for helping the bookies and the odds makers. It's to entice the bettors.

Does it hurt the integrity of the game? Of course not. But let's not kid ourselves; the NFL's popularity is built in large part from the action that comes to the bookies each week.

Back in 2003, we tried to advertise on television during the Super Bowl. It was something like $2.5 million for a thirty-second spot. We wanted to promote Las Vegas. The Convention and Visitors Authority came up with the idea, and I was wholeheartedly in favor of it, but Tagliabue said no way. He said, "We don't want our game to be associated with Las Vegas."

I went bonkers. In an interview with a reporter for the *Las Vegas Sun,* I said that I couldn't believe the double-standard. I said the NFL's image had been tainted by former and current players who have been accused of and, in some cases, convicted of crimes ranging from murder and child molestation to burglary and sexual assault. I added, "As far as I'm concerned, Tagliabue has the most deviant athletes in professional sports."

The paper went on to list various football players who had been the subjects of criminal investigations in several high-profile cases. The media all over the country picked it up, and the television networks played our proposed Super Bowl "ad" over and over. I was screaming and hollering about the hypocrisy of it all. I think I generated about $20 million worth of advertising for Las Vegas, and it didn't cost us a cent.

I even wrote an op-ed piece that the *New York Times* published. Here's what I said:

The National Football League has made another bad call: It has denied the city of Las Vegas the right to advertise itself during Sunday's televised broadcast of the Super Bowl. Why? Because we are Las Vegas.

The NFL has long had a policy that prohibits gambling-related advertisements during televised games. And even though our ads—promotional spots commissioned by the Las Vegas Convention and Visitors Authority—do not make direct reference to gambling, the league has said that the basic reason for their rejection is simply "because Las Vegas is so synonymous with sports betting and gambling." The ads—which have already been shown on several cable networks—are based on real-life tourist experiences, none of which involve gambling.

Are the commercials provocative—even racy? Sure. One features an alluring woman on a limousine ride through Las Vegas. But this is Vegas, after all. Will the ads, as the NFL says, "have a uniquely negative effect on the public's perception" of the game of football? I am willing to bet the NFL commissioner, Paul Tagliabue, that they won't.

At any rate, NFL telecasts are constantly interrupted by ads that aren't just negative but offensive. What about the beer ads that run during nearly every NFL broadcast? Does alcohol (or the bevy of scantily clad women who appear in so many of those ads) not have a negative effect on the public?

There seems to be a bit of hypocrisy going on here: To some degree, NFL games have and always will attract betting. Almost every newspaper in the country publishes point spreads. And the league's own web site is associated with CBSSportsLine.com, which lists the odds on upcoming major sporting events and tips on how to bet.

The NFL needs to face the reality of what is going on outside its stadiums. Some form of gambling is now legal in almost every state—and many states, like California, are hoping to balance their budgets by allowing an expansion of gambling. Nevada may be the only state where betting on sporting events is legal, but we have always been honest and consistent about what we are and what we offer.

On Sunday I'll be watching the Super Bowl from the comfort of a Vegas casino. I'm looking forward to an exciting game—but it would be more exciting if Mr. Tagliabue would allow the broadcast to include a taste of the city that is like no other.

Eventually we'll have a professional team here, and I say this knowing that it can be both a good and a bad thing. When I was promoting and lobbying and arguing for this, a noted college professor who studied the business of sports said that I was the only one who really got the point. There are economic benefits and there are economic burdens for any city that has a professional franchise; it's not a panacea or a cure-all. But what a professional sports team does for a city is create a sense of place and a sense of pride for the community.

That's the real reason to have a team. And if we have to fight the hypocrites who run the professional sports leagues to get that, I say bring it on. In this one, I'm betting on us, and I like our chances.

CHAPTER 17
BENEVOLENT DICTATOR

As I've been saying, I really enjoyed my time as mayor. But as I look back on it now, I think I would have preferred a different title: Benevolent Dictator.

I could have gotten more done and made Las Vegas a better city.

This thought occurred to me one day a couple of years ago when I walked into a casino-hotel for a breakfast meeting. As mayor, I served on the Las Vegas Convention and Visitors Authority and did a lot of speaking engagements promoting the authority and the city. It was a little before seven in the morning when I walked into the hotel, and all over the lobby were these beautiful women. Some were coming down the steps, others were getting off the elevators. Dressed to the nines. Very attractive.

One of them recognized me and smiled.

"Hello, Mister Mayor," she said.

"How are you, dear?" I asked.

"I'm fine," she replied.

I had represented her on a solicitation charge several years earlier. She was a beautiful girl, very articulate, and quite worldly. She could speak about wine, the theater, or craps. Think Sharon Stone in *Casino*.

We had beaten the case. She obviously was still out there working. That morning the thought occurred to me, as it has many times. Prostitution is a big business in Las Vegas. But it's illegal. And that, to me, doesn't make sense.

It's hypocrisy. We all know it's here. It's part of what Las Vegas is. If I had walked into the lobby of any of the major casino-hotels in town that morning, I would have seen the same thing. Beautiful women on their way home from work.

So why do we try to hide it? It's ridiculous to pretend it isn't happening. And it's a waste of time and money for the police to try to control it. Why not legalize it so that it's regulated and so that we can tax it?

My first act as dictator would have been to legalize prostitution.

And my second act would have been to make drugs—all drugs—legal as well.

Just imagine the headlines if I had been able to legalize the businesses of sex and drugs. The media, as they often did during my terms, would have gone nuts. When I suggested on a radio show that I favored legalization of prostitution, there was a great hue and cry. I said at the time that it was my personal position, but one that I realized I would never be able to get through city council or past the electorate. The funny thing is, most people think prostitution is legal in Las Vegas. It's not. You've got to drive about sixty miles out of town to reach the first legal brothel.

During my three terms in office, I saw a lot of changes in the city and in the casino industry. We tried family friendly, which I think was a bad fit. Then we came back to the more comfortable and appropriate "what happens here, stays here" pitch. That was in keeping with the attitude that made us unique. I liked that. We've got to be smart about the way we do business, but we can't let the accountants and bean counters take over. It's not always about the bottom line. It used to be that the great buffets and the amazing lounge acts were loss leaders. Now everybody's calculating and adding and using spreadsheets. Now all the different enterprises within a casino-hotel have to pay for themselves. I liked the old way better.

Look, I was right out there with everyone else saying how we have to diversify our economy, but now I'm having second thoughts. Maybe we emphasized change too much. I love Las Vegas. But we have to embrace what got us here. As mayor, I never would have had the political or public support for this, but as benevolent dictator, I would have advocated for the old, "anything goes" Las Vegas.

And prostitution would have been at the top of my list of priorities.

Maybe we could have changed the word to soften the connotation. Let's talk about the "brothelization" of Las Vegas. I'm talking about sexual contact between two consenting adults, a business run in a safe and hygienic atmosphere where there is respect for the workers who are well compensated and who willingly decide to pursue that career. I'm not talking about pimps and their hookers, girls strung out on drugs and forced to work the streets. I'm talking about a business approach to what they call the oldest profession in the world.

Why not at least talk about that? Why not have a discussion?

And when I think about the amount of taxes that could be raised, I'm even more convinced it's the way to go. We have it now and the city doesn't get a penny. Now I understand some people will have moral or religious objections. That's their right.

I'd frame it this way: the money raised from taxes on brothels would be used to fund teachers' salaries in the city. We'd aim to have the highest paid public schoolteachers in America. Imagine what kind of school system we could have and what that would mean for the community.

Our public schools are not very good. And unfortunately, I think public schools throughout the country are on the decline.

If you get the finest teachers, bribe them to come here by offering them a salary they can't refuse, think of what we could become. Everybody who came here in the early days came because they thought they could make a lot of money. Why not offer educators the same option? That's all I'm saying.

You think people come here for the beautiful environment? We're in the desert. It's 115 degrees. They say it's dry heat. I say it's hot. But people come because of what we have to offer or because of the opportunities that they see. Make it the same for educators, for doctors, for other professionals. Use the taxes from prostitution to do positive things for the community at large.

All of this would bring us a different level of respectability and take us to a whole different level as a community. I spoke with some casino executives about this one time. They agreed. They're not blind. They see what's going on in their hotels. I had one tell me if I could get prostitution legalized he'd build a gentleman's club that would look like a palace. I don't see a downside in this. We'd take the pimp out of the equation. We'd reduce the risk of sexually transmitted diseases. We'd create safe working environments. Women who voluntarily choose that profession shouldn't be ostracized, nor should they be taken advantage of, which they sometimes are, both physically and economically. Just make it a regular business.

In fact, that's the way the high end of the business operates right now. There are ladies who make calls to casino-hotel rooms. Doormen or security guards help set up what the eighteenth century novelists like to call "assignations." There's a degree of safety in that for both the girls and the customers, but there are still occasional problems.

But the lower end of the business is fraught with danger for everyone: girls working in alleyways strung out on drugs and controlled by vicious pimps; customers trolling the streets to get what they want and sometimes whatever the girl may have.

Common sense and the public good have to say there's a better way.

I've always been able to draw a distinction between my personal views and my obligations as an officeholder. I may personally believe prostitution should be legal, but I'm smart enough to realize that the public—my constituents when I was mayor—might not have the same point of view. To me, they need to be educated.

Had I been a benevolent dictator, I just would have ordered it, and if anyone said I was wrong I would have banished them from the land. Instead, we're living in a community where people can say we don't have prostitution. Yet it's rampant and you can see it all around you.

The argument that we can't have a world-class city if we have brothels is bunk. I wish we had the art and culture that Amsterdam has.

I never did opinion polls when I was running for office. I'm not sure you get an accurate read on what the public thinks. I used to conduct my own polls every Saturday or Sunday. I'd go to Costco or some other big store and talk to shoppers. I used to spend three or four hours just talking to the people. And when it came to the issue of prostitution, to be honest, I think women liked the idea more than men. They understood what it was all about. You make it safe and it becomes a legitimate way for some women to earn a living.

We'd also be able to educate the public with regard to lifestyle issues. It doesn't have to be this evil thing. It's a vice, sure. But so is gambling and smoking and drinking. We have all of that. Some of this is just nonsense.

Here's something to think about. In Nevada, the state constitution prohibits us from having a lottery. Does that make any sense? It's just silly. I'm just saying let's talk about it. I would have the biggest lottery in the country, bigger than Megamillions.

If I were the dictator, I'd say we're doing it.

Same thing with drugs. Legalize all of them and tax them. I come from the era when Nancy Reagan launched the war on drugs. If there was a war, we lost it a long time ago.

When I was a defense attorney, I represented a lot of drug dealers. Some of them I was able to keep out of jail. But most of them were convicted. And you know what? As soon as they were off the street, somebody else was out there taking their place. There were plenty of people willing and able, even anxious, to step in.

Regulate it and tax it. And I mean all of it. Not just marijuana. All the drugs: cocaine, heroin, methamphetamines. You can't go halfway with this. Even if we lose a generation in the process, I think it's something we ought to do.

The prisons will be empty and the amount of street violence will drop dramatically. Drug dealers have bigger guns than some third world armies. And they're always ready to use them. Violence is the way they settle disputes. It's armed conflict resolution. If they have a problem with another dealer—and when you look at it from one perspective what they have is a business dispute—they can't resolve the issue in a legal setting. There's no tribunal. So they resort to violence. And we all pay a price for this. Innocent people get killed. City streets are dangerous. People who can, flee our cities. It's a negative process that is helping to destroy the country.

It's helped create a cottage industry in terms of building and maintaining jails, but is that what we want? Is it worth it? Legalize the damn drugs and set up agencies to deal with the health issues.

We have drug laws and draconian sentencing guidelines and it's a travesty of justice. I've seen young men and women who were drug mules. They were literally at the bottom of the ladder in the drug underworld. And they're convicted and sent away to prison for ten years. What purpose does that serve? The next day there are ten more mules waiting to take their places.

I looked at the immigration debate and the vitriol of some citizens in our border towns and you know what it's really about. It's about drugs. They look to Mexico and they see the violence over there from the drug cartels and they're scared to death that it's going to come over the border. I don't disagree with their concerns. They're real. A drug war in Arizona or New Mexico could be devastating. But building a big fence isn't going to solve the problem.

I hear some people talk about the decriminalization of certain drugs, especially marijuana. That's bullshit. That's not going to address the real issues. I don't draw any distinction between pot or meth or coke or heroin. They're all drugs and they should be legalized.

It's like the Garden of Eden. If it hadn't been forbidden, nobody would have eaten the damn apple.

I can remember when I was actively practicing law, kids coming into my office with drug cases and they're sitting across the desk from me with their noses running, snot dripping on their thighs and knees. Nobody wants to see someone like that, but what we're doing now isn't helping. Let's educate and legalize. That's what the benevolent dictator advocates.

I've seen it work with my four children. Educated to the evils of drunk driving, they either don't drink or they really do have a designated driver. They don't smoke because it gives you lung cancer, heart disease, nothing good. Not a puffer among them.

We can't stop these things, but we can try to control them, talk about them, be sensible about them.

There was an issue when I was mayor over a rave concert that some promoters wanted to stage. The year before a girl had died at the concert in Los Angeles. The question was, did we want it here?

The concert was going to attract 300,000 people. I said, "You're damn right I want it. It's good for the city."

We policed it as best we could. We made sure the residents didn't see any negative impact, but I can't worry about what individuals do. It's a free society. If people going to the concert were taking drugs, that's their problem. If they want to kill themselves, I'm not going to stop them.

The war on drugs is nonsense. If you can't accomplish what you set out to do, and it's clear that we can't, then it's not worth talking about. You're just a blowhard.

If I had had the power, I would have legalized all drugs in Las Vegas. I think it's the right thing to do. I would have advocated for changes in the federal laws, too.

I'll tell you another thing I would have done, and this has nothing to do with prostitution or drugs. I'm concerned about young people in this country. Too many of them seem to lack a sense of community. They're devoid of feelings other than for themselves and their small group of friends. And I think part of the reason is an overall decline in personal interaction.

A benevolent dictator could do something about this. If I had the power, I'd make everyone who bought one of those social media conveyors—a smart phone, an iPad, those kinds of things—take a test before they could start using the product. They would have to shake a hand, look someone in the eye, blow someone a kiss. People have forgotten how to do this. All they do is use their thumbs to interact.

If Darwin is right, and I think he is, within the next couple of generations the thumb will become the largest appendage on the human body. This could cause all kinds of problems, not the least of which would be the ability to throw a pitch.

I already know a little bit about that. Just stay away from that rosin bag.

CHAPTER 18
ALL IN THE FAMILY

I t's been a great run, and the beauty of it all is that it's not over. As I look back, it occurs to me that only in Las Vegas could I have lived the life that I did. Carolyn and I made the right choice coming out here. My law career and my three terms as mayor are certainly a part of what I'm talking about, but there were other, greater accomplishments.

Carolyn is extraordinary. Would you believe that during fifty years of marriage, she's only asked me for three things? When we first moved to the desert, she asked me to buy her a horse. To me, that was a signal that she was ready to embrace the "western life" that I was exposing her to. I got her a horse, "Moon Lad." He was 7/8ths thoroughbred and 1/8th quarter horse, and he stood seventeen hands high; a real horse. She loved him.

When I started earning big bucks, Carolyn asked if I would buy her a Mercedes. I got her the car, and she treasured it. She kept the first one for sixteen years. She has another Mercedes now, but her favorite car is her 1990 Suburban, which is really good during the flash flood season. Anytime she parks that car, someone leaves a note under the windshield wiper asking if she's interested in selling it. No one ever leaves a note on the Mercedes.

Her third request was to meet the Queen of England someday. We've been to London several times for the Convention and

Visitors Authority, but so far, I've struck out. I haven't been able to deliver on that last request. If anyone has read this far and happens to know the Queen, please call me. I'll arrange a game of pool for you with Prince Harry the next time he's in Las Vegas if you can set up a curtsey for Carolyn.

Las Vegas also provided us with our four incredible children. As I said, Carolyn raised the kids while I was traipsing around the country representing people in trouble, but we both take the greatest pride in our sons and daughter, who they are and what they are accomplishing.

Carolyn had a rule. When the kids went off to college, she told them that once they earned their final degree and started their careers, they would have to live away from Las Vegas for three years. Because of my situation as mayor, she thought they should establish themselves somewhere else without the potential influence, for better or worse, of being the children of the city's top elected official.

Oscar Jr. is an MD with a PhD; an oncologist who's doing cancer research. He graduated from Swarthmore College and Thomas Jefferson University Medical School in Philadelphia, and then went to work at New York Presbyterian Hospital. He was recruited and came back to work at the Las Vegas Cancer Institute. The nicest thing in the world is to have someone say to you, "Your son is my husband's doctor, and he saved my husband's life."

Ross, our middle son, is a wonderful lawyer. After earning degrees at the University of San Diego and University of Tulsa Law School, he completed his reserve commitment as a Major in the U.S. Marine Corps, serving at Quantico, Cherry Point, and the Washington Navy Yard. Upon returning to Las Vegas he has achieved several multi-million dollar verdicts and has had the thrill of hearing verdicts of "not guilty."

Eric, our youngest boy, gave us all we could handle. At one point he dropped out of college and Carolyn said that was his choice, but he wasn't going to live at home. For a time he worked in a carpet factory here in town. I think he was the only employee who had a legitimate social security card; everybody else was a felon. He took advantage of those second chances I'm always talking about in Las Vegas and went back to college. He graduated from Ohio Wesleyan and then, of all things, went to the University of Pennsylvania Law School. He spent some time at a big Philadelphia law firm, then came back home. He was recently elected a judge in Las Vegas Township Justice Court.

Cara, our daughter and our youngest, went to Stanford after graduating from the Meadows School. She was the only one of our children to go to the Meadows; the others were too old. She stayed to get her master's at Stanford, and then worked for a time in San Francisco as a human resources consultant before coming back to Las Vegas, where she works as a family therapist.

When she applied to Stanford, she wrote, "I know you only consider the top ten percent of the class. I am the top third."

There were only three students in the first graduating class at the Meadows.

All four of our children came back. I'm not sure what that means, but it's great to have them and their families come over for Sunday dinner or to watch a football game with me. Carolyn cooks their favorite meals, and we just enjoy one another.

It all makes me wonder about that age-old argument of nature versus nurture; whether the environment or heredity determines how one turns out. No one wins the argument with our family; Carolyn says each of their personalities is distinct and unique.

Oscar Jr. was asked about that in an interview published in a local magazine, *Vegas Seven,* back in 2011. The interviewer noted that Oscar's parents were both highly accomplished individuals who had adopted four children, and that those four children in turn were highly accomplished in their own right. To what did he attribute that?

"It was the upbringing," he said. "It really speaks to the environment versus the genes [debate]. I think we're a case study . . . the environment . . . makes the difference, and particularly parenting. It's a huge part of upbringing. It's probably 80 percent, and schools are the other 20 percent. My parents really bestowed values on all of us. I heard the golden rule a million times: 'Do unto others as you would have them do unto you.' And whenever you decide to do something, don't just think of yourself, think of others."

When my final term as mayor was about to expire, Carolyn and I were looking forward to retirement and maybe traveling a little. She had stepped down at the Meadows after running the school for twenty-six years. But I could see that she was restless. One day she said to me, "I've cleaned the house once. I've cleaned it twice. I don't want to clean the house again. I want to do something meaningful." I wasn't sure what she meant or what she had in mind, but retirement wasn't in the cards for either of us.

On July 6, 2011, I swore in my wife as the twentieth mayor in the history of Las Vegas. The pundits joked about a dynasty, and Carolyn, as always, was ready with an answer.

"We've got four children and six grandchildren," she said. "You have no idea what a dynasty is."

When she first mentioned that she was considering running for mayor, I was less than encouraging. I didn't want her to have to deal with all the petty bickering, the squabbling, the treachery and chicanery. I have a thick skin, and it rolled off my back. But I didn't want her to be exposed to the meanness of some people. Politics is full of greedy, envious, and jealous individuals who are always playing games and looking for their own advancement. Carolyn isn't like that. Don't get me wrong; she's just as tough as I am, and in many ways tougher. I just didn't want her to have to go through that.

Her argument to me, however, was simple, and obviously aimed at the large ego that she, over the years, had come to recognize was part of my make-up.

"Who's going to finish what you started?" she asked. "Someone else will have a different agenda."

I couldn't argue with that. And to my mind, no one was better qualified to succeed me. She had raised our four children, gotten her master's degree, and founded the Meadows. Her accomplishments spoke for themselves.

A few days before the filing deadline, I told her that if she was going to run, she should do it now, and not on the last day because her announcement would get lost in the weekend news cycle. The next morning, when we woke up, I said, "I really don't think you should do it."

"I'm going for it," she said.

What else could I do? I became her biggest supporter.

There were eighteen candidates in the original field, and three were elected officials who had never lost a race before. One candidate was a multi-millionaire with deep pockets. Several others had ties to a variety of special-interest groups who were happy to fund their campaigns. But from the get-go, it was Carolyn's race. She won going away, capturing 61 percent of the vote. And she's been great. Like me, she didn't need the job, but she wanted it. That makes all the difference.

I moved on to the Las Vegas Convention and Visitors Authority, where I work as a spokesman and an ambassador-at-large for Las Vegas. My actual title is chairman of the authority's Permanent Host Committee. The committee's goals are to educate the public on the importance of tourism and to make tourists aware of how much we appreciate their presence.

The bottom line is that I'm a brand. I show up at events with a showgirl on each arm and a martini in my hand. That's Las Vegas.

I wouldn't want to be anywhere else. Among other things, I've licensed my persona to the restaurant at the Plaza Hotel downtown. The hotel was totally renovated as part of the renaissance there. The site is historic; it's where a land auction occurred on May 15, 1905, that was really the birth of Las Vegas.

As I said earlier, the restaurant is called "Oscar's Beef, Booze and Broads." It's become pretty popular, and I try to stop in as often as I can. They've got a giant martini glass always ready for me. I enjoy meeting the customers and telling them stories about my time as a criminal lawyer and my years in City Hall. Stop in and say hello the next time you're in town.

Life is still full for both Carolyn and me. She's working twenty-four/seven for the city. I'm trying to stay relevant, but I feel a little like Aesop telling my fables to anyone who'll listen. It's been a great life; I wouldn't change a thing. And I guess if you can say that, there's really nothing else that needs to be said.

People ask me if I miss being mayor. I tell them it's more fun sleeping with the mayor.

ACKNOWLEDGMENTS

Since this is the first book I've written, I'm not really sure how the acknowledgement part goes so I'm just going to wing it.

It goes without saying that my family was my mainstay and I can't say enough about all of them. But there also were a lot of other folks along the way who helped to shape Oscar, and those I also want to thank.

In elementary school two friends, Spinks and Hurst, made sure I walked back and forth to school without having too many fights with the boys from St. Carthage. Mrs. Cecelia Chevone was smart enough to have me skip second grade at Bryant School after I wrote and produced a play called "Felix the Cat." And the class of 206 students at Philadelphia's Central High School convinced me I was no genius but did have a ken for leadership.

The boys at the Main Line's Haverford School were socialites with whom I had little in common. But I did manage to conquer many of their debutantes. Haverford College, on the other hand, was an Elysium where Professors Desjardins and Reid and Coach Prudente made every day a pleasure.

The saving grace of Penn Law School was to come into contact with the most decent of men, Professor A. Leo Levin, and to have the opportunity to work as a bartender at social gatherings in the home of my criminal law professor, Louis Schwartz.

I learned how to practice law at the feet of some of the great defenders of citizens' rights while in the courtroom. Many are mentioned in this book, but there are legions of others to whom I am also grateful and indebted.

To the decent judges with whom I fought tooth and nail, only to show more class than I had when embracing me after a case, I say thank you. And the same to the handful of prosecutors who lived by the adage that achieving justice is more important than winning.

A special thanks to Tom Cochrane of the U.S. Conference of Mayors who guided me throughout my mayoral tenure, and also to his wife, Carlotta, with whom Carolyn and I became dear friends. The same to all the mayors I met along the way who loved the city they represented and weren't looking to seek "higher office." In my mind, there is no higher office.

Thank you, too, to George Anastasia, a real author, who folded all my stories into a book.

I'm also grateful to the members of City Council who supported my dream of creating a renaissance in Las Vegas and to the city staff that made it happen: Joel, and Joel and Keith who put Humpty Dumpty back together. Finally, to my office staff, Sherry, Joey, and Ericka, who worked with me and, more important, rooted for me, all along the way.

INDEX